The Haymakers, Unions and Trojans
of Troy, New York

ALSO BY JEFFREY MICHAEL LAING
AND FROM MCFARLAND

Bud Fowler: Baseball's First Black Professional (2013)

The Haymakers, Unions and Trojans of Troy, New York

Big-Time Baseball in the Collar City, 1860–1883

Jeffrey Michael Laing

McFarland & Company, Inc., Publishers
Jefferson, North Carolina

LIBRARY OF CONGRESS CATALOGUING-IN-PUBLICATION DATA

Names: Laing, Jeffrey Michael, author.
Title: The Haymakers, unions and trojans of Troy, New York : big-time baseball in the collar city, 1860–1883 / Jeffrey Michael Laing.
Description: Jefferson, North Carolina : McFarland & Company, Inc., Publishers, 2015. | Includes bibliographical references and index.
Identifiers: LCCN 2015043979 | ISBN 9780786494934 (softcover : acid free paper) ∞
Subjects: LCSH: Troy Haymakers (Baseball team)—History. | Baseball—New York (State)—Troy—History—19th century.
Classification: LCC GV875.T76 L35 2015 | DDC 796.357/640974741—dc23
LC record available at http://lccn.loc.gov/2015043979

BRITISH LIBRARY CATALOGUING DATA ARE AVAILABLE

**ISBN (print) 978-0-7864-9493-4
ISBN (ebook) 978-1-4766-1965-1**

© 2015 Jeffrey Michael Laing. All rights reserved

No part of this book may be reproduced or transmitted in any form or by any means, electronic or mechanical, including photocopying or recording, or by any information storage and retrieval system, without permission in writing from the publisher.

Front cover: The 1866-67 Lansingburgh Unions baseball team, also known derisively as the Troy Haymakers (National Baseball Hall of Fame Library, Cooperstown, New York)

Printed in the United States of America

*McFarland & Company, Inc., Publishers
Box 611, Jefferson, North Carolina 28640
www.mcfarlandpub.com*

To Chauncey,
who hit me all those
extra fly balls at Geer Field and
who taught me to throw a change of pace
and
to Jackie,
now and always

Acknowledgments

This work has benefited from the invaluable research and inspirational scholarship of baseball historians of the nineteenth century, especially the work of Peter Morris, Brian McKenna, and John Thorn and including (but not limited to) David Fleitz, Leslie Heaphy, Roy Kerr, Tom Melville, David Nemec, Dave Pietrusza, William J. Ryczek, and Geri Strecker.

Thanks are also due John Horne, Baseball Hall of Fame photo archivist; the Santa Fe Public Library staff, especially Barb Messer and Bea Smith of the Inter-Library Loan Department; and Kathryn T. Sheehan, Rensselaer County historian and registrar of the Rensselaer County Historical Society, who provided expertise in contextual photographs of nineteenth-century Troy and for a close reading of the text.

Jim Davey, former South Troy Little League teammate, freely gave of his great advice and efforts on my behalf, tirelessly working at the on-site research of non-digitized primary sources in the Troy Public Library.

Tom Church, an enthusiastic proponent of Troy baseball history, provided helpful comments on the text. Thanks, Tom.

Chris Chenes, media relations / production manager for the Tri-City ValleyCats, generously provided his photograph of Joe Bruno Stadium and information about Troy's current minor league team.

Table of Contents

Acknowledgments	vi
Preface	1
Introduction	5
ONE. Troy Baseball in the Amateur and Early Professional Era	9
TWO. The Collar City Rides High	45
THREE. The National Association and the Wilds of Independent Baseball	56
FOUR. National Leaguers at the Gates of Troy	96
FIVE. The Fall of the Trojans	143
SIX. A Minor League City on the Hudson	176
SEVEN. The Legacy of the Haymakers	187
Appendices	
A. Major Pitching Rules and Regulations Changes, 1863–1893	197
B. Won-Loss Records for Troy's Major League Seasons	199
C. Starting Lineups for Troy's Major League Teams	200
Chapter Notes	203
Bibliography	217
Index	223

Ilium fuit, Troja est
(Ilium was, Troy is)
—Troy, New York, City Motto

Preface

The term "Troy Haymakers" is actually a media-inspired and publicly embraced generic term for the Troy, New York, baseball teams that played from 1866 to 1878. In 1865, an all-local baseball team was created, the Union Base Ball Club of Lansingburgh (which was a village due north of Troy that was incorporated into the larger city in 1900). In 1866, the Unions ventured down to New York and defeated the heavily favored New York Mutuals. When Lansingburgh in a repeat encounter at Troy later that summer again defeated the Mutuals, the New Yorker players, fans, and newspapers all bemoaned the fact that their club lost to a "country" club of upstate farm folk. The Troy players and populace were bemused by the big city moaning and gripping. As far as the Trojan populace was concerned, its base-ballists were the "Haymakers" from that day forward, though the club was actually much more a representative of a striving, urban industrial city of mid-nineteenth century American corporate culture rather than an unsophisticated collection of rubes and hayseeds. Trojans reveled in their reputation as underdogs and outsiders who could compete with the best clubs in larger, more celebrated cities. The Haymaker era had begun.[1]

The officially named Troy Citys club was also referred to as the "Troy Trojans" during their 1879–1882 National League tenure. However, this team and all Troy organized professional baseball clubs over the first fifty years of organized baseball in the city were often also identified by the term "Haymakers." In fact, in the first two decades of Troy baseball, only the National Association major league club (1871–1872) and the short-lived League Alliance Troy entry (1877) were officially named the "Troy Haymakers."

The team name most frequently employed by Troy franchises was

Preface

the "Trojans," which was employed by Troy's minor league franchises in 1886–1893, 1895, 1899, 1901–1916. However, the "Haymakers" moniker never disappeared from the sports pages and the public consciousness. In fact, the term "Haymakers" became so ubiquitous that it was employed in games where no Troy club was directly involved. An 1878 sports reporter writing for the *Lockport (NY) Daily Journal* used the term in ironically commenting on a victory of the local Niagara Base Ball Club over the Erie Base Ball Club of Akron: "The Akron club while doubtless haymakers at home were not found to be Troy Haymakers on the road. The Niagaras beat their opponents by eighteen runs (49–31)."

An amateur/semipro "Haymakers" club has been Troy's entry in the Albany, New York, Twilight League for the past 32 years. In 1938–1941, there was even a "Troy Haymakers" entry in the American Basketball League and a "Junior Haymakers" hoops team, consisting of mainly recently graduated basketball players from Troy High School and neighboring schools.

All this discussion goes by way of establishing that Troy has long embraced the term "Haymaker" as an emblem for the tough-minded working class individual who becomes successful through a combination of grit, perseverance, and native intelligence. Toughness and doggedness are virtues for the Trojan whose battle cry is "[South] Troy against the World." As with the sporting crowd of the day, I use the term "Troy Haymaker" throughout this work to refer to any organized Troy or Lansingburgh baseball club from 1863 to 1916. This term serves to describe both the desired self-perception and historical reality of Troy and of its inhabitants' sports teams (and themselves) in the period under discussion.

This work grew out of a lifelong love of baseball and a fascination with the fact of the surprising preeminence of my hometown of Troy, New York, in the development of the national pastime. Troy in the mid–1800s had all the elements of a boomtown. The city on the Hudson was peopled with creative innovators, leading artists and educators, ambitious industrialists, unregenerate capitalists, shady politicians, and striving (predominantly Irish) immigrants looking for both a livelihood and a new life. Baseball served as a source of unification and civic pride that allowed all the disparate elements of the Troy community to coalesce in a pleasurable and identifiably "American" activity and to achieve a regional, and even national, notoriety.

Furthermore, the growth of newspapers became inextricably linked with the exponential growth of the popularity of baseball. In an age of increasing mass circulation and advertising, newspapers helped spread the gospel of baseball, and more particularly for Troy, aided in the development of the Haymaker mythology. Equally important, newspapers focused on the deeds and thoughts of individual players who, whether as heroes or villains, became celebrities. Finally, Troy newspapers latched onto the David versus Goliath nature of the city's games with larger metropolitan areas, which further extended the Haymaker legend.

Whenever possible, I have tried to allow the players, management, and loyal and casual fans of early baseball have their say, often in their own words, with regard to what quickly became a nineteenth-century cultural pillar and a national obsession.

Introduction

After a highly celebrated beginning with a strong and controversial amateur team in the 1860s, Troy has had a long and storied history of professional baseball. In 1869–1870, the Troy Haymakers were a member of the National Association of Professional Base Ball Players. They then were charter members of the National Association from 1871 to 1872. In July of 1872 they were forced to disband for financial reasons. From 1873 to 1879, the Troy Haymakers played as an independent club and in the League Alliance (1877) and the International Association (1878). Their ultimate goal was to return to major league play in the National League in 1879. What followed Troy's departure from the National League in 1882 was a long minor league tenure, beginning with the Hudson River League (1885–1886), the International Association (1888), the Eastern Association (1891), the Eastern League (1892–1894), and the New York State League (1895 and 1899–1916).

In an attempt to invoke the rich baseball tradition of the past, a mid-century amateur club reclaimed the name "Troy Haymakers" for an entry in the Troy Amateur Baseball League (1946–1962) that reflected the tradition of its historic namesake: local baseball talent and a progressive attitude with regard to its roster combined with scrappy play and fervid community pride: "The Haymakers, who joined the Troy Amateur League right after the end of World War II, were an innovative team and the first to incorporate black players from the Negro A. C. team in Troy."[1] This incarnation of the Troy Haymakers sent local talent to the major leagues, including Billy Harrell (four years with the Cleveland Indians and the Boston Red Sox) and Rip Coleman (five years with the New York Yankees, Kansas City Athletics, and the Baltimore Orioles).

Without a professional baseball team for eighty-five years, Troy

Introduction

welcomed the Tri-City ValleyCats, which began play in 2002 in the short-season New York–Penn League. This club continues to play and to flourish as an affiliate of the Houston Astros.

The immediate cause of Troy's loss of a major league franchise in the early 1880s was due, in large part, to the westward movement of industry to areas with rich sources of nearby natural resources and with lower labor costs. The growth of the railroads greatly aided this migration and hastened the decline of hydroelectric power as the chief element of industrial production. Furthermore, the overall boom-and-bust economic cycles of the Gilded Age with its unregulated speculation and resulting depressions and recessions dominated the national and Troy economies. Throughout the twentieth century, the city's continued loss of heavy industry and manufacturing jobs further displaced and weakened the local economy, forcing Troy to (finally) adapt to a service economy and to embrace non-industrial innovation while continuing to tap its strong educational resources.[2] Thus, the arc of Troy's baseball fortunes has been directly dependent on the Capital District's changing economic fortunes.

During the period 1840–1860, Troy underwent a period of sustained economic and population growth that was fueled by a shortage of skilled labor and technological innovation that mirrored the experimentation with rules and refinements and the increased participation of players as baseball developed during the same period. After a devastating economic depression from 1873 to 1877, in the 1880s, capitalists wrested control of its key Troy iron and collar-and-shirt industries by monopolistic and politically astute moves; likewise, baseball investors acted in similar fashion with the implementation of the Reserve Clause that tipped the scales in favor of management. By 1890, labor in both instances responded to the capitalistic cartels by labor unrest that led to violence in the foundries and mills and the creation of the Players League rebellion in organized baseball. The irony in both instances is that the success of union action led to manufacturers closing up shop and heading to newer markets with less expensive labor costs and to baseball investors lowering salaries and severely limiting player movement. Thus, industrial capitalism worked to benefit the power brokers and monied interests in the name of maintaining stability and establishing security. The resurgent nationalism that followed the Civil War and the many social progressive ideals that

Introduction

found a receptive home among Troy's working immigrant class, such as the Cooperative, Greenback, and Eight Hour movements, took a back seat to the basic economic needs of Trojans.[3]

Finally, the city's national preeminence and abrupt down turn in the mid- to late-nineteenth century mirrors the sharp rise and sudden and extended decline of Troy as a major player in professional baseball. While the game always claimed the devotion of many of its Trojan supporters, the ability to maintain and sustain a viable professional team was determined by social and economic factors that were emblematic of the Gilded Age as a whole.

What remains of the Troy Haymaker narrative is a rich legacy of tough, talented, perseverant teams and memorable, often notorious, individual players who created a rich baseball tradition, both mythic and historic, that reflects positively on the inhabitants of Troy and serves as an example of many such urban industrial nineteenth-century communities. That Troy's native Hall of Fame members—Johnny Evers and Mike Kelly—were win-at-all-costs, hard-driving ball players who were quintessential Troy Haymakers in spirit and who were indicative of the way Trojans wished (and continue) to be perceived.

This work, finally, is a discussion of a love affair with baseball in its earliest incarnation(s) in a small but ambitious city. Trojans of every age and ethnicity[4] embraced the game as the community was changing and attempting to find its identity in a United States that was expanding and developing in exponential fashion. The heroes, scalawags, and plain ordinary folk who organized, played, and rooted for the Haymakers and who reflect the spectrum of urban life in the nineteenth-century are the heart of this narrative and, ultimately, are acknowledged for helping to create and to define both Troy, New York, and its relationship to the national pastime.

Notes on the Text

The spelling, punctuation, and usage appear as they occurred in the newspapers of the day and are not corrected to conform to modern spelling and usage rules.

Introduction

What follows are a few spelling variants and conventions of nineteenth-century diction and usage that should be noted:

- "Baseball" was generally written as two words: "base ball."
- "Centre" was the standard spelling "center."
- Clubs were frequently referred to by simply adding an "s" to the city of the franchise, e.g., "Troys."
- Pitcher-infielder Charles Bierman was frequently referred to as "Bearman."
- Pitcher-utility player Asa Brainard was at times referred to as "Brainerd."
- Club names or nicknames ending in "City" simply added an "s," e.g. "Troy Citys" (the official name of the National League Troy franchise) or the "Forest Citys" (the nickname of the Cleveland franchise).
- The terms "Troy Citys" and "Troy Trojans" were used synonymously for the city's National League franchise from 1879 to 1882.
- The word "League" in capital letters, unless further identified, always refers to the National League.
- Total Bases were expressed simply as "total."
- "To-day" and "to-morrow" were the standard spelling for "today" and "tomorrow."
- Troy Haymaker (Lansingburgh Union) pitcher Andrew McQuide was most often referred to as "McQuade."
- Troy Trojan shortstop Eddie Caskin was frequently referred to as "Caskins" as first baseman Roger Connor was (less) frequently referred to as "Connors" in contemporary accounts.
- Troy Trojan Ed Cogswell was often referred to as "Coggswell" in contemporary accounts.
- Troy Trojan pitcher Mickey Welch was often referred to as "Welsh" or (less frequently) "Walsh" in contemporary reports.

ONE

Troy Baseball in the Amateur and Early Professional Era

By 1860, Troy, New York, had fully embraced the national pastime. A relatively small town (39,235 in the 1860 census), it nevertheless had a long, successful baseball tradition. This long, storied history of Collar City baseball began in earnest with the formation of the successful Victorys of Troy in 1859.[1] In 1861, the Rensselaer Unions were created by a merger of Troy's Priam Baseball Club and the National Baseball Club of Lansingburgh. When in 1866 this club was reconstituted after the end of the Civil War, the team changed its name to the Union Club of Lansingburgh, which became the direct antecedent to Troy's first major league entry.[2]

In the 1850s, baseball began its evolution from a middle class leisure time activity with the emphasis on participation by members of social clubs to the "working masses" who established teams from among coworkers. On January 22, 1857, the National Association of Base Ball Players (NABBP) was convened under the presidency of Daniel "Doc" Adams. Fifteen clubs, all from New York City, agreed to play by the revised 20 "New York Knickerbocker" rules, which were articulated and formalized in 1845 by William Wheaton and Alexander Cartwright. In 1858, the second NABBP convention was held with 22 clubs, all from New York City; in 1859 the number of participating clubs rose to 49, including teams from Upstate New York ("country clubs") and New Jersey. The following year 62 clubs became members of the NABBP.[3]

On July 3, 1860, Troy played an inter-city match at Weir's Course

The Haymakers, Unions and Trojans of Troy, New York

Baseball's growth in Troy was slowed in the early 1860s by the Civil War and the rebuilding of the city after a devastating fire that destroyed more than 500 buildings (collection of the Rensselaer County Historical Society, Troy, New York).

Field with the Victorys losing, 7–13, to the touring Brooklyn Excelsiors, who would travel by boat up the Hudson River to play the Albany and Troy nines during the 1860s. The Excelsiors outclassed the Troy team behind the pitching of the legendary Jim Creighton; however, the game report praised the Trojans' sound fielding. As was the custom of the day, post-game activities included a dinner at the Troy House and the awarding of the game ball and an inscribed bat to the conquering Brooklyn team.[4]

The 1860 Victory Club was the first memorable club during Troy's storied amateur baseball period. In fact, the loss to Creighton and the Excelsiors was the only loss for the Victorys in a 14–1 season. Organized on August 2, 1859, the club began play in September of that year with two loses in mid–September to local clubs: the Vanguard Club of Cohoes (29–39) and the Excelsior Club of West Troy (14–19). In October, the Victorys defeated the Troy Priams twice and won a rematch against the Cohoes Vanguard. The Victorys ended their 1859 season on a winning note with a 29–26 six-inning defeat of the undefeated Champion Club of Albany, which blamed its loss on having three starters report late to the October 26, 1859, game in outlying Greenbush. Troy quickly accepted

ONE. *Troy Baseball in the Amateur and Early Professional Era*

the Capital City's challenge for a rematch, but the season ended with the victory over Albany because of the unsupported claim that three Victory players were too injured to compete.

The Victory Baseball Club began the following season with key early wins against the Union Club of Whitehall and Albany. The attendance for the latter game was 400–500 fans. While the 7–13 loss to the Brooklyn Excelsiors prevented the club from securing an undefeated season, the Victorys gained local and regional respect for the competitiveness of the result and for their perseverance in battling back from a 1–9 deficit. The 1860 Victorys claimed road victories at Chatham, New York, 79–11, and at North Adams, Massachusetts,. Closer to home the Victorys defeated the Yorkville Champions, the Albany Champions (twice), the Beverwycks, the Albany Baseball Club, the Whitehall Unions, the Schenectady Mohawks, and the West Troy Excelsiors (twice, avenging a loss to the same club in the previous year). The Victory Baseball Club of Troy ended its season with a well-played win over the imposing Utica Base Ball Club, 18–14.

The Civil War limited the 1861 Victorys season to one game, a thumping of Saratoga. The Victory Club reformed in 1862, but the team was only a shadow of its pre-war stature. For example, after defeating the Knickerbocker Club of Albany, the Victorys were routed in a rematch with the Albany club on July 14, 1862, 35–74. In September, Utica visited Troy and defeated its host, 68–27. Furthermore, the club cancelled a proposed tour of Western New York cities. Though there were plans made for a silver cup game in Saratoga for a June 22, 1863, game with the Albany Knickerbocker Club, there is no record of the game ever being played. The Victorys played no further baseball games for the duration of the Civil War.

The Victory Base Ball Club of Troy reorganized in both the 1866 and 1867 seasons. In its last amateur games, the team won a $200 prize for winning a second division tournament at Rensselaer Park, defeating the Granville, New York, Eurekas, the Lansingburgh Griswolds, and the Cohoes Unions. When the Victory Club finally disbanded for good in 1867, it left an undeniable legacy to the Troy baseball community: The Victorys helped extend and popularize baseball in the Collar City at a pivotal time in the development of pioneer baseball and established a hunger for the sport that insured that future Troy amateur clubs would flourish in such an environment.[5]

The citizens of Troy were not left without baseball after the demise of the Victory Base Ball Club. As early as 1861, the Priams of Troy merged with the National Club of Lansingburgh to establish the Union Base Ball Club of Rensselaer County to form a strong team.[6] The onset of the Civil War stopped or severely limited the growth of baseball in areas where it was being played on a regular basis. However, as baseball was played in army camps and became part of military fitness programs for soldiers, baseball during the Civil War was introduced into sections of the country where it was previously relatively unknown.

On balance, the Civil War had a mostly deleterious effect among already established clubs and their supporters. As a result, in 1863, the NABBP membership fell to a low of 28 clubs. Troy's participation in the shrinking world of organized baseball was further affected by natural causes. In 1862, Troy suffered a devastating fire that destroyed upwards of 500 residential homes and buildings in the area just south of the main business district.[7]

After the cessation of hostilities between the states and the rebuilding necessitated by the Great Fire, the Unions of Lansingburgh were founded and almost immediately were branded as miscreants and thugs who engaged in such unacceptable behavior as gambling and hippodroming (throwing games). The Unions' reputation among their opponents, the sports reporting media, and, especially, the ticket-buying baseball fans was that the club "was competitively successful and organizationally corrupt."[8] Rumors were rampant that the Lansingburgh players, though members of an "amateur" team, received such perks as little or no-work employment in private industry or in no-show political appointments. On a more positive note, the Unions were recognized as a fence-busting group of hitters, including such early stalwart batsmen as Bub McAtee, Steve King, and William Craver, whose take-no-prisoners style led to their winning more than 80 percent of their games in the middle and late 1860s.[9] However, the winning baseball did little to dampen the persistent rumors of illegal activities that swirled around the Lansingburgh club.

It had long been believed by the public that the Unions were aided

ONE. *Troy Baseball in the Amateur and Early Professional Era*

and abetted in their suspect practices on and off the baseball diamond by suspect characters such as the Irish rogue John Morrissey (who was reputed to have a central role in the Haymakers' most notorious contest with the undefeated Cincinnati Red Stockings in 1869). Born in Tipperary, Ireland, in 1831, Morrissey came to America with his family two years later. Self-taught, poor, and with few opportunities for the future, Morrissey led a hard-knocks early existence as a bar tender, brothel bouncer, riverboat deckhand, and gang leader. He was also the U.S. heavyweight boxing champion for six years (1853–1859). On October 12, 1853, in a fight at Boston Corners, New York, against Yankee Sullivan, Morrissey won a controversial decision on a technicality. Having clearly proven his superiority, Sullivan left the ring after the 37th round and did not return within the time allotted by the referee. Morrissey was then declared the winner in a fight in which he was soundly beaten. Morrissey was elected to the International Boxing Hall of Fame in 1996.

John Morrissey's checkered gambling career and suspected ties to Haymakers players and management helped further the scandalous public image of the Troy club (courtesy of the National Baseball Hall of Fame Library, Cooperstown, New York).

John Morrissey also parlayed his notoriety in the sporting world and familiarity with the Upstate New York criminal underworld into a successful manufacturing career that led to a career in local politics where he again worked his way up the ladder from ward heeler to Tammany Hall leader (and eventual opponent of Boss Tweed as the vagaries of political change(s) dictated) to state senator and, ultimately, congressman for two terms in the House of Representatives (1867–1871). As a friend of the political and economic upper crust, Morrissey made much of his fortune by gambling, both legally and illegally, on sports. Morrissey had a number of mobster friends and protégés, including, for example, Trojan John Daly, who was a noted mob gambler for over thirty years and was discovered to have made payoffs to New York City officials in the Lexow Committee Investigations in 1894–1895. While only circumstantial evidence suggests his direct involvement with the Haymakers' shady dealings, Morrissey's questionable behavior and suspicious dealings appealed to the average Trojan's desired self-image: a self-made battler who succeeds on his own terms through a combination of talent, grit, and perseverance.

Alleged to have employed some of his gambling profits to infiltrate the sports world, John Morrissey became an owner of the Saratoga Race Track (the oldest thoroughbred racing track in the country) and a follower of the local baseball team, the Troy Haymakers. Though popular with the large Irish immigrant population of Troy, Morrissey was the epitome of the ambitious man of boundless energy and dubious character who the guardians of the early game felt it necessary to prevent from direct inclusion in the sport for the long-time survival of baseball.[10]

The 1866 Unions of Lansingburgh were an entirely local team with the entire starting nine born and raised in either Lansingburgh (L) or in neighboring Troy (T): Andrew McQuide (L), pitcher; Bill Craver (T), catcher; Sonny Leavenworth (T), first base; James Ward (L), second base; Bub McAtee (L), shortstop; Cal Penfield (T), third base; Steve King (L), left field; Thomas Abrams (L), center field; and Peter McKeon (L), right field.[11]

Urban dwellers and workmen, the Unions were erroneously but commonly viewed as an 1860s "country club" of unsophisticated rubes whose baseball prowess was looked upon with disdain by the strong clubs among the more renowned Brooklyn and New York teams. Some of the earliest Union games were monumental routs of Capital District teams, including wins over the Champions of West Troy (146–9), Ancient Citys of Schenectady (107–2), and Cohoes Base Ball Club (127–8). The Unions also defeated a favored Williams College nine in Williamstown, Massachusetts,, and the losers referred to the winning Unions as "countrymen" in one of the first references to the team as an unsophisticated and unlettered (and, therefore, "lucky-to-win") group. As the team won

ONE. *Troy Baseball in the Amateur and Early Professional Era*

and garnered popular support, the Unions raised a subscription fund to travel to New York City to face the sport's most renowned clubs. It was in the New York metropolitan area where the legend of the out-of-town rubes who were smiled on by fate was first created.

Arriving at the Capitoline Grounds in Brooklyn to play the homestanding Atlantics, the Burghers could not run or slide on the clay field. It was reported that the Trojans had never seen spikes and that the Upstaters played in their bare feet. In this same report of the Brooklyn club's victory, the term "haymakers" was first attached to the Lansingburgh nine. It has been alleged that Union player William Craver tried to buoy his losing teammates by referring to them as "hay rakers" and that the admonition was misheard as "haymakers" and thusly reported in the newspaper accounts of the game.[12]

Far from their media image as doltish farm boy, the players on the Lansingburgh Unions, living in an emerging industrial city, were urban dwellers and industrial workers who had the time and opportunity to develop their game skills on the many ball fields of the Capital District. One such player was team leader and standout infielder Bub McAtee.

James "Bub" McAtee played shortstop and first base for his hometown Lansingburgh Unions from 1866 to 1869. He signed with the 1870 Chicago White Stockings along with fellow Union teammates Clipper Flynn, Bill Craver, and Mart King. The 1870 Chicago Baseball Club was composed entirely of players from the East Coast and finished the season with a 65–8 win-loss record. Bub McAtee entered the NA in 1871 as a member of the Chicago club. After the October 1871 Great Chicago Fire led to that franchise's withdrawal from the league for two years, McAtee returned the following year to play for Troy, as did his fellow Trojan and Chicago teammate Mart King. He retired after the close of the season with a NA batting average of .249 and a fielding average of .945. As with many of the original Lansingburgh Unions club, McAtee died young, in his case from a long bout with tuberculosis.[13]

Despite the sudden loss of star hurler Andrew McQuide in a November 22, 1866, accident in which he was killed when his carriage was struck by a passing train, 1867 was another successful year for the Lansingburgh Unions on the playing field. Thomas Abrams took up the mound duties, Clipper Flynn started at first base, and Mart King, Steve's brother, joined the club as a catcher/outfielder. More important for the Haymaker narrative, 1867 was the first time the term "Haymakers" was in wide use by fans and reporters alike and continued in use throughout the many ownership and name changes of the local club in the nineteenth century.

The Haymaker moniker had its birth during an 1866 road trip of the Unions to New York City and New Jersey. Lansingburgh Unions secretary James H. Spotten planned a trip to New York City with $37 dollars allotted for travel expenses. On August 7, 1866, at the Capitoline Grounds in Brooklyn, the Lansingburgh club lost to the Brooklyn Atlantics, 11–46. However, on August 9, 1866, at the Elysian Athletic Field in Hoboken, the Unions defeated the New York Mutuals in a close match, 15–13.[14] The stunning nature of the game's outcome is reflected by the fact that the Haymakers were such overwhelming underdogs that the pre-game betting odds were $100 to $5 for the Mutuals.[15]

The New York City club was mortified by having been "beaten by country boys," and in their post-game comments to reporters referred to their victorious rivals as "hicks" and "haymakers." Eager for revenge, the Mutuals travelled upstate in a rematch against the Haymakers on August 28, 1866, held in Lansingburgh at Rensselaer Park (now Knickerbocker Park), but the game resulted in another, more decisive defeat for the Gotham club, 18–32. The Mutuals continued their bad sportsmanship by refusing to attend the social supper that was to have followed the game. Among the din of the Mutuals' complaints, excuses and self-recriminations, one fact was firmly established: The Union Base Ball Club of Lansingburgh—now popularly referred to as the Haymakers—was clearly able to compete with and defeat the best baseball teams in the 1860s. Always a cantankerous bunch, the Troy Haymakers often found themselves to be their own most formidable opponent with unexplained (and suspicious) on-field behavior:

> The Union Club, with their friends, leaves this evening by boat for Washington and Philadelphia, where they play this week. The match on Saturday between the Unions and the Hampdens of Springfield resulted in the success of the Haymakers by a score of 28 to 35. The playing on both sides was very good, although the Unions did not appear to be in their happiest

ONE. *Troy Baseball in the Amateur and Early Professional Era*

mood, unaccountably wrangling among themselves, which lost them some runs. During the sixth inning, it absolutely seemed as if they were trying to lose the game, by allowing the Hampdens to score thirteen runs against them in that inning, and placing the Springfield club four runs ahead. However, during the seventh and eighth innings, they recovered their lost ground—giving two blinders successively to their opponents, while they ran up their own score [by] eight runs.[16]

No matter how the club received and adopted the appellation, the 1867 Unions fully embraced the name "Haymakers." At their home field, the club flew "a white flag in the center of which was a large yellow sheaf with a sickle struck through it and underneath the word 'Haymakers.'" A logo was created with "two rakes and a bale of hay along with the words '"Hay Makers' and 'Lansingburgh, N.Y.'" Legends abounded sur-

The 1866–1867 Lansingburgh Unions won 80 percent of their games and embraced the derisive moniker "Troy Haymakers" (courtesy of the National Baseball Hall of Fame Library, Cooperstown, New York).

rounding this term, including the fact that the entire starting nine was at least six feet tall, that the players were uniformed in blue jeans and work shirts, that these farm boys played in bare feet, and that they used hickory saplings as bats. The players soon appeared in team photographs with some members holding pitchforks. Such publicity stunts seemed to overshadow the club's play on the field, which could be mystifyingly uneven but was essentially top-rate.[17]

Having national ambitions, the 1867 Lansingburgh Unions played few games, refusing to meet many local clubs. When they did take the field they were quite successful. On July 4, 1867 before 4,000 fans at Vail's Lot (Lansingburgh), the Unions achieved a dramatic comeback victory by scoring 18 unanswered runs in a 29–26 victory over the Hudson Rivers of Newburgh. Five days later the Unions walloped the Union Club of Morrisania, 51–23, inflicting that club's worst loss in their history. The Unions earned other impressive wins against Morrisania a second time later in the year and against the strong Eureka club in Newark, New Jersey. Lansingburgh had another near-impossible comeback victory against the National of Washington (DC) when they scored nine runs in the ninth inning of a 16–15 thriller.[18]

The 1867 Troy Haymakers continued to play winning baseball into the fall and seemed to have cleaned up their act. The club was the model of comportment in a 28 to 9 home victory over the [New Jersey] Irvingtons: "The admirers of the 'national game' were treated to one of the most exciting and brilliant games of base ball, yesterday, ever witnessed in this section. [Clearly, hyperbole was a basic element of the earliest sports reporting.] There were over six thousand spectators on the grounds, among whom were several ladies. The police arrangements on the grounds were of the most perfect character, and the best of order prevailed throughout the game." The game was a rout with every Haymaker player scoring at least two runs. The post-game festivities included "a present of twenty-five dollars to [left fielder and star hitter] Steve King, for the best score, by P. G. Marsh. Steve was taken by surprise, and extends his most sincere thanks to the donor for his most generous gift."

Yet the 1867 Lansingburgh Union ball club was maddeningly inconsistent in losses to Irvington, New Jersey, by 32 runs before defeating

ONE. Troy Baseball in the Amateur and Early Professional Era

them by 19 runs in a rematch. Rumors abounded about dissension on the team and some suspiciously uninspired play.

Yet, on balance, the 1867 season must be accounted a very successful one for the Lansingburgh Unions, whose two victories over the 1867 powerhouse Union Club of Morrisania (Bronx), the disputed national champion of baseball, only heightened the Unions' national profile and popularity.[19]

Eighteen sixty-seven was a breakout season for the Lansingburgh Unions hometown boy Bill Craver. He was a Civil War veteran with the Thirteenth New York Heavy Artillery Battalion; however, he deservedly earned the title of the" most notorious individual" in all of Troy Haymaker history. His flouting of baseball rules and traditions and his desire to gain any edge over his opponents, often by violating the written and unwritten codes of baseball, were as instrumental as any one individual's actions in creating the commonly accepted reputation of the Troy Haymakers as a renegade, outlaw club. As early as 1867, Craver was the center of controversy and debate over his rude ungentlemanly behavior on the diamond. On September 27, 1867, the *Brooklyn Eagle* printed a reader's letter, signed "A Brooklynite," that defended Craver's offensive behavior and the editor's response, which held the Trojan to be at fault and claimed, in addition, that he was overrated as a catcher:

> "A Brooklynite"—In your issue of the 25th inst., I notice that you speak in severe terms of Mr. Craver, now, although I cannot justify in full the action of which he was guilty in the late match with the Union, still I think that you ought not to have been quite so severe, because there was undoubtedly great provocation for the act. Among the crowd of people that occupied the seats in the rear of the catcher's position were a number of the rough element, who embraced every opportunity of annoying Mr. Craver by insulting remarks; and at the time the action occurred Mr. Craver was running to catch a very difficult foul fly ball; these persons were shouting and hooting in order to confuse him, so that he would lose it; under these circumstances, I think there was some extenuation for his fault. In regard to his play, I cannot agree with you, as I think the he made was decidedly superior to that of Mr. Birdsall of the Union Club.

A day later, the editor of the *Eagle* responded in what was soon to be a near-universal appraisal of Craver as an unprofessional, hot-headed tough:

The Haymakers, Unions and Trojans of Troy, New York

In all respect to the comments of "Brooklynite," we can see no excuse for the act of Mr. Craver. No matter what the crowd did or said, he should have preserved his dignity as a base ball player and as catcher of the celebrated Haymakers' Club. His policy should have been to have paid no attention to the roughs, but by his disgusting action he put himself on a level with those who insulted him. With the regard to the relative merits of the two catchers, Birdsall and Craver, it is a mere matter of opinion. Mr. Birdsall catches from a swift pitcher, while Mr. Craver catches from a slow one. With everything in favor of Mr. Craver, in the late game, we still feel that Birdsall's catching was far superior to that of Craver's.

Craver was a solid player who hit .290 for seven major league seasons, batting .322 for Troy in the initial season of the National Association (1871). He was a better-than-average catcher and shortstop but a mediocre second baseman; his record as a manager was 70–66. A serial revolver, Craver jumped to the NA Baltimore Canaries in 1872 where he had 55 runs batted in 35 games. In 1874–1875 with various Philadelphia NA franchises, the Trojan had career highs in doubles (13), triples (13), and runs scored (68). In the National League, Craver hit .224 (1876) and .265 (1877).[20]

In spite of his success as a player, Bill Craver carried some heavy baggage for whatever team he was on: "Bill Craver had a prominent role in every allegation of scandal from 1867 to 1877" and his involvement in such schemes culminated in his being banned for life from the National League for his refusing to cooperate with authorities in the Louisville Grays gambling and game-fixing investigation.[21]

Bill Craver was a heady baseball player who is credited with being among the first catchers to stand immediately in back of the plate to improve his fielding chances. As for personal failings, Bill Craver would jump contracts whenever a better offer was presented to him; even worse, Craver was noted for betting on (or against) his own team in a rather obvious attempt to supplement the era's rather low yearly salaries ($800–$1,200).

Though there had been "heaving" scandals from the earliest days of the sport—the 1865 New York Mutuals had their starting catcher, shortstop, and third baseman permanently banned for illegal gambling—the first and most pervasive National League scandal occurred when Bill Craver was a member of the Louisville Grays, who in rather open

ONE. *Troy Baseball in the Amateur and Early Professional Era*

and transparent fashion—losing ten of their last twelve games after being in first place before the skid—violated the league's prohibition on betting and were widely suspected of dumping a number of late season games in a flagrant manner. Craver was never proven to have entered into a conspiracy to throw games or to have received any gambling bribes; however, he refused to cooperate with the commission as well as refusing to reveal to the investigators his Western Union telegrams. When the committee considered his checkered baseball past and his lack of cooperation, the members gave Craver along with three of his Louisville teammates lifetime bans from major league baseball.

In 1878, though he never played in the league, William Craver was reinstated into the ranks of professional baseball by the International Association, a short-lived sometime rival of the National League for baseball supremacy. Upstate New York newspapers were supportive of Craver and even suggested that he would return to the Haymakers: "Craver's expulsion from the Louisvilles last year is now looked upon as unjust. His record last year in batting and fielding was very high. He is engaged to play this year with the Troy Haymakers as second baseman and captain of the nine." The contemporary newspapers, for the most part, took the Haymakers to task for their rumored attempt to reinstate their favorite son: "An effort is being made of the Troy Haymakers ... to bring up again the Craver case before the International [Association] court. This is quite serious. Were the International Judiciary Committee to try the case and reinstate him it would do no good. They have no justification whatsoever in any court the fates of the players by the Louisville club in 1877."

Bill Craver filed for a Civil war pension in 1892 and the following year served on the Troy, New York, police force for eight years until his death in 1901.[22]

The 1868 season began with the Unions/Haymakers playing their home games at Rensselaer Park, a 42-acre horse park located in Lansingburgh between 108th and 110th streets and 5th and 9th Avenues. The significant roster changes revolved around the mound. Abrams, who pitched in 1867, became the tenth man, with Cuban RPI student Julian de la Rua doing the early season pitching before leaving the team. The departed Rua was then replaced by New York Mutual hurler Charles Bier-

The Haymakers, Unions and Trojans of Troy, New York

William Craver was a Troy native and pioneer in post–Civil War baseball. Praised for his play and his savvy on the field, Craver was also excoriated for his actions off the diamond, which are believed to include game fixing and illegal gambling. To this day, Craver possesses the most notorious reputation of any Troy Haymaker of any era.

man (who reportedly was the first Unions paid player from outside of the Capital District). For the second year in a row, the Unions defeated the national champions—in 1868 the New York Mutuals—twice during the season. Their most resounding win was a 48–11 destruction of Mutuals at Rensselaer Park. Yet, at season's end, the Haymakers were still judged as a step below the first tier clubs—the Philadelphia Athletics, the Brooklyn Atlantics, and the Cincinnati Red Stockings.[23]

A local stalwart of the 1868 Haymakers was Lansingburgh native Clipper Flynn, who was a key utility player of the 1867 Unions in his rookie season at the age of 18. He became a slick fielding and dependable hitting starting first baseman in 1868–1869 before following many of his teammates to Chicago for the 1870 season. His major league career consisted of the 1871 NA season for the Troy Haymakers (29 games), during which he hit .338 with 27 runs batted in, and his 1872 NA season with the Washington (DC) Olympics (9 games before the club disbanded on May 24, 1872), in which he hit .225. Flynn fielded .955 in 1871 with Troy (third best in the league) and led first basemen in assists with eight and in outfield double plays with two. Flynn worked in a Lansingburgh brush factory when he retired from baseball and died in his home village at the age of 32.[24]

The hometown Lansingburgh brother duo of Steve and Mart King were the heart of the 1868 Unions with the former leading

ONE. *Troy Baseball in the Amateur and Early Professional Era*

the club at the plate and the latter providing the hard-nosed attitude that became synonymous with Haymaker teams.

Steve King played with the Unions in 1866 and his brother joined the team in 1867 when both started in the outfield for the club. The older brother Steve was a superior batter for the 1867–1872 Troy baseball teams. He hit .396 in 1871 (which was fourth highest in the NA) with a .400 on-base percentage and a .596 slugging percentage. He was the 1871 Haymaker leader in hits and runs with only one strikeout for the entire season. Steve King was also a productive hitter for Troy in 1872 with a .305 batting average. However, Steve King was not a complete player. His fielding percentage was shockingly low, even for the era, at .807, and his range was even worse. He never left his local club as did many of his fellow Haymakers, and he retired after the Troy team disbanded in August of 1872.

Steve's younger brother Marshall ("Mart") was an outfielder and backup catcher who was notorious for his toughness on the diamond and his disdain for any effete behavior or fashion that countered his he-man image. Part of the Haymaker mythology has Mart King playing without a baseball cap or shoes. Mart King accompanied Bill Craver to the 1870 Chicago White Stockings. When his fellow Trojan was dropped from the club for supposed contract violations, King caught many games in a season when Chicago defeated the renowned Cincinnati Red Stockings twice in September and October of 1870. King left Chicago in early 1872 and played a few last games with the NA Troy Haymakers. He retired from baseball after the season, complaining of the less rough-and-tumble style the sport was embracing. He lived in the Capital District area and worked as boater and gardener until his death in 1911.[25]

One final interesting note of the Haymakers' 1868 season was the brief career of Rafael Julian de la Rua, who it is claimed threw baseball's first screwball. Rua was Cuban-born and attended Rensselaer Polytechnic Institute in Troy in 1868 and began pitching for the local Haymakers: "Rua's pitching was the acme of perfection—not too swift to be unreliable, and with just enough of the 'twist' to prevent the Mutuals from making their heaviest batting."[26] After withdrawing from RPI, Rua's brief stint in Capital District baseball apparently ended his American baseball career, as no mention of his ever playing again in the United States has been uncovered.

Troy's Early Professional Days (1869–1870)

Prior to December of 1868, when the NABBP allowed 1869 baseball clubs to declare that they were "professional" and openly pay their players, the game of baseball was supposed to be a purely amateur endeavor. However, from the sport's earliest days in the 1850s, there were persistent rumors and whispers that star players were being paid. There was even an 1866 investigation and mini-scandal involving among others future Haymaker manager and slugger Lipman Pike of Troy's entry in the 1871 National Association. The Haymakers, who were reputed to owe much of their financial support to gamblers and other

The 1869 Lansingburgh Unions, also called the Troy Haymakers, were Troy's first professional baseball team and competed with the country's best clubs (courtesy of the National Baseball Hall of Fame Library, Cooperstown, New York).

ONE. Troy Baseball in the Amateur and Early Professional Era

undesirables, were widely believed to be open violators of the NABBP amateur clause.

A disheartening 8–26 loss to the best-of-the-West Cincinnati Base Ball Club during the 1868 season seemed to galvanize Haymaker ownership to upgrade its roster and to officially embrace professionalism for the following season. The Haymakers followed Cincinnati's lead and signed non-local players, including reserve infielders Mike Powers of Utica and Steve Bellán from Cuba by way of the Bronx. More important, Troy signed as their first major openly professional non-local, Cherokee Fisher, one of the hardest throwers in the game, to pitch for the 1869 season. With Fisher on the mound and Trojan Bill Craver behind the plate, the Haymakers had an imposing battery along with a solid cast of returning locals led by McAtee, Flynn, and the King brothers. The 1869 baseball season looked promising for the revamped Troy club. Though the team lost eight games, they defeated the New York Mutuals twice and had a 2–1–1 record against the powerful Brooklyn Atlantics.[27]

William Charles "Cherokee" Fisher was a hell-raiser who fit right in with the Haymaker ethos. He was a fastball pitcher who played for seven teams in seven years, including a two-year stint with Troy (1869–1870). He was erratic on and off the field, compiling a 56–84 record on the mound and a .256 batting average at the plate as a below average fielding utility player (third base and the outfield). However, Cherokee Fisher had a dominating short stretch when he was the top NA pitcher in the 1872–1873 seasons. In 1872 with the NA Baltimore Canaries he went 10–1 for a .909 winning percentage with a 1.80 earned run average. The following year with the NA Philadelphia Athletics he again led the league with a 1.81 ERA.

On the debit side, Cherokee Fisher also admitted on February 3, 1877, that as a member of Milwaukee's West End club in 1876, he had taken a $100 bribe to throw a game. As with his old battery mate Craver, Fisher on retirement became a member of the uniformed services as a fireman in Chicago.[28]

The arrival of the vaunted Cincinnati Red Stockings to "cross bats again" with the Haymakers at Lansingburgh's Bull's Head Tavern field on June 7, 1869, was splashed across the pages of the local newspapers. Previews of the invading baseball champions of the West

25

were unrestrained in their praise of the visiting team, the first open and totally professional team (players received seasonal salaries from $800 to $1,200) organized by early baseball pioneer Harry Wright: "Lansingburgh was again the scene of a raid by the tribe of savage hitters known as the Red Stockings.... They have struck blows with the bat with a vigor of old Tecumseh himself. All nine are cool and accurate throwers, sure and heavy batters, and tall and strong and swift of foot are they."[29]

The game itself was a nail-bitter with the undefeated Cincinnati Red Stockings squeaking out a 32–30 win. The day was defined by heavy hitting, disputed umpire calls, and great swings of fortune, with a furious Haymaker comeback falling short in the last inning:

> The Haymakers were deprived of a run in the opening inning when Steve Bellan was called automatically out for stealing home on "three called balls" to Fisher, according to a new rule that season. When one considers the outcome of the game, this run would have been a vital one. In the bottom of the second, with the score tied at two all, Leonard "took the ash" for the Red Stockings and hit the ball "furiously" over right field," but "Clipper" Flynn was there and compelled him to "drop out."
>
> Brainerd [Asa Brainard] sent a "daisy cut by first base, but was put out" at second splendidly by Jim Ward and Gene Bonker. Sweazy, after passing first and second, was put out at third. The favorites were pounding the ball but could not score against the Haymakers.
>
> The fourth inning decided the contest as the local boys took a "don't-care-if-you-do" attitude and let the visitors tally 10 runs, but the Unions pulled themselves together and their score continued to "bloom up" until they entered the ninth inning trailing only 32–30 [the actual score at this juncture of the game was 32–29 in favor of Cincinnati].
>
> Bill Craver, up with two outs and one run in with two men on base, fouled out to Gould on a check [sic] swing to end the game. It was generally agreed that, excepting the blunders in the fourth inning, the Haymakers outplayed the visitors, and felt the loss of injured Mike [Bub] McAtee very much.[30]

By mid–June of 1869, the leading baseball clubs in the New York City area—the Mutuals, Unions, Eckfords, and Atlantics—were threatened by the success of "foreign clubs," or teams from outside of Metropolitan New York, such as the Red Stockings and the Haymakers. The New York City reporters defended their local clubs with a harried logic presented in fulsome detail:

ONE. *Troy Baseball in the Amateur and Early Professional Era*

> Then they [Cincinnati supporters] brag that either of the two "foreign clubs," the "Haymakers" and the "Red Stockings," "can easily beat the Mutuals in the second game" [is a statement that] may convey a meaning of some significance. Does it mean that the Mutuals would not have a chance to win if they went to Cincinnati? Do the Cincinnati people so terrify visitors as to give the impression that a club to play against the "Red Stockings" in that town would be obliged to play against the entire city? Of Lansingburgh the author of the above scintillations cannot speak officially, so he must speak only for his own village folks. If it be meant that the "Red Stockings" and the "Haymakers" can defeat the Mutuals easily, simply on the merits of the game, then the [clubs have behaved] at this time with a very bad grace. The "Red Stockings" have found in the Mutuals their toughest opponents so far, and did it "easily." The victory of the "Haymakers" over the Mutuals the "Haymakers" themselves must acknowledge was gained not so much by their own good playing as by the poorer playing of their opponents ... they [Cincinnati fans] are not foolish enough to reckon on anything as being safe in base ball.[31]

The Haymakers, in preparation for their major Western tour, played the formidable Brooklyn Atlantics nine at Saratoga Springs, New York, on August 9, 1869. Led by three key future members of the early professional Haymaker teams—Bob Ferguson, George Zettlein, and Lip Pike—the Brooklyn club defeated the Trojans handily: "The Atlantics out batted their opponents, but their fielding was only mediocre. The batting of the Haymakers was poor, except in the sixth inning [when the Haymakers scored five runs] and Craver's home run in the fourth inning. Their fielding was at times good and at times bad.... About 2,000 persons were present among whom was a crowd of noisy individuals."

However, the Haymakers got revenge later in the summer by beating the Atlantics, 17–10, and battering Zettlein, who had never previously lost to the Lansingburgh club. Before hitting the road to play in the Midwest and South, Troy also beat Harvard University, the best baseball collegiate nine in the country and faced down a local challenge in near record fashion: "The reputation that the Haymakers had made got the 'goats' of the Ancient City Club of Schenectady (although "goats" were not known at that time) and the Schenectadians [sic] issued a challenge to Troy's famous team.... The Haymakers accepted the challenge and went to Schenectady to play the Ancient Citys on their own grounds. The result was 107 to 2 in favor of the Trojans."[32]

The Haymakers, Unions and Trojans of Troy, New York

The Haymakers began their famous Western tour in late August, winning a "plucky uphill game" at Cleveland against the Forest Citys, 34–21 on the 23rd and defeating the Mansfield Independents the next day, 44–20. On Wednesday, August 25, the Troy club arrived in Cincinnati to play the 49–0 Red Stockings the next day. The odds were 2–1 in favor of the home team, the field was in superior condition, and the day only a bit warm, so the stands were full with a crowd estimated at between 8,000–12,000 partisan Red Stocking fans. The Haymakers were an impressive contrast sartorially to the homestanding club with uniforms of dark blue trousers, light blue shirts with tight collars, long sleeves with ruffled cuffs, and large "U" for Unions "emblazoned on a button down shield. Back in Troy, approximately 1,000 Haymaker supporters "packed the streets of downtown Troy to hear inning-by-inning dispatches at the stores of Col. Egolf and Tom O'Brien."[33]

It is a salient fact that 1869 was the first year of professional championship play, so the outcome of the August 25th game would further the national reputation of the winning club. Troy would finish the 1869 season in fifth place (of twelve teams vying for the professional championship) with a 12–8–1 record.[34] Troy's first professional team was a successful one on the diamond, but it is the Haymaker tie with Cincinnati that is the most celebrated (and infamous) single game in Troy baseball history.

The game itself was a seesaw affair with some odd, even suspicious, events occurring in the early innings. In a surprise move, Troy started junk ball pitcher Charlie Bierman rather than fireballing ace Cherokee Fisher. The Haymakers scored six runs in the bottom of the first inning off ace Asa Brainard (whose first name was purported by a few baseball advocates to be the source of the expression "ace of the staff"). In the second inning, the Red Stockings solved the slow deliveries of Bierman, who was relieved by Fisher. The Upstate New York club felt the umpire—W. R. Brockway of the Buckeye Club—was biased: "Harry Wright attempted to steal second and Fisher, covering the area well, put him out by 10 feet, but to the chagrin of the Lansingburgh team, Brockway declared Wright 'not out.'"[35] However, the Haymakers continued to light up Brainard and went ahead 13–10, a lead the Red Stockings chipped away at for a 13–13 tie at the end of the fourth inning. Each club traded four spots in the next inning with the most impressive blast being an

ONE. *Troy Baseball in the Amateur and Early Professional Era*

In the nineteenth century, Troy had many successful baseball clubs other than the Haymakers. One of them, the 1870 Putnams (above), played its way to a 23–2 record and was generally acclaimed as the best junior team in the country (courtesy of the National Baseball Hall of Fame Library, Cooperstown, New York).

over-the-fence home run by Trojan Steve King. So the sixth inning began with the teams locked in a 17–17 tie.

The game ended with the first batter in the sixth inning and the reasons for such an abrupt halt in action have been analyzed, debated, rehashed, and questioned for the past 145 years:

> Every close decision was given to the Red Stockings; the Haymakers demanded a new umpire but were refused. McVey led off the 6th inning for the home club and struck a foul which was apparently caught by Craver before it had reached the ground. [Most every unbiased report states that Craver's play was a very close one that could have been called either way.] The umpire, looking the other way, decided it was "not caught."
>
> "Cherokee" stormed off the mound and had to be restrained by his teammates. President James McKeon of the Haymakers Club again requested a new umpire and was denied. McKeon then ordered the team to "pack up bats" and leave the field, convinced they could not win with such a wretch for an umpire.
>
> The police had their hands full with the rowdy, turbulent crowd, which

felt like tearing the Unions apart. As our team left the field for the Gibson House where they were staying, their omnibus was followed by a multitude of hooting bootblacks and other Cincinnati roughs, at whom McKeon was swearing back "vehemently." Umpire Brockway mounted his chair and shouted: "I declare this game in favor of the Cincinnatians, because the Unions of Lansingburgh refuse to continue it!"

After midnight on August 27, the growing crowd outside the Gibson House became so menacing that the Troy Haymakers left Cincinnati under cover of darkness, spending the next two days in Louisville.[36]

The Midwestern response to the Haymakers' actions was swift and unequivocal. The local Buckeye Baseball Club cancelled its scheduled game with the Troy club on August 27th, and the Red Stockings refused to play the Haymakers during the New York State Fair in Elmira during a September Cincinnati tour of the East. The Red Stockings also withheld the visitors' share of the purse (40 percent of which was approximately $1,000) unless and until the Haymakers' management apologized for their behavior on the field and to Brockway, which the Troy club did after the season. The dispute was finally decided the next season in Troy's annual visit to the West: "All agreed that their [Haymaker] treatment in Cincinnati was *par excellence* itself, and all recollection of former troubles was buried in the present era of good feeling. The amount of money received on account of last year's game was $700."[37]

Serious allegations from both baseball camps about the actual reasons for the petulant behavior of the Trojans began almost immediately after the August 26 fiasco. Cincinnati supporters believed that *"l'affaire* Craver had been staged" to save Troy bettors from losing a bundle. Haymaker supporter John Morrissey ran a national betting syndicate and rumors arose that he had bet an enormous sum (figures ranged upwards of $17,000)) on Troy to defeat the Red Stockings. With the game ending in a 17–17 tie, all bets would be declared void (which was the ultimate result of Troy's actions).

The debate over who was at fault in the contentious tie was fought out in the newspapers, barber shops, and gin mills of both cities. Haymaker supporters thought that John Brockway was bought off to counter fears of the Troy club's reputation as a strong, tenacious nine and to insure, ultimately, a Cincinnati victory. Troy defenders believed that the

ONE. *Troy Baseball in the Amateur and Early Professional Era*

three debatable calls that went against Craver were too many to be considered mere chance and that the club had no reasonable expectations of a fair and unbiased outcome, thus justifying the Haymaker walk-off.[38]

The newspapers had a field day with the incident with the Troy team receiving the majority of the brickbats. Even in rather even-handed accounts of the game, Haymaker president McKeon was singled out for his foul-mouthed and contentious behavior; he was attacked by a number of his own players for pulling the Troy team off the field for what appeared to be a minor reason and for continuing to pursue the matter to the point that the local police needed to provide an escort to safely return the players to the Gibson House.[39] Moreover, the consensus media response of the day further condemned the Haymaker actions: "The Haymakers ... took offense and left the grounds. They got the sulks and wouldn't play anymore. Small children have just such scenes in their play every day. But what astonishes us is the fact that a good part of Cincinnati went out to see the play ... and paid their money for the privilege.... [The controversy was] all over a little dispute between grown-up children whether it was a 'tip' or a 'miss.'"[40]

The final action regarding the disputed August 26, 1869, game was a pyrrhic victory for Troy. Umpire Brockway's decision to award the Red Stockings a 9–0 forfeit win was overturned by the NAPBBP and the game officially declared a 17–17 tie. However, the gambling and bribery allegations that persisted about the contest further cemented the Troy Haymakers' scandalous reputation as game-fixing hooligans and, more generally, threatened the public trust and belief in the integrity of nineteenth-century baseball.[41]

The irony of the public scorn heaped upon the Troy club was that many neutral reporters felt the New York club was "shamefully" treated" and were actually victims of crowd assaults and of financial shenanigans by the Cincinnati club. One such reporter referred to the Troy players as "lively, rollicking, full-of-fun, and good-natured" men (the reporter even described them as "good vocalists") who were willing to give their withheld gate share to charity![42]

In spite of an impressive Western tour that saw the club go 9–2–1 with both losses coming by one run, and their 9–5–1 record against elite clubs in its debut season as a professional team, 1869 cannot be viewed as an unqualified success in light of the persistent rumors of gambling and game fixing that dogged the Haymakers. Such criticisms were not confined to the Red Stocking tie. For example, the Trojans' one run loss, 14–15, to the underdog Baltimore Pastimes raised eyebrows since the betting odds were 100–25 in favor of the Haymakers. This situation would provide Morrissey, who was uncharacteristically traveling with the club on the western trip, with the opportunity to recoup any loses he had incurred from the cancelled Cincinnati bets. However, the newspaper reports of the game do not reveal any suspicious behavior, only that "Bearman [Bierman], McAtee, and King deserved credit" and that "Craver was suffering as usual with a sore hand." Equally important, there is no verifiable proof of any irregularities concerning the game and the Baltimore Pastimes became a solid winner against other strong clubs as the 1869 season progressed.[43]

The post-mortem on the Haymakers' western tour suggested that the entire trip was uneventful: "With the exception of the unfortunate affair at Cincinnati, nothing occurred on the trip worthy of note. Mike [Mart] and Steve King led in hits; Mike [Mart] King and Craver led in runs." The returning Haymakers were treated as heroes and 2,000 supporters saw their team defeat Buffalo 34–9. The banquet at the Mansion House following the game became the swan song for both the 1869 season and for the victorious Haymaker teams of the 1860s.[44]

In fact, while having a successful season in the win-loss column, the Troy team in 1869 continued to be defined as a good hitting, poor fielding club. For example, Fisher and Bierman were lauded for their stellar batting—each had five hits—in a thrashing of the Boston Tri-Mountains. As for a game against the Brooklyn Eckfords, the game was described as "not a good fielding exhibition. Both sides did some tall muffing, the 'Haymakers' extolling in this respect. Craver was not in a condition to play, his hands being banged up and sore."[45]

The Haymakers' season actually ended on October 1, 1869, in a "social" game between the home-standing champions the Brooklyn Eckfords and the visiting Haymakers, who lost 19–23 in eight innings. In a rare baseball occurrence, Eckford pitcher Alphonse "Phonney" Martin induced 23 of the game's 24 outs to be made through the air. In a pattern of players revolving that was all-too-common in early baseball, Martin

ONE. *Troy Baseball in the Amateur and Early Professional Era*

played for the Haymakers in 1872 in the National Association of Professional Base Ball League (NAPBBL) until the Troy team folded, at which point he then returned to his former Eckford team.[46]

The 1869 championship baseball season ended in a manner that spurred many in the game to search for a simpler system to crown a national champion. Uncharacteristically for a recently crowned champion, the 1869 Eckfords opened a championship series with both the dethroned New York Mutuals (September 1) and the Brooklyn Atlantics (September 6). After much jockeying for supremacy among the Eckfords, Atlantics, Mutuals, and Philadelphia Athletics, the 1869 season ended with the Brooklyn Atlantics coming from behind to claim the crown from the Eckfords on November 11, 1869.

The awarding of the championship to the Brooklyn club was rather hollow in that it was generally accepted among the populace that the Cincinnati Red Stockings were clearly the best team in organized baseball in 1869.

The hot stove league season in the winter of 1870 was tumultuous for both owners and players. One such series of events that colored the competitive and financial fortunes of the Chicago and Troy franchises resulted in a tug-of-war over revolving players and management raids of the rosters of rival clubs. Such a situation is representative of the often byzantine and opéra bouffe–like twists and turns that were common in compiling a successful team before the institution of the reserve clause:

> The finances of the Haymaker club at the close of the season of 1869 were at such low ebb that the managers decided not to carry a professional nine through the season of 1870, and advised their players to make the most advantageous arrangement possible with other clubs. The decision of the Haymaker Board flooded the market with "bully" players. Craver went to Boston, Fisher to Philadelphia, and the lesser lights took a Micawber-like view of the situation.
>
> The heavy skirmishing by the ball-tossers in the early part of the season awakened the war-like spirits of the old Haymaker board, and they determined to recruit their forces and bear the brunt of the battle again. The old vets had gone, but they followed them to their new homes, and sang in the sweet tones "Auld Lang Syne" and "Home Sweet Home," keeping excellent time with batons of greenbacks. Craver's eyes filled with tears as he listened to these sweet melodies, and he was about to reach forth his hand to

take in friendly grasp the hands of his old Troy friends with a $2,250 baton in them, but Tom Foley of Chicago sang a different tune, covered the Troy pile, and went $250 better. Craver determined to sacrifice his love for Trojan honors and take Chicago's $250.

Next was the gentle and handsome Fisher, but they came at him in a most inopportune moment. He had been a regular of the [Philadelphia] Athletics for several months, and was still a member, drawing his salary for the season of 1870 in advance, like a little man; therefore at the time was obligated to them financially. Tom Foley, who was quite ubiquitous at that time, about February last, had been playing sweet to Fisher for his city's great Chicago's sake. Powers, the old Haymakers' short-stop, who knew the ground well, had been detailed from Albany, which strategic point Tom had made his base of operations, to Troy, with the intention of picking off the old "Cherokee," and, if possible, bring him captive to the headquarters. The work was well done, and Fisher was the recipient of royal favors at the hands of his captors. He yielded to their persuasions to break his allegiance with the Athletics of Philadelphia accepted, it is said, an advance of salary for 1870, and was to be a full-fledged Chicagoan. The Haymakers then approached him, when he had been metamorphosed into an Athletic-Chicagoan, and knew not how to encounter such a being. But mightier power than they accomplished the work. Fisher, while a Trojan, had conceived a passion for an interesting lady of that city, who brought him back to Troy. His financial obligations to the Athletic club were settled, and on May 3 his resignation was accepted by the Athletics, of which the Haymakers received official notice. His Chicago contract, if there was one, was not considered to be very binding, having been made under circumstances of a very peculiar character, and the Haymakers reelected him. Foley had been keeping a close watch upon him, and endeavored to outwit the Haymakers, but Fisher stood firm in his last resolve, and Foley was outplayed. A personal friend of Fisher, in his behalf, tendered the amount drawn from the Chicago ball tosser, who was refused; "Fisher, not money" was Foley's lament. He got neither and returned home. The lake breezes revived him, and he then wanted the money. He drew on the Haymaker club for the amount. The draft was returned, protested; a letter from the club followed, with the advice that the Haymaker club [should attend] to its own business and Fisher to his, and by so doing, both were getting along nicely. The inevitable goose quill was called into requisition, yet no settlement was made.

The Haymakers with old "Cherokee," arrived in Chicago last week, and played a game on Friday with the Chicago club. Foley guaranteed that the Haymakers should have their share of the gate money, without any deduction for Fisher's account. When the game ended the report showed 1,064 tickets sold, from which the printing bills, the ground rent, the revenue tax and Fisher's account were to be taken by order of the Chicago club.

ONE. *Troy Baseball in the Amateur and Early Professional Era*

McDonald, the gentlemanly manager of the present Haymaker nine, repeated the former explanations, and informed the Chicago club that he would await the time when they decided to treat the Haymakers in a business transaction as the Haymakers had treated them when they played in Troy on their late tour. Chicago therefore retains the Haymakers' share of the gate money.[47]

In 1870, the Chicago-Troy relationship continued to sour as four of the Haymakers' key players—Bill Craver, Clipper Flynn, Mart King, and Bub McAtee (and future Haymaker player and manager Jimmy Wood, who also played for Chicago in 1870)—headed west to play for the Chicago White Stockings, who in a disputed contest with the New York Mutuals were declared that year's national champion.[48]

In spite of this mass exodus, the reorganized Union Club of Lansingburgh was considered to be a solid professional club, though they lost their local flavor with only Steve King and Bill Craver remaining with most of the rest of the roster filled out with professional players from the Philadelphia area. Entering the season, the Haymakers were thought not to be on a level with the four recognized powerhouse teams: Brooklyn Atlantics, Cincinnati Red Stockings, Philadelphia Athletics, and the New York Mutuals. The next tier of possible championship teams were all to some degree in the process of rebuilding, including the usual suspects: Troy Haymakers, Brooklyn Eckfords, Boston Tri-Mountains, Baltimore Marylands, Morrisania Unions, and the Washington D.C. Olympics and Nationals.

The wild card in the upcoming season proved to be the newly formed Chicago White Stockings, who had a club composed of strong players wooed from long-established professional teams. They were recognized as a talented collection of all-stars who would need time to jell as a top club:

> In addition to these [the aforementioned first tier professional clubs] there is the new Chicago Club nine, which contains Craver of the Haymakers of Lansingburgh; Pinkham, late of the Olympics, of Washington; McAtee, of the Haymakers; Wood, of the Eckfords; Meyerle, of the Athletics; Hodes, of the Eckfords; Treacy, ditto; M. King, of the Haymakers; and Cuthbert, of the Athletics in regular positions. This composes the new "$10,000 nine" of the Chicago Club. It is a strong team: but after all, it is only a "picked" nine, and not a *Club* nine as the Red Stockings now are. The Chicago party may be very successful, but we think that it'll take them at least a season to

get into training. Unlike the Cincinnatis, they have not yet to stand the ordeal of a season's defeats.[49]

The pre-season reports for 1870 focused on two major changes for professional baseball. The first such change was an amended rule on the "delivery of the ball to the bat": "Last year the umpire could require the pitcher to deliver a ball low or high to any degree the striker chose to call for.... All that the pitcher can now be required to do is to send in a ball within fair reach of the striker." Equally important, a "Grand Tournament" was planned for the Capitoline Grounds in Brooklyn to determine a professional champion on the field in head-to-head matches:

> One of the great events of the coming season will be the grand Tournament which will take place early in September, on the Capitoline Base-ball Grounds, Brooklyn, the object of the tourney being to settle the question of the championship for 1870. In this tourney, the four clubs who hold the leading position at that time will be the contestants, and the games will be six, one a day, thus having a gala week of first-class play. The club which wins will be the champion club. The four clubs which have lost the fewest series of games—best two out of three—up to September will alone enter the lists.[50]

On November 1, 1870, at Dexter Park before 6,000 fans, the New Mutuals were leading the Chicago White Stockings by a score of 13–12 in the top of the ninth inning when the New York pitcher Wolters walked the bases loaded and the next batter would not swing at any delivery. Wolters stomped off the mound and the umpire had the final score revert back to the last full inning, which Chicago led, 7–5.

Since this was the Midwestern club's second win over the Mutuals, the White Stockings won the championship from the Brooklyn Atlantics. Chicago was awarded the 1870 baseball championship, though they had fewer professional victories (22) than the Mutuals (29), the Cincinnati Red Stockings (27), and the Philadelphia Athletics (26). This second questionable title after the undefeated Red Stockings did not win the 1869 championship appears to have been at least a small impetus to the creation of a more formalized league with more delineated regulations for 1871.[51]

The Haymakers might have had only a so-so record in 1870, but they had some memorable and dramatic moments on the diamond. In

ONE. *Troy Baseball in the Amateur and Early Professional Era*

late May, the Troy club lost a contest in Troy to the Rockford Forest Citys by a score of 3–21: "The President of the Haymakers said the Forest City did some of the most terrific batting ever seen in Troy. During the game they [Forest City] made a beautiful triple play."[52]

The most bitterly fought contest of the year was a grudge match between the upstart Chicago White Stockings, who had raided the Haymaker roster in the 1869 off-season and the homestanding Trojans, who made an all-out effort to be competitive at the highest level of the game:

> The hardest fought game of base ball that has taken place in this country since the origin of the national game came off here [Troy on June 26, 1870] between the Haymakers and White Stockings. There were 6,000 people who witnessed the game. Ever since the Rockford club gave the Haymakers a severe drubbing in the course of the eastern trip of the former club, it has been generally supposed that the city of Troy, the great baseball centre of America, and the school which has graduated its scores of first-class players no longer had a ball club which could be called first-class in any respect. But that defeat set the managers of the Haymaker organization to working, and the result is that the city now has a club fit to compete with any in the country. [The only 1869 starters for the 1870 Haymakers were Bill Craver who was accused of violating his Chicago contract and revolved back to Troy and Steve King with the bulk of the roster being former Philadelphia pros.] When it was definitely learned that the White Stockings were to come to Troy, $5,000 were at once raised to put the Haymakers in a condition to defeat them. To this end, York, of the Rockfords, McMullen, of the Athletics, and McCarty, of another Philadelphia club, were paid liberally to join the organization. McMullen, [who is] a change pitcher from Fisher, the old pitcher in that position, made the club as strong in that direction as it could possibly be.
>
> The White Stockings arrived in Troy on Sunday morning, and met with the most hospitable reception. The Managers of the Troy Club talked very confidentially, and expected to give the Chicago men a very close rub, which they certainly did. When the Chicago management found out that the three new players above alluded to above had joined the Haymakers, they were at once objected to, on the grounds that they had played match games in other organizations within the last sixty days. As the Haymakers refused to play without these men, the managers of the White Stockings drew up a protest to be forwarded to the National Association. These preliminaries being settled, the time for the game set at 3 o'clock this afternoon. The game resulted in favor of the White Stockings—score 25 to 21.[53]

The Haymakers faced other imposing foes in 1870 and were bested by superior clubs. One such important contest was a rematch with the

The Haymakers, Unions and Trojans of Troy, New York

Cincinnati Red Stockings at the Union Grounds. This was one year after the 17–17 tie game debacle that was the only blemish on Cincinnati's undefeated season in 1869. On June 13, 1870, at the Capitoline Grounds, in what was almost universally described as the "best game ever played," the Brooklyn Atlantics defeated the Red Stockings, 8–7 in 11 innings, to end Cincinnati's 84 game winning streak. While the Red Stockings were proven human in 1870, they were still a very formidable baseball club and, on August 8, routed the visiting Troy Haymakers at the refurbished Union Grounds, 34–8. The only important result of the game was a serious knee injury to Cincinnati shortstop Harry Wright who was put out of action until October.[54]

The Haymakers began June on a winning note defeating the Atlantics in Brooklyn in a squeaker (32–31) and the Keystones in Philadelphia in a rout (41–20) with the consensus of press and fans that the Troy club was a force to be reckoned with and a source of pride for Troy:

> [The Haymakers] vanquished them [the Keystones] to the tune of 41 to 20. This result was gained by some tremendous batting, the Haymakers striking hard and sending balls in all directions over the field so that it was impossible to top their scoring. After the third inning the Haymakers handled the willow in superb style, and by terrific batting added 33 to their score.
>
> The Haymakers thus far have covered themselves with glory, and their friends in this city and vicinity may now indulge in a just pride in the success of their favorites. The present nine have proved itself immensely superior in batting qualities, and if they can keep up the work as they have begun the result of this tour will bring up the old-time reputation of the club. The general play of the nine was very fine, Steve King doing himself great credit by his superb play in left field; Hollister, King, and Wolverton each made home runs.

A day earlier at the Capitoline Grounds in Brooklyn, the Haymakers won a slugfest, 32–31, over the vaunted Atlantics that was described as "one of the finest and most exciting which has taken any place on any ball field this season": "Both clubs worked hard for victory.... The Atlantics scored 33 clean first bases and the Haymakers 38, while the totals [total bases] ran into the fifties." A reprint from the *New York World* provides further game detail(s) and a possible reason for such a high-scoring contest:

ONE. *Troy Baseball in the Amateur and Early Professional Era*

> The game resolved itself, before three innings had been played into the heaviest batting contest of the season. The ball was a lively one, and as every player on both sides threw all his weight and muscle into every stroke, the fielders found plenty of work to do, and the ball was generally found to be a hot one.... Many will think that with so large a score there must have been much muffing. The contrary was the case. With the exception of two or three bad throws and a couple of dropped fly balls, there was really nothing to find fault with.... The Haymakers played well in the field and excelled the Atlantics at bat, and thereby won the game. Wolverton's third base play was sure and accurate; Dick was efficient as captain of the nine and at second base; Hollister [1B] and Penfield [SS] played their positions capitally, while Foran [RF] and King [LF] took everything that came their way.[55]

The Troy Haymakers continued their mastery over the New York Mutuals, as demonstrated in a July 3 game on the Union Grounds in the Collar City:

> The Haymakers for the second time this year [got] away with the "invincible" Mutual club of New York—winning the game by a score of 37 to 16. The Mutuals came up, accompanied by a large crowd of their betting friends, very confident of winning, in three innings were freely offered and quite freely taken. About 3,000 spectators were in attendance. Both nines were promptly on the ground and amused themselves by tossing the ball around while the preliminaries were being settled. The Haymakers demoralized the Mutuals by the heaviest and safest kind of batting, while their fielding was simply superb, but very few errors being committed either in the out or in-field. Craver did splendidly, making several fly catches and some splendid stops. Bellan and Flynn did finely at third and first, as did also McGeary behind the bat. McMullin pitched very effectively, and he never filled his place with more judgment. [Outfielders] Pike, York and King each made good catches in the field, although Steve [King] dropped one fly—an excusable error. Flowers, at short, did finely, making some pretty difficult stops, and some beautiful throws. In fact, the whole nine are deserving of great praise for the fine playing. The ball was one of Van Horn's dead balls, although the way that it was batted led many to suppose it was a lively ball.[56]

The issue of which baseball was used in a game is a clue to the Haymakers' uneven performance on the diamond and was much commented on by the contemporary sporting press:

> A dead ball was used. The game occupied two hours, and was won by the Morrisania club, by a score of 12 to 10. We had expected to chronicle a victory for the Haymakers, as we knew they went away in good shape and felt

confident of winning. As it is, the defeat is not a bad one, but bad enough to disappoint the friends of the club in this city and vicinity. We presume, however, the secret of their [Morrisania's] success may be found in the fact of a dead ball having been used. The Haymakers are accustomed to playing with a lively ball, and when compelled to use a dead ball, as they were in this game, and also the Harvard game a short time since, they cannot master it with their usual effectiveness, and consequentially came out second best. As the leading clubs of the country are fast abandoning the lively ball, we think it is about time for the Haymakers to do likewise, and commence practicing immediately with the dead ball, so that when they engage in a match where it is sure to be used, they will be better prepared to handle it. We are confident that the superior batting powers, and excellent fielding qualities can be turned to as good advantage with the one as the other after a little practice.[57]

The 1870 season continued to be a roller coaster ride for the Haymakers, who would lose a game to the Harvard College club (13–25) and soon thereafter defeat the mighty Chicago White Stockings (16–11) in the Windy City:

Yesterday was another poor day for the Haymakers. Something seemed to be the matter. What it was no one could tell. The wind was high, the College ball was soft and the Haymakers were out of sorts generally, and allowed themselves to be defeated in a contest in which their friends counted on certain victory. Everyone expected that the well trained nine of Harvard College would show good qualities on the ball field. Their record hitherto has been good, but that they would be able to "get away" with the Haymakers in the manner which they did yesterday quite surprised all who were present at the game, and caused much chagrin among the supporters of our home club. There were some errors in umpiring which had their effect on the total score, but making all due allowance for these we are compelled to say that the visitors outplayed our boys, and fairly won the game.

Their batting was safe, and their fielding was sharp and sure. They insisted on playing with a light soft ball, furnished by themselves, and that together with the very effective pitching of Goodwin, told fearfully against the batting style to which our boys are accustomed. [The Haymakers were notorious for their wild hacking and slugging.] Our best batters rarely sent the ball beyond the infield, and we attribute the defeat to their inability to bat Goodwin's pitching. The Harvards have earned a splendid victory, and we look upon the defeat as the most damaging in many respects which the Haymakers have sustained this season. Still we do not lose confidence in our home champions. The best clubs have their poor days, and we know that ours is among the best. We are disappointed and

ONE. *Troy Baseball in the Amateur and Early Professional Era*

we dismiss the subject with the oft repeated remark that " base ball is mighty onsartin [sic]."[58]

When the Haymakers showed some life in August, the newspapers were enthusiastic backers of the club, but the sporting press also hinted at some (unnamed) dark doings and bad luck that dogged the team the entire season:

> There is no cloud without its silver lining. The victory of the Haymakers over the Chicago club yesterday was the silver fringe to their defeats which the Haymakers have recently sustained, and it may prove, moreover, that their hard luck has been converted into better fortune. That they won this game is not strange, for it is difficult to find nine better men in circles than the Haymaker players. That they have been unfortunate in the past is owing entirely to causes over which they had no control, and it would be well if members of the club themselves should remedy the evils [gambling? game fixing?] at which we hinted yesterday. The game with the Chicago club was a very closely contested affair. It was a hard struggle all through, and the fortunes of the day wavered from club to club up to the very last innings.[59]

The 1870 Haymakers did have their moments of greatness, as in their early season win (27–18) over the well-respected Morrisania Baseball Club of the Bronx, which had fallen on hard times with a 7–18 record for the year. Following a disastrous defeat by the Rockford, Illinois, team, Troy won a decisive contest over one of the East's long-established clubs:

> The announcement of a game between the Haymakers and the Morrisania club brought together an assemblage of about three thousand persons to witness the sport. The day was fine. The sun shone out bright and the atmosphere was clear and invigorating. In all respects a splendid day for haymaking, and the way Steve King raked in the balls in left field was a caution and a terror to the ball tossers of the other side. The Morriosania club entered he grounds confident of victory. Having won games this season from a number of crack clubs of the country, they thought they had a sure thing on the Haymakers, who were so badly beaten last week in the game with the Rockford club. This feeling was shared by their friends, who backed them in betting a considerable extent. The odds before the game commenced, were about a hundred to sixty in favor of the Morrisania club, and we understand the friends of the Haymakers gobbled up enough at these chances at these rates.
>
> The crushing defeat of last Monday instead of demoralizing our club, as many supposed it would, has proved beneficial. The managers have been working over it until now it is conceded it has a remarkably strong nine.

The Haymakers, Unions and Trojans of Troy, New York

The most of the players on the Haymaker nine did well, but Steve King is entitled to go up ahead. We presume a finer exhibition of skill on the part of a single player, was never witnessed than that made by Steve yesterday. He is credited with a clean score at the bat, and not a single miss in the field. One running catch of his was so fine as to elicit a second round of applause.

Bellan, who was placed behind the bat, gave unbounded satisfaction in that position. When he improves a little in throwing to second base, which he can doubtless do, he will give credit to the position which gave fame to his "illustrious predecessor." Hollister, was "out of sorts," and disappointed his friends. Something seemed to be wrong with him. He made two wretched blunders, and muffed several times on good throws. He batted well, however, and presuming that yesterday was one of his "blue Mondays," we predict for him a more brilliant career henceforth. Wolverton's play on third was praiseworthy, and York did finely in centre. Flowers, on account of the injury to his hand, was compelled to leave his position as shortstop and take right field. There he did nobly, and Foran did very well at short, though an entirely new position for him. Dick's play on second base was an improvement on the last game. One catch of his, taken while running in the same direction of the ball, was very fine, and deserves especial commendation. Fisher's pitching, we think, was superb. He used good judgment, and disconcerted the visitors about as much, or perhaps more, than anyone whom they have faced this season.

The Morrisania club is by no means a second-rate institution. Their catcher, Birdsall, is a safe and steady player, and accomplished all that could be expected of him under the circumstances. Pabor, who is a left-handed player, has the reputation of being a first-class pitcher, and it was expected he would "bother our boys to death." But his pitching yesterday was very wild, and when the Mowers handled the willow they managed usually to "knock it into smithereens." A large number of balls were called upon him by the Umpire, and the defeat of the visitors was measurably attributable to his unsteady pitching. Austin and Gedney [who was to play with the Haymakers in the NA] are splendid fielders, and Bass is a number one shortstop. There was some muffing on both sides—more than we have a right to expect on the part of first-rate clubs, but still the gamed was an interesting one, and was enjoyed by all who witnessed it.

[The newspaper account ends with a bit of levity in discussing some bone-headed play by the Bronx club.] The profitable little game played by the Fisher on the seventh innings furnished some amusement, and is worth relating. Fisher was on third base, Foran on second, and Bellan on first. York at the bat struck a foul ball on the right. The pitcher and first baseman both went for it, but neither secured it in time. The ball was given to Pabor, who marched leisurely along towards his position, tossing it up quite carelessly. This, being observed by Fisher, he started for home

ONE. *Troy Baseball in the Amateur and Early Professional Era*

base. Pabor seeing the movement threw to [the] catcher's position, but Birdsall not being on guard, the ball went bounding past the plate, enabling Fisher to get in, and also Foran and Bellan, thus securing three tallies and a hearty laugh all around at the expense of the boys who were so innocently "caught napping."[60]

The season also saw the revival of the Haymaker-New York Mutual rivalry that underscored the improvement and strength of the New York club. In a game in New York on August 26, 1870, the Mutuals defeated the Haymakers handily, 24–13. Troy's replacement second baseman was signaled for poor play in the field and at bat while third baseman Bellán was praised for a "fine stop" early in the match. In a game that "was only pretty good," two odd happenings, however, were memorable, one event at bat and one on the base paths:

> A point which all present could not understand occurred one time when Martin was at bat and E. Mills on first base. The ball was pitched so as [to] oblige Martin to "duck" his head to avoid it, In doing so he held the bat up over his right shoulder, and the ball, hitting the bat, glided off, and Mills, taking advantage of the accident, ran for second base. It was intimated that Martin had held up his bat to hit the ball more by design than accident; if so Martin was guilty of obstructing the catcher in catching the ball and should be declared "out." As it was rather dubious, however, the umpire (Mr. Wildey) gave a compromising decision, declared Martin "not out," and ordered Mills back to first base, so that there was no advantage gained by the accidental—or otherwise—back stroke.
>
> In the ninth inning an amusing incident occurred. McMullen hit to centre field, helping two men around, but did not start for first base himself. He supposed one of the other players would run for him, as had been done throughout the game; the others thought he wanted to run for himself, so nobody started. The ball was passed around the field, badly thrown to head off McGeary, and passed back to the benches, when it was discovered that McMullen was quietly lying off and watching the fun instead of taking advantage of several errors. Then there was a call: "Go to your base, Mac; what are you doing?" The Mutuals were also astonished, and C. Mills threw the ball so wildly to E. Mills that Flowers, who had started to run for McMullen, got clear to second base. This created a general laugh all around, which continued to almost the end of the game.

On October 6, 1870, the Haymakers and Mutuals met again at the end of a mediocre season for the Trojans. The game was again played on Brooklyn's Union Grounds before 3,000 people. The game was not memorable in any respect and the Haymakers put in an indifferent, desultory performance: "The game was not as good as many expected to see, although there were a few fine individual plays. The result should have been three to nothing in favor of the 'Mutes' instead of twelve to nine, as the Haymakers did not earn a run during the entire game."[61]

Surprisingly, the most-debated baseball story for Troy baseball in 1870 did not involve the Haymakers but another local team and a disputed national title. The Troy Putnams junior team finished the season with a 23–2 record and was generally acclaimed the country's best junior club. It was the New York Flyaways, however, who were awarded the Junior Association of Base Ball Players championship silver ball. The Putnams, who had the trophy in their possession, refused to give the silver ball to the Flyaways because that team had lost to the Putnams twice earlier in the season, by scores of 21–10 and 17–13.[62]

While a member of the National Association of Base Ball Players professional division for two years, the Troy Haymakers/Lansingburgh Unions ranked just below the top tier of baseball clubs with pitcher Cherokee Fisher going 24-9-1 in 1869. In 1870, though finishing with a mediocre 11-13-1 record in pro games (30-15-1 overall), the club continued to upgrade its roster by adding such strong players as McMullin, York, and McGeary (as captain). The spirits of Troy's supporters and players were buoyed by the team's ability to compete with the top tier baseball teams in the country. With an improved roster, solid financial backing, and an enthusiastic fan base, the Troy Haymakers desired to compete on a national level and were instrumental in forming and competing for a year and a half in the newly formed (and first) major league, the National Association of Professional Base Ball Players (NAPBBP).[63]

Two

The Collar City Rides High

The 1840 census revealed that Troy, New York, "was the fourth wealthiest city in the nation on a per capita basis."[1] Within two decades, this Upstate New York town was one of the country's leading industrial cities that became a model for other such communities with its urban markets, new technologies, abundant labor force and central transportation links in an age of hydroelectric power. Not only was Troy an economic powerhouse, but it helped define the social transformations that were affecting the region and the nation as a whole.

Troy owed its prominence as a transportation hub and as a manufacturing and trade center, primarily, to its geography. It was at the center of a diamond with Buffalo to its west, Montreal to its north, Boston to its east, and New York City to its south. More important, it was located at the "northernmost navigable reaches of the Hudson River" and "the easternmost end of the Erie Canal."[2] Equally important, the Champlain Canal to the north merged with the Erie Canal on the way to the Albany, thus avoiding the natural barrier of the rapids north of Waterford, the many abrupt changes in elevation along the Wynantskill and Poestenkill Creeks, which feed into the Hudson River, and the nearly impassable Cohoes Falls. In 1823, with the creation of a dam at the juncture of Troy-Green Island (the southernmost island in the Mohawk River), Lansingburgh[3] was opened to sloop traffic.[4]

Thus, Troy with the neighboring communities of Waterford, Cohoes, Green Island, and Watervliet (originally called "West Troy") became a prosperous manufacturing center and a trade destination in an age of hydroelectric power and water transport.

The Haymakers, Unions and Trojans of Troy, New York

Troy also had further natural advantages to bolster its early economic development. The area was rich in natural resources, had a nearby canal and river system to move both raw materials and finished products, and was close in proximity to mineral deposits of elements needed for iron production, including limestone, coal, pig iron, and dark magnetic ore:

> Iron ores from the Adirondacks were shipped down the Champlain Canal to Waterford and West Troy. Charcoals for heating the furnaces came from the charcoal maker, or collier, from the hill towns of Rensselaer County, from Albany's Pine Bush area and other parts of the Hudson Valley Sand Belt. Finished goods easily found their way west on the Erie Canal, or south to New York City and beyond.[5]

With its strategic Hudson-Mohawk Gateway location, Troy soon outstripped its already established neighboring communities of Albany, Schenectady, and Lansingburgh due to its access to inexpensive waterpower, which encouraged industrialists to establish companies in Troy. These manufacturers, in turn, proved to be a spur to population (especially European immigrant) growth as needs for labor rose sharply. Furthermore, Troy, with its impressive general and technological educational institutions, provided these industrial entrepreneurs with the necessary scientific and managerial work force to successfully run their companies.[6]

Two early voices that championed Troy's status as a first-rate nineteenth-century industrial and cultural city of prominence were Arthur James Weise (1886) and Rutherford Rayner (1925):

> Troy is not only noted for the manufacture of collars, cuffs, shirts, horseshoes, iron, steel, stoves, cars, railroad rails, surveying instruments, church bells, chains, knitting and laundry machinery, but enjoys the distinction of distributing her products in more countries than in any other city in the United States of like population and wealth.
>
> Troy has been first in many movements of national import and the achievements of Trojans form a proud heritage. There has long existed a saying that wherever one goes there is a Trojan to be found, and it is even truer that Troy products circle the globe for Troy collars, Troy laundries and Troy bells, stoves, and valves are now everywhere.[7]

From its mid-nineteenth century position as a rising industrial power and progressive city, Troy was considered a modern and desirable

Two. The Collar City Rides High

place to live with its quality-of-life amenities and intelligent and hard-working populace:

> It is the theatre of a very extensive business. The remaining portion of the place generally exhibits the quiet aspect of country. Many of the buildings, both public and private, are spacious and elegant. The court-house, built of Sing Sing marble, is a splendid edifice.... Troy is indebted in a great measure for its prosperity to its advantageous situation, and the enterprise and industry of her inhabitants.[8]

By 1825, Troy was a bustling industrial center with much of the river traffic done by ferries—the first steamboat used the canals in 1826. When the Eire Canal was completed, Troy served as the easternmost port of the waterway at West Troy (Watervliet) as did the Champlain Canal, "which emptied into the Hudson at Waterford and joined the original Eire Canal at Juncta [Cohoes] and provided a water route to Lake Champlain and Canada."

As transportation technologies developed, the ferries were replaced by area bridges to decrease costs and to increase speed. In 1835, Troy built the Saratoga and Rensselaer Railroad. The first passenger train, pulled by horses until 1853, crossed the Hudson and facilitated the movement of raw materials and people. By the 1870s, the improved railroads wee dominant; they increased the speed of transfer of goods even further and the trains cut deeply into the canals' freight industry.[9]

In the nineteenth century, Troy was the second leading producer of iron in the United States trailing only Pittsburgh. One of the leading nineteenth-century Troy iron industrialist and manufacturer was Henry Burden. He oversaw at his Troy Iron Works the creation of the largest waterwheel in the country (60 feet in diameter and 23 feet wide), the production of railroad spikes, most of the horseshoes for the Union Army during the Civil War, and the erection of local Rensselaer Polytechnic Institute's (RPI) graduate George Ferris's 36-bucket Ferris wheel. Perhaps Burden's greatest scientific achievement, however, came near the end of his career in 1865 with the development of the first American converter for the Bessemer steel process that radically changed the United States iron industry.[10]

By the mid-nineteenth century, Troy developed a reputation for scientific and commercial discovery, innovation, and success that was

The Haymakers, Unions and Trojans of Troy, New York

Burden Iron Works (above) was owned by Henry Burden, who introduced the Bessemer steel process to the United States and was a leading inventor, innovator, and industrialist of the era (collection of the Rensselaer County Historical Society, Troy, New York).

reflected in other companies, such as the Gilbert Car Company (Green Island, 1852–1895), the W and L. E. Gurley Company (maker of precision instruments, 1845 to the present), and the Meneely Bell Company (Watervliet,1826, and Troy, 1870), which produced nearly 100,000 bells until it closed its doors in 1952.[11]

A key development in nineteenth-century communications had an early presence in Troy. In 1846, the "first Morse magnetic telegraph line" was established between the Collar City and Whitehall (New York). Within four months lines were completed and messages sent from Troy to Saratoga Springs (New York), Buffalo, and New York. A turn-of-the-century observer notes the stir that this mode of communication made in the city: "The operations of this mysterious apparatus created a widespread interest in Troy and were even more inexplicable to the wondering masses than was the telephone, introduced thirty years later."[12]

John Griswold was a competitor of Henry Burden in the iron production business and with John Winslow and A. L. Holley built a two and a half-ton plant to first employ the Bessemer steel process in America. He

Burden Iron Works was powered by the Burden Water Wheel, which at 60 feet in diameter and 23 feet in width was the largest in the country. It was also said to be the most powerful vertical water wheel ever built (collection of the Rensselaer County Historical Society, Troy, New York).

was instrumental in gaining financing for the ironclad USS *Monitor* and his Rensselaer Iron Works produced some of the iron products on the war ship. Griswold also was one of the few major industrialists who supported Troy baseball in its infancy. He was the supposed financial backer for the Troy Haymakers' 1867 tour to Washington and Philadelphia[13]

The Haymakers, Unions and Trojans of Troy, New York

As water transport was being replaced by railroads in the Gateway Area in the 1870s and iron and stove production in Troy was declining with the movement of companies to the Midwest to be closer to both needed fuels and ores, Troy turned to employing its hydroelectric power sources to the manufacture of textiles, including the production of the first cotton handkerchief. However, what made Troy a national leader in the manufacture of textiles was the creation of detachable collars and cuffs. In the 1830s, 85 percent of the nation's detachable cuffs and collars were made in Troy, which was referred to as "the collar and cuff capital of the world."[14]

Furthermore, the unused textile cuttings were made into paper, felt, and shoddies [woolen yarns made from reclaimed cloth]. In 1837, the A and W Orr Company became the first paper maker to print paper with wood fiber in it, following the lead of the earliest Northern New

The Meneely Bell Foundry cast more than 100,000 bells in its century-long history (collection of the Rensselaer County Historical Society, Troy, New York).

Two. The Collar City Rides High

York paper manufacturers, who date their origins to 1792. Other Troy leading industries included breweries, brush makers, oilcloth factories, and paint factories.

All of this industrial activity in the 1860s and 1870s helped create a working class in Troy that had sufficient capital and leisure to spend on amusements, including baseball, which was championed as a particularly American activity that was outdoors, exciting, easy to understand (and play), inexpensive, and relatively short in duration with most contests lasting two hours. Troy had a successful baseball team from the 1860s onward. The Troy Haymakers were mentioned first among nine pre–1876 teams that "could compete with crack organizations of the great cities, including the Noisy Nine of Taylorville (IL), Binghamton (NY) Crickets, Rockford (IL) Forest Citys, Fort Wayne (IN) Kekiongas, London (Ontario) Athletics, Guelph (Ontario) Maple Leafs, Ogdensburg (NY) Pastimes, and the Lynn (MA) Live Oaks."[15] Troy amateur baseball was at its peak in this era among not only with the nationally celebrated Troy Haymakers but also in the schools, professions, labor organizations, and social clubs. Troy's large Irish immigrant population played for many of these clubs and also provided the devoted fans who became such a part of the Haymaker narrative.

As Troy's economic fortunes declined in the 1880s, the city's professional baseball club(s) suffered as well, with plunging attendance and shaky management, poor business plans, and insufficient funding that didn't allow the team(s) to compete for first rate baseball talent on the open market with larger and more prosperous metropolitan areas such as New York and Philadelphia.

Troy's primacy in the textile began to wane in the 1880s with the movement of manufacturing mills to the South to lessen production costs and to be nearer to its industry's cheaper and more abundant raw materials. Troy's once competitive advantage of cheap labor—at one point in the 1850s, 40 percent of the city's population was employed by local manufacturers (34,000 out of a total census of 76,000)—was undercut by many Trojans in the skilled labor force moving to more lucrative positions outside the Capital Region. Matters worsened as many of the well-established local industries refused to change as technologies in production and distribution improved and evolved.

The Haymakers, Unions and Trojans of Troy, New York

An equally significant reason for Troy's decline from its influential position as a major force in the national and regional economies was, ironically, due to what was once a major factor in its rise as an industrial power—its geographical location. A victim of its own success, Troy began to lose companies to the Midwest, which provided more spacious and less challenging terrain as industries grew and needed to expand to meet consumer demand(s). Such movement westward was also the zeitgeist of the United States in the nineteenth century, a spirit that was predicated on the inevitability of change and the desire for more self-determination and increased individual freedom(s).[16]

A further irony of Troy's late nineteenth-century economic decline was the success of its labor movement. As a new middle class emerged from the unskilled labor of the 1840s-1850s, the working class's influence was replaced by professionals, financiers, and entrepreneurs. With the growing strength of labor and craft unions, manufacturers simply abandoned Troy and moved their business to more favorable locations.[17]

Troy's rapid economic development in the nineteenth century also fueled notable achievements in both education and the arts. The Rensselaer School (later to be rechristened as "Rensselaer Polytechnic Institute") was founded by Amos Eaton (1824), a geologist and natural historian, and became the first degree-granting engineering school in the English-speaking world.[18]

In keeping with Troy's tradition of championing women's rights, Emma (Hart) Willard, who wrote one of the first histories of the United States (1828), founded a school for girls in Waterford, New York (1819), and the "Troy Female Seminary" (1821), which was the first school in the nation to teach young women the same mathematics science and social studies curricula as men experienced.[19]

Troy also was noted for and recognized as a supporter of the literary and performing arts in the nineteenth century. Herman Melville lived in Lansingburgh (1838–1844) when he published his first two novels, *Omoo* and *Typee*. On December 23, 1823, the *Troy Sentinel* first published Clement Moore's "Account of a Visit from Saint Nicholas" (better known as "Twas the Night before Christmas").

In the performing arts, the first performance of the stage version of *Uncle Tom's Cabin* occurred at Peale's Museum on River and Fulton

Two. The Collar City Rides High

The Troy Music Hall, on the second floor of the Troy Savings Bank, was established in 1870 and considered an acoustic marvel. Many famed musicians and theatrical companies performed there in the nineteenth century. It is still in use today (collection of the Rensselaer Historical Society, Troy, New York).

Streets on November 15, 1852, and ran for 150 consecutive nights. Furthermore, the Troy and Cohoes Music Halls became stops for such touring luminaries as Lillian Russell, Eddie Cantor, Al Jolson, Buffalo Bill Cody, John Philip Sousa, Sarah Bernhardt and Harry Houdini. Dedicated to the citizens of Troy in 1875 with a concert organ added in 1890, the Troy Music Hall (which today remains virtually unchanged from its original state and is located on the second floor of the Troy Savings Bank) is internationally praised for its perfect acoustics and is in use to this day.[20]

One final note that underscores Troy's progressive nature in the nineteenth century is its important historical position in the nation's civil rights movement. In 1804, Troy had an African American population of 159 (80 freed blacks and 79 slaves) in a population of 3,200. A leader in the national emancipation movement, the Reverend Henry Highland Garnet was the first minister of the first African American Troy church—Liberty Street Presbyterian Church, which was a stop on the Underground Railroad. He was also the publisher of the national abolitionist weekly newspaper, *The Clarion*. In 1841, Troy was the host of the first Negro New York State Convention, from which the NAACP evolved.[21]

By the mid-nineteenth century, Troy, New York, was an economic and industrial success story whose rapid development, growth, and achievement(s) reflected the nature of a fiercely competitive and energetic society composed of successful scientists, inventors, innovators, sportsmen,[22] and businessmen with a burgeoning (and necessary) work force that was fed by European and economic immigrants. As a prosperous city, Troy had the wherewithal to attract financial investment and quality-of-life amenities, such as superior educational institutions and a vital and thriving performing arts and literary milieu. Moreover, it had a populace with sufficient money and leisure time to support the civic status symbols and activities of any city with pretensions to national acclaim.

In the nineteenth century, one of the social and cultural amenities an ambitious citizenry and a prosperous investor class found it necessary to possess in order to lay claim to first-rate civic status on a national level was, as it remains to this day, a professional sports franchise. The Troy populace with its working immigrant class with money and leisure time, an educated populace geared to accept new challenges and changes, and capitalists eager to increase their markets throughout the nation and abroad, were all enthusiastic about acquiring a professional baseball team that would reflect the importance of their community.

By 1860, baseball was fewer than four decades old, but it could stake a claim to be the country's "national pastime." The sport acted as a unifying American experience that cut across all strata of society and provided a sense of individual and community identity to a culture that was changing at a break-neck pace.

Furthermore, baseball was attractive to many Americans because of its fast-paced nature, especially when compared to America's only other popular team sport—cricket. Spectators reveled in the many abrupt changes and surprising happenings that the sport presented.

Moreover, baseball at its core is both competitive (defeat your opponent) and cooperative (win by working together). While psychologically reassuring in providing an ideal and coherent life narrative, the national

Two. The Collar City Rides High

pastime also replicated the emerging business work model where "the common workplace shared by the ball players ... created a set of values that included a scientific world view, an appreciation of rationality, and competitiveness between groups with cooperation within them."[23] Baseball, finally, could be perceived as an extension of the developing industrial mindset, which was congruent with the tenets of industrialization and urbanization.

Thus, the United States adopted baseball as its national pastime because of its similarities to and differences from everyday existence in a fast-paced society that was challenging America's sense of individual identity. Troy with its sudden prosperity, diversified economy, and progressive nature was a modern city with national ambitions, making it an attractive location for a baseball franchise. Baseball adherents lauded the game for its supposed American nature at a time of nationalistic fervor, manifest destiny, and the melting pot. With the added pleasures of gambling and drinking while attending a game under summer skies, it is little wonder that Troy embraced baseball with such fervid devotion and enthusiasm.

Three

The National Association and the Wilds of Independent Baseball

1871

By 1871, baseball was firmly established as the national pastime, appealing to Americans' love of excitement, chance, and physical action both on the diamond and in the stands. Baseball was an amusement shared by all levels of society that had culturally-defined patriotic connotations, as revealed in the following lyrical description of a game on the Fourth of July:

> The attractions at the ball fields to-day are many and interesting, and the thousands who will seek them will do so for a two-fold purpose—to amuse themselves or be amused and escape the horrid din of exploding firecrackers, pistols, guns, and cannon which the city walls reverberate from early morn till night. Every ball field in and around the city has been engaged, and the superfluous national enthusiasm which will be worked off in this way will be greater than in any other line. There is no game that offered to our people an amusement so fitting to their tastes as base ball on this natal day. By a slight stretch of the imagination one can perceive in it the elements of pyrotechnic display. The faces of the throng, according to their sympathies, are lit up or darkened—some white, some red, some blue—according to the fortunes of this side or the other, rise and fall. And as fortune ever plays a fickle part in these contests, the crowd's visage is constantly changing hue. The ball follows the curved lines of the rocket or goes ricocheting like a hot shell upon the water. The players themselves perform gyrations that a pinwheel might imitate with honor, while all go in, go off and go out as would so many Roman candles.[1]

THREE. *The National Association and Independent Baseball*

The economy was riding high as the decade of the 1870s began. Having weathered the Panic of 1857 that was caused primarily by a European speculation bubble in the United States railroad industry and the post–Civil general deflation period during Reconstruction, Troy was eager to return to its former spendthrift ways to retain (and to improve) its position among prosperous cities in the nation. This profligate mind-set found its way to the baseball diamond where the city fathers were determined to field a winning baseball team. With committed and enthusiastic fans a supportive political class and a well-heeled and eager-to-spend ownership group, Troy was instrumental in the founding of the National Association of Professional Base Ball Players (NAPBBP or NA) in 1871.

Founded in part to have an undisputed championship to help further nationalize the game, a meeting regarding the concept of a national baseball organization (on the suggestion of Nick Young) was held in New York on St. Patrick's Day (March 17) in 1871. John W. Schoefield from Troy opened the meeting that lead to the creation of the National Association, and the Trojan was elected as major league baseball's first Secretary.[2]

With an entry fee of only $10, there was no strong commitment by the communities in question to devote much energy to the success of the endeavor. Organized as a "joint stock company," the Troy club possessed a solid business plan, which was atypical for the NA. In fact, the league in general lacked a strong organizational structure and was too dependent on gate receipts for economic survival that would insure a lasting stability for the league. However, the National Association (NA) did last five years with a total of 26 teams. Only the New York Mutuals, Philadelphia Athletics, and Boston Red Stockings fielded a team for the entire tenure of the NA, but the league did serve its stated goal of further developing public interest and extending national attention on baseball.[3]

The 1871 Troy Haymakers opened their season with a non-league tilt against another Trojan team, the Putnams. According to local reports, the retooled Lansingburgh Unions club did not make a favorable impression as they prepared for the initial NA season: "About four-hundred persons wasted three hours and a half yesterday afternoon in watching an uninteresting game between our crack local clubs. There were no extraordinary good plays, and but few even noteworthy."[4]

Troy's first major league game was on May 9, 1871, at Haymaker

Grounds (also named "Rensselaer Park") on Center Island in Lansingburgh near the confluence of the Hudson and Mohawk Rivers. The Haymakers played before an estimated 2,500 spectators. After racing to a 5–0 lead against the Boston Red Stockings, the Haymakers lost, 9–5, with what would be the team leaders in hitting and stealing demonstrating their skills in the opener: Steve King had four singles and Mike McGeary had three steals. The Haymakers' first NA victory came at Roxbury, Massachusetts, on May 16, 1871, before 3,000 disappointed fans of the Boston Red Stockings, 29–14.[5]

The Haymakers began the season well with decent fan support and victories on the diamond, though their reputation as an error-prone nine was clearly in evidence. On April 19 at home, the Haymakers drew 1,000 partisan supporters to see their club defeat the Brooklyn Athletics, 23–11, on the basis of two big innings—the first (10 runs) and the ninth (five runs): "There was some good playing and bad muffing on both sides. The Athletics earned two runs and the Haymakers seven."[6]

The 1871 Troy Haymakers, a member of the National Association, were Troy's first major league baseball club (courtesy of the National Baseball Hall of Fame Library, Cooperstown, New York).

THREE. *The National Association and Independent Baseball*

A rematch with the Brooklyn club took place a week later on April 26, 1871, before 300 fans at the Capitoline Grounds and resulted in another Haymaker victory, 17–7. In spite of winning a decisive victory against a solid club, the Haymaker play was uneven, indicating a season-long problem for the Trojan club:

[T]he fear of rain, which threatened to fall every hour, [kept] a large crowd away.... The Trojans fully anticipated returning home victors in two contests; but the match with the Atlantics which was to have been played today [April 26, 1871], is off for the present, as their club uniform was not ready for one thing and a match with the Haymakers will be played in Troy in May.
  The game yesterday [April 25, 1871] proved to be quite an interesting one, and had all of the Atlantics played their positions as well as the majority did, the Haymakers would have had difficulty in winning. But the Brooklyn nine proved to be weak at short-field and third base, and hence runs were scored by the Haymakers which were not earned ... [In the first inning] on the Haymaker side, Flynn, Megary [McGeary], and McMullin earned bases by good hits, and 2 runs were scored before the side was put out.... Thus far the game was closely contested. In the fourth innings, however, the Haymakers ran up a score of 8 runs, chiefly by the loose fielding of their opponents, the Athletics having previously broken the ice by scoring a single [run]. This deprived the game of much of its interest; but afterward the Athletics rallied in the field and at the bat, and in the ensuing four innings they not only added 5 runs to their score, but they disposed of the Haymakers for a couple of singles, thus leaving the total, at the end of the eighth innings, at 12 to 6 only, not a bad score under the circumstances. In the last innings the Brooklynites were disposed of for a single, and by as good dash at the plate for the Haymakers ran up a score of 5 in handsome style and thereby came in the victors by a score of 17 to 7. The Troy team showed want of practice, and if they do get it between now and the 9th of May, Harry Wright [captain of the Cincinnati Red Stockings] will take home a trophy from Troy, sure. The game was satisfactorily umpired by Mr. Ferguson [of the New York Mutual Club, who was to be a key member of Troy's National League entry, 1879–1882], and the contest proved to be quite a pleasant meeting.[7]

The Haymakers were always looking for the edge in their contests and were notorious for complaining and baiting both the umpire and their opponents. In a mid–June league game with the Fort Wayne Kekiongas in Indiana, the Haymaker "kicking" resulted in their being awarded a 9–0 forfeit win over the home club. The issue involved the

The Haymakers, Unions and Trojans of Troy, New York

suitability of the game ball and the Fort Wayne supporters were irate at decision of Umpire Isaac Leroy.

After complaining throughout the game about the calls of the umpire, the Troy club took another tactic to unsettle the opposition. In the top of the seventh inning, Captain Bill Craver questioned the quality of the ball. Under NA rules, the home team needed to provide a suitable ball; however, Fort Wayne denied the Haymaker charge and refused to either let Troy provide a ball or provide another ball themselves. It is reported that Trojan Lip Pike stayed at the plate for fifteen minutes until the game ball was inspected and found a "bit loose at two seams."[8]

Fort Wayne declared that they deserved a forfeit victory over Troy, arguing with great specificity that the NA rulebook favored their position:

> The game in Troy yesterday had rather an unsatisfactory termination. During the progress of the contest the ball they had been using became ripped, and the Haymakers demanded that the Kekiongas furnish them another. The Western men very promptly refused to do so, and in consequence, the umpire, Mr. Isaac Leroy, at the close of the sixth inning, declared that the game was won by the Haymakers by a score of 9 to 0. Such action on the part of Mr. Leroy was wholly unwarrantable and is without a precedent, Section 1, rule 6, governs the matter, and is as follows:
>
> "The game shall consist of nine innings to each side, when, should the number of runs be equal, the play shall be continued until a majority of runs, upon an equal number of innings, shall be declared, which shall conclude the game, unless in such cases it be mutually agreed upon by the two captains of the two nines to consider the game as drawn. But in case of no such agreement, the parties refusing to play, no matter from what cause, shall forfeit the ball, and a game thus forfeited shall be recorded as a won game by a score of nine runs to none. All innings must be concluded at the time the third hand is put out."
>
> At the time the dispute occurred, the game stood six to three in favor of the Kekiongas.[9]

On June 28, 1871, the Troy Haymakers were involved in another controversial game that set the major league record for total runs scored by both teams. The Philadelphia Athletics defeated the homestanding Trojans, 49–33, in a slugfest with each player in the game garnering a hit and run scored and all but one player having a run batted in. Both teams combined for 74 hits and 20 errors. Three Athletics' players com-

THREE. *The National Association and Independent Baseball*

bined for nineteen hits: John Radcliffe (7), Levi Meyerle (6), and Al Reach (6). (These three players are best known for other reasons: Radcliffe was banned from baseball in 1874 for trying to bribe an umpire to throw a game to the Chicago White Stockings; Levi Meyerle was the leading hitter in the NA's debut season with a .492 batting average, a .500 on-base percentage, and a .700 slugging percentage; and Al Reach was a left-handed shortstop who is best remembered for the establishment of a sporting equipment enterprise.)

Ironically, the ever-contentious Haymakers were offered a 9–0 forfeit win by the Philadelphia captain, but in deference to the large home crowd, which they did not want to disappoint by accepting the win, Troy played to the conclusion of the contest. The details of the event are as follows: Both sides were upset with the umpiring of Edward Tighe, who left his post when he was bombarded with profanity. Coaxed back to continue the game by the Trojans, Philadelphia refused to take the field unless Tighe was replaced. At this point, they offered Troy a forfeit; however, Troy management inquired if Samuel Holly (a member of the Niagara Baseball Club), who just happened to be at the game, would consent to umpire the contest. Holly agreed to do so, the Athletics concurred, and Philadelphia went on to a record-setting victory.[10]

The question of the use of regulation baseballs in Haymaker games continued throughout the 1871 NA season and was often an area of intense scrutiny and even potential violence by the offended parties. On July 3, 1871, in Troy, the Haymakers won rather handily in a contest with the visiting New York Mutuals. The outcome of the game was a forgone conclusion by the middle innings, but the Mutuals protested the use of the game ball provided by Troy:

> The Haymaker-Mutual game here [Troy] today was won by the former by a score of 37 to 16. Mr. Chapman, of the Eckfords, was umpire. The Haymakers won by a wonderful display at the bat, knocking the ball all over the field in safe positions, making second and third base hits repeatedly. The Mutuals were whitewashed five times, and the Haymakers not once. Pike made the only home run, and made a remarkable running catch, as also did Craver.
> After the game the Mutuals claimed that the ball was not regulation. It was one of Van Horn's make, and on being cut open by the umpire, the rubber was weighed in the presence of Chapman, Ferguson, and the Presi-

dent and Secretary of the Mutual Club, and found to weigh just one ounce, the regulation weight.[11]

The rematch between the Haymakers and the Mutuals took place in Williamsburg on July 13, 1871, at the Union Grounds. The game was a nail-biter, hotly contested, and ended in acrimony and near-violence by an unruly Brooklyn mob. The New York newspapers, which provided the specifics and context for the July 13 face-off, focused on the overconfidence and lack of professionalism on the part of the New York club:

> While the nine [The New York Mutuals] opened play, their first grand match was with the new and strong nine of the Haymaker Club at Troy. Like a brilliant rocket, the Mutuals went up the river, astonished the natives with a brilliant display, and marked their inaugural match of the season with a noteworthy victory. Flushed with their success, and erroneously imagining that with such a strong corps of players of note, they could ignore the fatigue and annoyance of regular training, they entered upon a series of gate-money contests, first with inferior playing nines and then with nines not thoroughly organized, and of course met with a degree of success that only confirmed them the more in the previous notion that they possessed an invincible nine. But they were doomed to have a rather painful awakening to the real state of the case, and the first notice that they received was at the hands of the self-same Haymaker nine, who, after getting well into practice, came down to the City and polished off the "invincibles" by a score of 25 to 10. This lesson should have been profited by, but it was not, and so things went on in the same old way, until the Mutuals lost their prestige of being the coming champions, and within the past three weeks the crack team of the Metropolis has gradually fallen step by step in the ranks of the championship contestants.[12]

A competing daily newspaper focused on the long-standing enmity between the clubs that reached incendiary heights at the July 3, 1871, game in Troy:

> [There has been] considerable ill feeling for a long time between the Mutual base ball players and the Haymaker players, and the matter has been taken up by their respective partisans. The Mutuals on various occasions have met with somewhat hard treatment in Troy, and having been whipped in every contest with the Haymakers' nine, excepting one, which has taken place in Troy, has not tended to increase their pleasant recollections of the classically named city. On the last occasion of their visit that city there was undoubtedly a pretty considerable muss, and although there

THREE. *The National Association and Independent Baseball*

was no blow struck, matters wore a very threatening appearance. The "Mutes" on their return, stated how they had been *threatened with bats*, and some of the newspapers having commented in pretty severe terms on the conduct of the Trojans, the public came to the conclusion that the 'Mutes" had been very badly treated.[13]

All the reports of the day emphasized the rancor and unacceptable violence of a few spectators, the restraint displayed in the measured protective crowd control of the police, and the threat of such behavior on the future viability of baseball itself. Such unacceptable rowdy behavior when coupled with an ineffectual league structure and rampant gambling was a serious threat to the game:

> The game of yesterday was witnessed by a large crowd of deeply-interested spectators, and so confident were the Mutual betting crowd of the success of the nine that they invested at the odds of $100 to 60 on the Mutuals. Their chagrin may be imagined when they saw the game terminate as it did, with a [9–7 run] victory for the Haymakers, and they took the petty revenge of gratifying their ill temper at the expense of the visiting Club, for at the close of the contest, some of the members of the Club attacked those of the Haymaker Club, and but for the protection of the Police the Haymakers would have been roughly used. The Officers of the Club interposed, but the "heelers" were bound for mischief. This is the first time the Union Grounds have been disgraced by such a scene. It is to be hoped that the Club will promptly punish those of their members—but two we believe—who participated in the attack on the Troy nine, for it is too their pecuniary interests as well as for the good name of their organization that it should be done.[14]

The post-game antics of the July 13 Brooklyn spectators were the real story of the day, though all the sports reports stated that while the Haymakers were out hit 8–13, the game "was won by the fielding." The *New York Herald* provided a more detailed and impassioned reprise of the day's events:

> At the conclusion [of the game], however, some East New York rowdy, either embittered by the loss of his stamps or inflamed by some yarn of the Mutual partisans [the New York Mutuals' player Dick Higham is the chief suspect as the one who sucker-punched the Troy player], attacked Flynn, the Haymakers' first baseman, in the *most cowardly* manner, cutting his mouth open. Considering the inflamed state of the public this was the spark which was wanted to create a riot second only to the bloody scenes which took place in New York Wednesday,[15] and had it not been for the

energetic and prompt movements of the police, assisted by several respectable members of the crowd, there would undoubtedly have been a grand free fight, which would have been a disgrace to the Mutual Club and every one [sic] connected with it. Fortunately the police were prompt in their action, and as many of the Troy players as were in the vicinity of the reporters' box were collected together and marched, under the escort of the police and a number of private citizens, to their coach, which was at the lower side of the grounds. The decided manner in which the police acted prevented the row from spreading any farther, although an ex-officer of the club showed very little sense in striking one of the directors of the Haymaker Club, Mr. McDonald, in the face, and using disgraceful language to him. Such conduct on his part was very likely to have created such a melee as would not easily have been stopped. Mr. Flynn completely exonerated the Mutual players from having any hand in the assault on him, and so far the affair is more satisfactory than it might have been. Such conduct, however, is disgraceful to the extreme, and if indulged in often will put a stop to the game entirely.

Violent crowd behavior lessened quantitatively in the 1870s but increased in intensity with Troy supporters being perceived as the most partisan and disruptive: "[The Troy club] was reputed to be the worse for visiting teams, acting as perfect hosts before and after, but ruthless hucksters, during, every game 'like the South Sea Islander, who fattens his victims, and then eats him, the Trojan has always allowed the baseball visitor to be cordially treated to a game, and then to be artificially flayed."[16]

A further controversy in the Haymakers' first season of play in the NA was the continuing saga of Bill Craver, who was the center of a lingering contract dispute between the Chicago White Stockings and the Troy club that was not settled until late October, after the 1871 Great Chicago Fire left the Windy City team homeless and Troy hosted two money games to help the orphaned Chicagoans:

The White Stocking Difficulty—The White Stockings have informed the Haymakers that they will not suffer Craver to play in any game against them, nor will they allow the Haymakers to play any other club on the Chicago grounds if Craver is one of the nine. The directors of the Haymaker club held a meeting Saturday evening to consider the ultimatum, and adjourned until Tuesday without taking decided action. It is understood that Craver refuses to play in Chicago anyhow, and he has excellent reasons for this refusal. The *Chicago Times* takes ground against the White Stockings for retaining the Haymaker money, and very properly stigmatizes

THREE. *The National Association and Independent Baseball*

the act as robbery. It says that a corporation may escape punishment for doing what an individual would be sent to break stone at Joliet.[17]

The Craver controversy continued to fester and remained unresolved throughout the summer of 1871:

> The Chicago-Haymaker Difficulty—Chicago Declines to Play Craver—The managers of the White Stocking club persist in their determination not to play the Haymakers with Craver in the nine and all chance for a series of games between these clubs this season seems to be beyond the range of probabilities. The Haymakers having, as they claim, presented a legal nine, and one which has been accepted by all the clubs in the country except the Chicagos, will bring the matter before the championship committee of the National Association, and demand that they be credited with the series which the Whites have refused to play. The correspondence between the two clubs culminated in a dispatch received here from Chicago on Saturday. The Whites first demanded to know whether the Haymakers would play them without Craver. To this a negative answer substantially was refused; whereupon they replied that they had leased the grounds to the Brooklyn Stars for the days set down in the Haymaker programme [sic] to play in Chicago.[18]

In a grudge match in Brooklyn in early October, the New York Mutuals concluded their season series with the Troy Haymakers with a solid victory that in the eyes of one game reporter may have been influenced by inexplicable betting trends prior to the contest:

> Yesterday afternoon [October 2, 1871], the Union Grounds, Williamsburg was the scene of the fifth and last game of the series between the Mutuals, of this city, and the Haymakers, of Troy. As a whole the contest was a fine one, sharp fielding and good batting being the rule rather than the exception. It will be remembered that of the four games previously played by these clubs the Haymakers won three and with that, too, with apparent ease: but for some reason, which is as yet unexplained, the betting was greatly in favor of the Mutuals—almost two to one—and that, too, in face of the fact that Wolters was quite sick with chills and fever. However, the result justified the outlay which the backers of the New Yorkers laid: for they won the game most handsomely, by a score of sixteen to six.... At the bat Start and Keeler took the lead for their club, while Flowers and Craver led the Haymaker score. In the field all, with the exception of King and Flynn, did very well. McGeary filled his position behind the bat as creditably as ever, which is, indeed, saying a great deal, for McMullen was at times quite wild in his delivery.[19]

Troy finished in sixth place in the 1871 NA season with a record of

13–15. They won championship series from New York and Rockford, tied Cleveland and Chicago, and lost to Boston, Philadelphia, and Washington D.C.

The Haymakers experienced a season-long, win one-lose one pattern. The last week of July was emblematic of the Trojans debut NA season with Troy's reputation for unruly crowd behavior and disreputable play frequently being commented on by their opponents and the sporting press. On July 28, 1871, the Haymakers won a match (10–6) against the Washington (DC) Olympics:

> Both nines with their managing directors left Troy on the *Neversink* last evening, while a number of the Haymakers' friends departed at a later hour on the *Vanderbilt*. Both boats arrived in good season in New York. During the morning it was reported by some New Yorkers that some of the rowdies who frequent the Union grounds were intending to whip Pike and Craver, but the report was not believed. To guard against contingencies, however, an extra squad of policemen was kept upon the ground until the match was over.
>
> About fifteen hundred spectators were present during the game, and they had the satisfaction of witnessing a game in which both nines did their best to win, and yet managed to keep on the best terms with each other. The fielding was almost if not quite up to the standard of Thursday's game in Troy [a 3–3 tie]. The only important error on the Haymaker side can be attributed to Bellan and Flowers, and this was to some extent excusable....
>
> The outfielders had more work than usual, but fielded well. No two clubs in the country can surpass the Haymakers and Olympic outfielders. King, by two terrific hits, did much to win the game. He brought in three runs by these hits.
>
> The betting at the commencement of the game was about even, but afterward Haymaker stock grew in favor, and odds of one hundred to eighty were offered and accepted upon them.[20]

A week later, the Haymakers travelled to Brooklyn, and amid the now commonplace controversy over what type of baseball to use in the contest and an injury to the starting catcher, the Upstate club lost to the homestanding Eckfords, 7–10:

> The Haymakers can't bat [Phonney] Martin's pitching. There is some peculiar twist in the ball as thrown by him that they cannot overcome. Being unable to bat the ball, of course the Mowers were defeated by the lads with the orange-hued stockings. Luck was against the Trojans from the start. All

Three. The National Association and Independent Baseball

of the fatal errors and accidents told against their score. In the second inning Flynn was disabled by having one of his fingers broken in catching a ball thrown hot by Bellan. Connors was substituted, and although he managed the base effectively and even brilliantly, he was worthless at the bat. In the eighth inning McGeary was struck in the mouth with the ball and knocked down. This unfortunate occurrence gave the Eckfords a run which they were not entitled. McGeary played second base during the rest of the game, while Craver stationed himself behind the bat.

The umpire did not decide according to the rules in the ninth inning, and the Haymakers lost at least two runs thereby. York and Flowers were on second and first; Connors was at the bat. Instead of giving the last named his base on called balls, and thereby advancing both of the others, the umpire ruled him out on three strikes when he was entitled to first. Connors [Ned Connor] for the Haymakers and Martin of the Eckfords did the lion's share of the work for their respective nines, and did it well. Two very pretty stops were made at third, one by Bellan and one by Nelson. About sixteen hundred people were present.

Before the game commenced a dispute occurred as to which club should furnish the ball. Both ostensibly offered Ryan a dead ball, but neither was inclined to accept the one offered by the other. At last the ball proffered by the Haymakers was accepted by the Eckfords.[21]

A final benefit November 2, 1871, exhibition game between the Troy Haymakers and the NA 1871 runners-up Chicago White Stockings, who lost in October to the Philadelphian Athletics, 1–4, was played in Troy after the Great Chicago Fire destroyed the Windy City's entire franchise. The game drew fewer than 100 fans.[22]

It had been a year for firsts and the Haymaker players contributed a number of outstanding performances on the diamond with Lip Pike leading the club as its most proficient hitter and as its first manager. Formerly with the 1869–1870 Brooklyn Atlantics, right Fielder Lipman Pike was the first Jewish player and the first Jewish team captain (who served as field manager in nineteenth-century baseball) in major league baseball history. (Pike was replaced as a manager after a 1–3 start by teammate and Troy native Bill Craver, who finished the season going 12–12.) Pike was also a bust as a manager in three brief minor league stints in the 1870s with a total win-loss percentage of less than .300).

Pike was the 1871 Haymaker team leader in a number of batting categories: doubles (10), triples (7), RBIs (39), and slugging percentage (.654); he was second in batting average (.377) to team leader Steve King

(.396). Lip Pike was also professional baseball's first great slugger, leading the NA in home runs from 1871 to 1873 with totals of 4–6–4 circuit blasts. He also was second in the NA in slugging percentage (.654), third in total bases (85), fourth in runs batted in (39), and sixth in batting.[23]

Lip Pike was a legendary slugger for many years prior to his 1871 debut with the NA's Troy Haymakers. As early as July 16, 1866, he was being acknowledged for prodigious feats of power hitting: "Lipman Pike of the Athletics of Philadelphia hit six home runs, five in succession, against the Alerts of Philadelphia. Final score is 67–25." That same year Pike along with two Philadelphia Athletics players was accused of receiving payment for play in strict violation of NABBP rules. Neither Pike nor his teammates attended a hearing to address the claim that they received $20 a game and nothing came of the NABBP's directive. Thus, Lip Pike indirectly helped move baseball from a much ignored and abused status as a stated all-amateur endeavor to a professional business in a matter of a few years.[24]

The major leagues' first Jewish player, Lip Pike, was also the Haymakers' first manager and hitting star (courtesy of the National Baseball Hall of Fame Library, Cooperstown, New York).

In his pre–major league days, Lipman Pike played for strong East Coast baseball clubs, including the New Jersey Irvingtons (1867), the New York Mutuals (1867–1868), and the Brooklyn Atlantics (1869–1870). His numbers as a part-time player in 1868 are off the charts with a .497 batting average and a .661 slugging percentage. Pike topped those numbers

THREE. *The National Association and Independent Baseball*

in 1869 in his first year as a starting player with a .610 average at the plate and an eye-popping .883 slugging percentage. As an outfielder, first baseman and second baseman (though he was a left-handed thrower), Pike held his own in the field in 1871 with a .898 fielding average. However, Lip Pike's status as an elite ball player rests on his batting prowess that was evident in his first NA game (which was his one and only victory as a manager): "The heavily favored Mutuals were soundly defeated by the Haymakers of Troy, in Brooklyn, 25–10. Lipman Pike, the Troy second baseman, collected six hits."[25]

Lip Pike's playing career ended the same way it began in 1866, with a controversy over a pay-for-play scheme. Pike was banished from the NL for suspicious play with the Worcester Ruby Legs. After another productive season with the bat in 1878 (.324) for the Cincinnati Reds, Pike drifted to the minor leagues where he played for Springfield, Holyoke, and Albany, which was directly across the Hudson River from his former club, the Troy Haymakers where he made his impressive professional debut in 1871. Pike played for Albany until the club folded in July of 1880; he then hooked on with the Brooklyn Unions and the New York Mets, the country's last two white independent baseball teams in the country.[26]

Pike then caught on with another old team—the Brooklyn Atlantics (now a minor league team)—until he was recalled to the major leagues on August 27, 1881, with Worcester. Hitting a woeful .120 for the Massachusetts club, Pike was suspended on September 3, 1881, for three errors in the ninth inning of a game with the Red Stockings that led to two runs and a 3–2 Boston victory. At the September 29, 1881, owners' meeting at Saratoga Springs, New York, Pike with eight other NL players (including former Troy Trojan Ed Caskin) was placed on a black list that was to remain in effect until a unanimous vote of the clubs would declare the player in question be eligible to be reinstated. After a year's banishment, Pike declined offers to return to professional baseball.[27]

Lipman Pike was lionized as one of the first great stars: "Pike was the center fielder of the Atlantics of Brooklyn in their palmist days and as an all-round batsman, fielder and base runner he had few if any superiors. He was a left-handed batsman and in his day could hit the ball as hard as any man in the business. He was a right field hitter and during his career had sent balls over the right field fence of nearly every park in which he had played in."[28]

In their initial NA season, the Troy Haymakers finished second in fielding (.845) for the season and replacement infielder Ned Connor—a .212 hitter with only two RBIs on the season in seven games as a utility infielder—had 20 putouts at first base on August 6, 1871, in a non-league game versus the Brooklyn Eckfords. However, fielding was a major weakness of the Troy club, which committed 209 errors in league games. Inconsistency was the hallmark of the Haymaker defense. For example, when Connor was pressed into duty in the outfielder, he committed four errors in nine total chances. The 1871 Haymakers achieved what success they did on the diamond because of their aggressive base running and batting prowess. In fact, Troy was a hitting machine with a .308 team batting average.[29]

One of the Haymakers leading fielders in 1871 was catcher Mike McGeary, who broke into organized baseball with the Lansingburgh Unions at the age of 19 in 1870 when the team was a member of the NAPBBP. The young backstop led the 1871 NA catchers in fielding percentage at .897 with no passed balls for the entire 29-game schedule. McGeary was a productive hitter with a .262 batting average; but he reigned supreme on the base paths, leading the NA with twenty steals. McGeary went on to have a solid 11-year career in the NA and NL possessing a .276 career batting average as a catcher and, in later years, as a standout infielder, playing most frequently as a second sacker. It is curious to note that the diminutive player never hit a single home run in his professional baseball career.[30]

John "Lefty" McMullin was Mike McGeary's battery mate with the 1870 Lansingburgh Unions and with the 1871 Troy Haymakers. McMullin had a 12–15 won-lost record with a very high 5.53 earned run average. In fact, McMullin led all NA pitchers in hits allowed (430), runs (352), earned runs (153) and walks (75). On August 17, 1871, McMullin set a major league record for pitching futility that has been unmatched to this day: he threw ten wild pitches in the ninth inning of a loss to the Brooklyn Eckfords, 13–15. In spite of his inconsistency on the mound in 1871, McMullin pitched 249 of the 250 innings the Haymakers played that season. (Haymaker starting shortstop Dickie Flowers pitched the

THREE. *The National Association and Independent Baseball*

one inning not pitched by workhorse McMullin. Flowers was a middle infielder who hit .314 with 18 runs batted in in 21 games and fielded at a .767 clip for the 1871 Troy club.) Playing in the NA until its demise in 1875, McMullin had only two more pitching decisions (both wins) and played in the outfield, hitting a respectable .284 for his career.[31]

The 1871 Troy Haymakers roster reflected the rather progressive nature of the city itself with, for example, the inclusion of major league baseball's first Latin player, Cuban Steve Bellán. May 9, 1871, marked the debut of Haymaker third baseman Esteban ("Steve") Bellán, the first Latin American ball player in major league history.[32] Bellán ("the Cuban Sylph") arrived in America in 1863 during the island's unsettled days of seeking its independence from Spain. He studied at St. John's College on what is now the Rose Hill Campus of Fordham University. Bellán competed in schoolboy interscholastic and collegiate baseball[33] as well as playing on the NABBP 1868 national champion Morrisania Unions; in 1873, he played for the NA New York Mutuals until June 9, 1883 when he returned to Cuba. The bulk of Bellán's career in the United States was his four-year tenure with the Lansingburgh Unions (1869–1872). Steve Bellán's best day as a hitter took place for the Troy Haymakers in an August 4, 1871, tilt with the Boston Red Stockings at Troy's Center Island Field in which the young Cuban had five hits, five runs batted in, two runs scored and a stolen base.

After becoming a naturalized citizen of the United States in 1874, Bellán returned to his native Cuba for the rest of his life. He was a .252 contact hitter in the NA with no career home runs in 1871–1872. However, on December 27, 1874, the Cuban Sylph hit three home runs for Havana in the first organized baseball game in his country that resulted in a 51–9 victory for Havana over Matanzas. Bellán was a player-manager for Havana from 1878 to 1886, winning Cuban championships in 1878–1879, 1879–1880, and 1882–1883.

Esteban Bellán's influence on baseball went far beyond his on-field and organizational accomplishments. During its long fight with Spain for independence, Cuba rejected the Spanish traditional violence and bloodletting of bullfighting and embraced another more cooperative sport from a neighboring country. It was from this modest beginning initiated by Bellán in Cuba that baseball became a "frenzy" that spread throughout the Caribbean, where even today the sport is second only to soccer in participation and popularity: "The baseball fever is spreading in Cuba and nearly all the leading towns will be represented in the contest for the championship in 1879–1880 which will commence next October.... A prominent club of Havana contemplates importing a first-class pitcher and other professionals from the United States." Baseball was becoming an international sport in Latin America.[34]

Another newcomer to organized baseball who contributed to the Trojans debut season in the NA was left fielder Tom York, who had a solid fifteen-year major league career in the NA, NL, and the American Association (AA) and a decade-long minor league East Coast managerial career from 1888 to 1898, including the NL Providence Grays from 1888 to 1891. In 1871 for the Haymakers, Tom York batted .255 with five doubles, seven triples, nine walks, and two home runs (second on the club) with 23 runs batted in 29 games. For his career, York had a .877 fielding average that was 40 points above the average player, and he hit .273.

Tom York was also not a person whom controversy dogged except for his turbulent year in 1886 as a major league umpire. He was hired by the AA to umpire for the 1886 season. However, after a May 22, 1886, game in Baltimore in which the home team lost 1–2 to the Louisville Colonels, the *Baltimore Sun* reported that York had abruptly quit umpiring: "He telegraphed his resignation... for the abuse he received from some of the spectators of Saturday's game. In fact, he was nearly equal to that of John Kelly, 'the king of umpires.' He declared Browning's hit near the foul line a fair hit. He was in the best position to know, but, as it was made at a critical point, some of the audience objected, and York came in for pretty severe abuse."

In a few weeks, York was hired to umpire in the National League. On June 30, 1886, the Kansas City Cowboys lost a home game to the New York Giants, 5–11, and according to the *Chicago Inter-Ocean*, York "was escorted from the grounds by the police on account of disapproval manifested over his umpiring." The final straw for York was a game at the Polo Grounds between the Philadelphia Quakers and New York, and after the game he sent a telegram to NL president Nicholas Young in which he resigned his position: "I'm have been badly treated in the West,

THREE. *The National Association and Independent Baseball*

but to be hissed and hooted at in the East is too much. I have often heard that an umpire's position was a thankless one, but I have never realized it before. It is bad enough to be hissed and called a thief, but in the West when the local club loses the umpire is fortunate if he escapes with his life." Tom York never umpired another baseball game in his life.[35]

In spite of the signing of such 1871 players as Pike, McGeary, McMullin, Bellán and York, the Troy management was tireless in attempting to upgrade their roster. At times, the pursuit and contract signings of top players became morally and ethically dubious. In their continual quest to upgrade their roster at any cost, the Troy Haymakers were involved in a messy contract dispute with pitching star Candy Cummings, who was a notorious serial revolver (contract jumper). In September of 1871, Lip Pike signed a contract for $2,000 dollars to be paid in twelve equal payments. Having previously signed with Troy, Cummings demanded a $400 advance after learning of Pike's financial arrangement. At a meeting with Haymaker representatives in New York City during the first week of October, Cummings stated that he would sign with the Philadelphia Athletics as Troy had violated his contract. Declaring that they signed Cummings in good faith, Philadelphia withdrew its contract offer because it was reported that Mrs. Cummings wished to live in New York City. The New York Mutuals then signed Cummings for the 1872 NA season.

Such complicated involvement with talented but unscrupulous baseball players heightened Troy's reputation for duplicity and gamesmanship. Cummings's late and *pro forma* apology included a disclaimer that the Haymakers were not at fault in this matter, but such a ploy did little to change the public perception of either the star pitcher or the Troy organization:

> The Haymakers recently relieved Cummings from the contract which he had entered into with them and received from him a suitable apology. After the release, Cummings with the lack of sense which has distinguished all his sayings and doings in regard in regard to this affair, published a card in the *New York Clipper*, reflecting on the ability of the Haymakers to pay him. Director Egolf replied in this week's *Clipper* and gives a complete narration of the affair, given with Cummings's written apology [reprinted in full in this article] which he indited [sic] on the 5th of this month in order to secure his release.

Haymaker Director Egolf added the following note after Cummings's apology:

> Now, Mr. Editor, my purpose is to vindicate the Haymaker Club against the false charge of having acted dishonorably. Our officers and directors are well known men of business, who mean to transact all matters pertaining to the management of the club in a fair and honorable manner; and I feel assured that the public, after reading this statement, will decide that in the matters therein referred to we have pursued throughout and honorable and straightforward course.[36]

1872

The 1872 Troy Haymaker season began with high hopes for a successful year both on the field and at the box office. The community was eager for the season to begin. This enthusiasm even extended to the Troy Public Library, which created a logo for the club that embraced the "Haymaker" name and included a haystack, scythe, pitchforks, and water jug. Backed by a management team with $30,000 in capital stock and a willingness to spend to replenish and to improve a depleted roster — only Steve King and Steve Bellán returned from the 1871 club—Troy built an imposing team with Chicago players—Jimmy Wood, Bub McAtee, George Zettlein, Charlie Hodes, and Mart King.[37] Troy also raided the Washington (DC) Olympics for star players Davy Force and Doug Allison and developed two rookies—Count Gedney and Alphonse ("Phonney") Martin—who made major contributions to the club on the diamond.

A Civil War veteran with the 9th New York Infantry, Alphonse Martin had a brief, rather undistinguished major league career as a pitcher and right fielder. He played for the 1872 NA Troy Haymakers until they disbanded in July. After Troy folded, Martin and his fellow Troy teammates Doug Alison, Candy Nelson, Count Gedney, Jimmy Wood, and George Zettlein finished the NA season with the hapless Brooklyn Eckfords (3–26), a team he played for previously in more successful times. Some researchers posit that Martin even had a brief and unsuccessful managerial stint (1–8) with the 1872 Eckfords. In 1873, Martin played for an old opponent, the New Mutuals, before retiring from the game at the

THREE. *The National Association and Independent Baseball*

end of that year's schedule. His NA career statistics are a .243 batting average (though he did hit .303 in his brief stay in Troy) and a subpar .747 fielding average; on the mound, he had a career 3–10 record with a 4.03 earned run average.

Phonney Martin's best years were prior to the establishment of major league baseball and culminated in the Brooklyn Eckfords 1869 illustrious season, in which they laid claim to the United States championship by winning a series with the New York Mutuals, the reigning pennant holder. On July 3, 1869, Phonney Martin surrendered five runs and 10 hits in a July 3, 1869, rout of the New Yorkers, 31–5.

An unsettling pattern became apparent in Martin's mound appearances in his career: he would first baffle and dominate a club's hitters the first time he faced a team, but he would be soundly defeated in subsequent meetings. For example, on June 6, 1869, Martin limited the New Mutuals to one run and three hits in five innings in a rain-shortened game. In a return match a week later, the Mutuals turned the tables on Martin in a 24–8 victory.

This roller coaster pattern of early victories and subsequent losses is in all probability due to the slow pace of his pitches, which kept hitters new to his throws off-balance at the plate. He is believed to be among the first nineteenth-century hurlers to throw a curve ball, and it is claimed he did so as early as 1862. The *New York Clipper* of April 3, 1869, described Phonney Martin as follows: "His style is peculiar, being neither slow nor swift, but a 'happy mean.' He is an extremely hard pitcher to hit for the ball never comes in a straight line, but in a tantalizing curve." This ability of Martin's to keep batters off-stride, especially a team of free-swingers, is evidenced in an exhibition game on October 1, 1869, at the Union Grounds between his Eckfords and his future employers the Troy Haymakers, Martin was the winning pitcher for the Brooklyn club, 23–19 in 8 innings. His curve resulted in 23 fly outs.

The year 1872 also saw the quiet but immeasurable influence of Troy's new backstop Doug Allison on the fortunes of the Haymakers. Recognized as "…the best and most sure-handed ball-catcher in the land," Allison was the starting catcher for the 1869 Cincinnati Red Stockings club that completed that season undefeated and had an accomplished ten-year major league baseball career. Doug Allison was a strong candidate for most valuable player on the 1872 Haymakers, hitting .307 and fielding his position at a .883 rate, which was second in the NA. He also placed second in the league in games played (40) and putouts (182) and third in assists (30). As with many of his Troy teammates, Allison finished the 1872 NA season with the Eckfords. He continued his superior play that year, hitting .337 and fielding .863 for the woeful Brooklyn club.

With such a talented roster, Troy found itself in first place in the NA as late as May 24, 1872, with an 11–3 record. By July 7, the Haymakers were 12–10 and the team was disbanded for financial reasons on July 24, 1872. Other compelling reasons that have been offered as contributing factors to the failure of the 1872 Haymakers, include too many "money" games played in the Capital District and a non-existent NA pennant race with the runaway success of the Boston Red Stockings.[38]

In 1872, the Troy club again was strong at the plate with a .300 team batting average, good for third highest in the NA. Gedney at .412 and Force at .398 paced the Haymakers (third in the NA), and all Troy regulars with the exception of Bellán and McAtee hit above .300 with seldom-used utility player Candy Nelson hitting .350.

Force was more than a top-of-the-order table-setter for the Haymakers; he was a sure-handed fielder and savvy base runner. In fact, in later years, Haymaker shortstop Davy Force was considered by some baseball observers to be an earlier, pint-sized version on all-time great Honus Wagner (standing 5'4" and weighing 130 pounds). In 1872, Force played for Troy, and, after the Haymakers folded in mid-season, for the Baltimore Canaries. Force led the NA with a .412 average. Davy Force averaged .334 in his two-year NA career; however, he was less successful at the plate in a ten-year NL career, hitting only .211. Davy Force was known primarily as a slick-fielding middle infielder who was often said to be in a class with Cincinnati's George Wright, the premier shortstop of the early 1870s. His career fielding average was .896, which was 48 points above the NL average.

Davy Force played a prominent if unintended role in the death of the NA and the birth of the National League (NL). In 1874, Force signed two NA contracts. He signed first with the Chicago White Stockings and then with the Philadelphia Athletics, who provided the shortstop with

THREE. *The National Association and Independent Baseball*

a financially more attractive offer. National Association president Bob Ferguson, who would soon play for and manage the NL Troy Trojans, declared that the Chicago contract was null and void because it was tendered before the 1874 NA season was completed. The Chicago newspapers excoriated Force and the NA decision in a classic case of sour grapes: "He [Davy Force] is a base-ball hack who has seen his best days as was amply demonstrated last season. He is intemperate, a constant kicker, a grumbler and a constant source of trouble to any club that employs him. Let him go by all means." White Sox owner William Hulbert was so upset with the decision against him that he began making plans in earnest to establish a new major league. Those plans came to fruition with the establishment of the National League in 1876.[39]

William Hulbert was the owner of the famed Chicago White Stockings, co-founder of the National League, and National League president from 1876 to 1882. Hulbert accepted Troy's application to enter the NL in 1879 and protected the franchise until his death in 1882 (courtesy of the National Baseball Hall of Fame Library, Cooperstown, New York).

The Trojans were much improved defensively with a team fielding average of .861 (third in the NA) with Gedney and Force leading the league at their positions. Likewise, the Haymakers were much improved on the mound with a team ERA of 2.60 (second in the NA), almost three runs fewer than they surrendered in 1871.[40]

The Troy Haymakers were "the offensive surprise of the league" in 1872. On an individual level, the hitting surprise of the season was provided

The Haymakers, Unions and Trojans of Troy, New York

by the spectacular nine-game debut of Haymaker left fielder Alfred "Count" Gedney. On April 27, 1872, Gedney began a hot streak at the plate that lasted until the Haymaker's withdrawal from the NA for financial reasons in mid-season. In his nine appearances with the Troy club, Count Gedney had 20 hits in 47 at-bats for a .426 batting average with 18 runs batted in and a .681 slugging percentage. He also had three of his five career home runs during this streak. These numbers were astronomically higher than his four-year NA career totals of a .251 batting average and a .319 slugging percentage. Count Gedney also had his highest fielding percentage of his career at .933, which was significantly higher than his career average of .846. While Count Gedney was a serviceable NA player, he burst on the scene with a notable bang in his brief tenure with the Troy Haymakers.

As with many team and individual accomplishments, however, there was a backstory that undermined The Haymakers' reputation as an unmatched hitting team. The Trojans continued to be almost unbeatable when using their "lively" baseball; their opponents, however, considered them an average offensive team because of their swing-from-the-heels approach to hitting and their lack of "scientific" batting. However, this reputation does not bear close scrutiny. Some 1872 Haymakers had strong on-base percentages and were willing to work the count to get a base on balls. Perhaps the most proficient such Trojan was John "Candy" Nelson, who broke into major league baseball by playing four games in the middle infield for the 1872 Troy club. He hit .350 with seven hits and four runs batted in before joining his teammates' exodus to the Brooklyn Eckfords after the Haymakers folded in mid-season. In his twelve-year major league career (which was almost equally divided among the NA, NL, and AA), Nelson was an average player with a .251 batting average and a .872 fielding average. However, he had a very good batting eye with league-leading walk totals in 1874, 1884, and 1885 and second-place finishes in 1875 and 1883. Nelson returned to Troy in 1879, the Trojans' first season in the NL, and enjoyed a season that closely approximated his career numbers.[41]

The Haymakers were a good club in 1872, a fact reflected in their battles with the formidable Boston Red Stockings team throughout the season. On May 29, 1872, for example, Boston won a see-saw affair

THREE. *The National Association and Independent Baseball*

against the Haymakers in Troy, 10–7: "[The game was] very unevenly played on both sides, one inning being distinguished by extra good fielding, and another by brilliant muffing. The errors were about equally balanced, but those of the Bostons were generally made when they could best afford.... [T]he game was won by the superior judgment and discipline of the Boston nine." Among the highlights of this contest were three Boston double plays from George Wright (SS) to Ross Barnes (2B) to Charlie Gould (1B). The Trojans had three hits by Steve King and 16 putouts at first base by Bub McAtee.

Troy newspaper reports of the May 29 Troy loss were in agreement with those of the downstate regional papers in reviewing Troy's first home loss of the season, though Captain Jimmy Wood was taken more directly to task for his poor field generalship:

> The Troy Haymakers [did not add] any fresh laurels to their record in the game yesterday. The game at the bat was fairly played. In the field it was a variable exhibition. At times the fielding was perfect, at others there was a looseness about it that would have done discredit to third rate clubs. The Red Stockings won due to superior discipline and judgment. This discipline the Haymakers seemed to lack and at times they became seriously demoralized. Captain Wood in the game gave remarkable exhibitions of poor judgment. He showed an ignorance of the points almost equal to that of the gentleman who occasionally writes and prints for the *Troy Press* about the national game to a Mr. Chadwick. In the first inning he placed his fielders too far out, an error which gave the Red Stockings four runs. In the sixth, when the visitors were having trouble punishing Zettlein, he sent that individual to right field, and placed the ball in the hands of Martin. This change, through bad playing, resulted in three runs for the Bostons.

Wood was also taken to task for his own sloppy play in the field, which highlighted a comedy of miscues and uninspired and inattentive play:

> Wood also missed two chances for double plays and ran his men around the bases with poor judgment. If the Haymakers had not batted stronger than in any previous game, their defeat would have been total. Allison failed to secure several easy fouls, and on one occasion threw the ball to second base when that position was vacant; Zettlein pitched with less than his usual deliberation in the first inning; Force, the incomparable, made a couple of errors; Hodes was not quick enough; two flys [sic] fell between King and Bellan, which either one might have had, had they not been so near South Troy. Martin, while he was pitching, was hit in the hand by the

The Haymakers, Unions and Trojans of Troy, New York

ball, and commenced to examine the injury thereby inflicted while the ball was at his feet and while the batter was going to first.

The Haymakers played so poorly that the reporter saw only a dire future for what he felt was an over-praised Troy team:

> There is no disguising a fact that is not apparent to all who are interested in base ball: The Troy club thus far has been a delusion and a snare; none of its members have played up to their previous reputations and they have showed but little ability in coping with first class clubs. They lack the discipline and steadiness which characterize the Bostons and the Athletics, and which are so necessary to success. Their short comings are excused by their friends, on the ground that Gedney and Nelson have not been able to play, and we are told that when the nine is perfected the record will change for the better.[42]

The attendance that day was still respectable—between 2,500 and 2,000—but the Troy club was fighting major financial pressures and were forced to play many money games, seemingly against all comers including the Ilion (New York) Clippers on the day following the Red Stocking loss. By mid–July, with attendance shrinking and players worrying about their paychecks and their future in the game, the Haymakers were playing lifeless and indifferent ball, including Haymaker batting star Steve King:

> The game between the Mutuals of New York and the Haymakers yesterday was not witnessed by more than five hundred persons, and it is evident that baseball in Troy had about received its quietus. The game was a good one [6–10 Troy loss], the playing on both sides being very fair, if we accept the utter inefficiency of the Haymakers at the bat, which has been the cause of their seemingly inevitable defeats this summer. For five innings it was "pop up and go out," and not a run was made until the sixth inning. Martin made a two base hit and got around. Three times successively that S. King went to bat double plays were made off his hits. [Catcher] Allison played much better than usual yesterday, and actually seemed to have some life in him.

The Haymakers travelled to Boston on July 20, 1872, to play the Red Stockings prior to the Massachusetts team's "contemplated trip through Canada and the West." The game sparked a great deal of interest as Boston led the NA with 22 victories while Troy was fifth with 13. Both clubs were singled out for not having been shut out during the season:

THREE. *The National Association and Independent Baseball*

"The Troy nine lost one game when the score was 8–1 ... [, but they have not] thus far been 'Chicagoed [shut out].' The Bostons have made one score as low as three, but the game was won by them on this occasion. The Bostons have defeated the Roths of Philadelphia 25 to 0, and the King Philips 32 to 0, in the course of the present season."[43]

Losing only their second NA game of the year, the Red Stockings were defeated by the Troy Haymakers, 10–17, at the Boston Grounds before 3,000 spectators. Boston was the heavy betting favorite with 100 to 30 odds, but the Trojans took the game directly to their opponents and jumped out to an insurmountable lead: "The whitewash was given to the Reds for four innings, while the Troy boys ran up one on the second, one on the third, and five on the fourth, this inning being marked by some very loose fielding on the part of the Reds. Despite trailing by a score of 15–2 after five innings, Boston 'showed grit' in outscoring the Haymakers 8–2 over the last four innings." The club was flat and deserved the loss: "The play of the Bostons was hardly up to their average, and it is difficult to say why it is so, as the club has just returned from a vacation and should have done their best. They were, however, outplayed throughout the game, and the runs earned stand 7 to 4 in favor of the Haymakers."[44]

On July 23, 1872, in their last NA game, the Troy Haymakers won their fifteenth game of the season, 7–0, against the Middletown (CT) Mansfields at Hampden Park, a racing track in Springfield, Massachusetts,. The team disbanded the following day as the club's coffers were bankrupt and the stockholders would (or could) not agree to raise monies to pay players who voted to stop play for the rest of the schedule.

One frequently overlooked reason for the weak team support of Troy baseball teams in 1872 was the continued boorish behavior of the spectators, which kept many potential fans from attending Haymaker games: "The Olympics of Brooklyn defeated the Putnams by a score of 20 to 10. There were about 100 spectators present. The visitors were a rough crowd, and their loaferish [sic] conduct on the boat coming up the river ought to have given them lodgings in the station house upon their arrival here. We hope never to see them again."[45]

Troy petitioned to finish the NL Eckfords' 1872 schedule. The

The Haymakers, Unions and Trojans of Troy, New York

Brooklyn club was pitiful often losing games by 20 or more runs and committing at least 13 errors in each game. They had high turnover with the 25 players on their roster, of which many were disaffected players with less than stellar professional reputations. Since the team was co-operatively paid rather than salaried, few Eckford players were of the highest caliber. Perhaps the nadir for the Eckfords was a 6–24 loss to Cleveland, which fielded only eight players that day. After the Haymakers disbanded, Troy players Phonney Martin, Jack Nelson, George Zettlein, Jimmy Wood, and Troy-native Doug Allison all joined the Brooklyn Club to help the team finish the season by at least losing in a more competitive fashion.[46]

A review of the short season of the 1872 NA Troy Haymakers finds that the club's most valuable player was second base man and team captain Jimmy Wood, who led all starters in extra base hits (11 doubles, four triples, and two home runs), RBIs (27), and slugging percentage (.558) while hitting a robust. 336. In three NA seasons, Wood hit for a batting average of .332 and was a top-fielding second baseman, leading the NA at his position in 1871 in putouts (105), assists (83), double plays (11)(which tied him with former Haymaker Bill Craver for the most in Troy history), and fielding average (.887). As a manager, Wood, who was denigrated as a leader for his disorganized clubs and his boorish behavior and temper on the field, was less successful, ending with a 76–76 win loss record in four NA seasons. His best season at the helm was 1871, when he led the 19–9 Chicago White Stockings to a second-place NA finish. Wood is also generally acknowledged to have invented spring training when he took his Chicago club to New Orleans to get ready for the 1870 season. A baseball lifer, Wood even managed to umpire two games each in the NA (1871) and the NL (1876).

Late in the 1872 season, Davy Force joined the Lord Baltimores (also known as the "Canaries") and, as previously stated, Wood, Nelson, Gedney, Martin, and Zettlein signed on with the Brooklyn Eckfords.[47]

The success of the 1872 Haymakers was dependent on a marked improvement on the mound. When fireballing pitcher George Zettlein joined the Troy Haymakers for the 1872 season, he was already an experienced pitcher who was at the top of his game. He began playing organized baseball in 1866 with the Brooklyn Eckfords and then signed on

THREE. *The National Association and Independent Baseball*

with the Brooklyn Atlantics from 1867 to 1870–1870. Zettlein was encouraged to sign with the 1870 Chicago White Stockings by playing manager Jimmy Wood, who brought his ace pitcher along with him when he served brief stints with the Chicago White Stockings, the Brooklyn Eckfords, the Troy Haymakers, and the Philadelphia White Stockings. In 1871 for Chicago, he led the NA in earned run average (2.73) with an 18–9 win-loss record. His whip-like fastballs led to two 1871 major league firsts regarding home runs allowed: On May, 6, 1871, Zettlein surrendered the first NA home run to the Cleveland Forest Citys' Ezra Sutton, and, on September 5, 1871, he also was the victim of the first and only 1871 grand slam home run hit by the Boston Red Stockings' Charley Gould.

As his career wound down, George Zettlein was mired in game fixing controversies with both the 1875 Chicago White Stockings where his long-time manager and friend Jimmy Wood had a falling-out over the pitcher's supposed lack of effort and the 1875 Philadelphia White Stockings. His Philadelphia teammates found his play in a game against the Hartford Dark Blues less than inspired. Finally, in October of 1875, in the post-season annual ten game series between the Philadelphia clubs, Zettlein walked off the mound in the sixth inning against the Athletics in the tenth game with his club losing, 3–7, claiming his club was trying to lose the game.

But he was still a dominant hurler with the Haymakers with a 2.16 earned run average and a 14–8 won-loss record. Zettlein was a star in the five years of the NA's existence but was a bust in the 1876 NL debut season going 4–20 with the worse earned average of his career (3.88).[48]

The Troy Haymakers attempted to stay together in 1872 by reforming as a cooperative club and they played their rivals, the New York Mutuals, with their NA starting lineup intact. On July 30, 1872, at the Williamsburg Union Grounds before twelve hundred fans, the two teams faced off in a much anticipated battle, especially in light of Troy's defeat of the league leading Bostonians a week earlier:

> The Haymakers, late of Troy, played their first game as a co-operative nine on the Union Ground yesterday against the Mutuals of this City, a crowd of 1,200 individuals being on hand the former a good "send-off" in their new venture. Strange to say, although the Haymakers were supposed to be

partly demoralized, the betting men on them at even, and in many instances at slight odds, but as the game progressed, it was manifest that they stood little chance against the fine fielding of the Mutuals, who, on the eighth inning, settled the game by scoring 6 runs, which added to 2 in the seventh and 3 previously scored , brought their total to 11, and gave them the victory, the Haymakers scoring only in the third and fifth, both runs being earned.[49]

Other reports of the July 30, 1872, match between Troy and New York, provided details about the curious betting pattern on the game, the on-field play, and the rumors about the Haymakers' supposed plan(s) for the future:

At the Union Ground, Williamsburg, yesterday afternoon, the Mutuals and Haymakers, late the Troy Club, played a friendly game. The Mutuals were short of Bechtel's services, but Dickie Pearce filled his position [right field] and played it well. The Haymakers were also short one of their nine, Force, who had poisoned his hands by touching a species of ground-ivy and could not play in consequence. The prestige attaching to the Haymakers from their handsome win over the Bostonians was sufficient to make them warm favorites in the pools at the rate of 100 to 80 on them. The day was a most agreeable one, and had it not been for the clouds of mosquitoes which were flying around, the pleasure of watching such a quick [the game took only 75 minutes] and prettily played game would have been unalloyed.

The Mutuals appear to be improving with almost every game they play, and although the game yesterday was not a championship game they played with as much zeal and vim as if the pennant had depended on it. Excepting in the sixth inning the Haymakers also played a fine fielding game, Bellan's play at shortstop being of the very highest order. His throwing to first was the best that had been seen on the Union Grounds in some time. Allison also played with a great deal of his old time form. On the Mutual side Fulman [Fulmer] and Hatfield played their respective positions [shortstop and second base respectively] splendidly, as indeed did all the nine. The fielding on both sides was brilliant, double plays being quite the order of the day. Should the Haymakers amalgamate with the Eckfords, as is most probable, there will be a lively [fight] between them, the Atlantics, and the Mutes.[50]

This game was the last hurrah for the 1872 Troy Haymakers, who suffered so many player defections, so little financial backing, and so little fan support, that the club was a shadow of its opening day self and further underscored the Haymaker reputation for "loose" play. The team

THREE. *The National Association and Independent Baseball*

that faced the Mutuals on September 10, 1872, was the Troy Haymakers in name only:

> The Troy people appear to be determined to earn for themselves as bad a reputation as possible in connection with base ball matters. Not only did they organize a professional club at the beginning of the present season, and turn the players adrift without their money in the middle of it, but after organizing a newly-organized Haymaker Club—consisting of McAtee, Flynn, Bellan, and the three brothers King, with three members of the Putnam Club—[that] would play the Mutual and Atlantic clubs here, they sent down a nine of the old Putnam Club, and not one of the above named six players, whose participating in the game would alone have given it any interest. Such a scandalous imposition on the club they had to play with, as well as the public who paid their money to see the Haymakers play, cannot be too severely reprobated. The game was so utterly worthless [a 37–6 Mutual rout] as far as the Troy players were concerned, that a description of the game would only be time and space wasted.[51]

The Troy Haymakers hit bottom at the conclusion of the 1872 baseball season. It would take seven years before the Collar City once again had the opportunity to compete at the highest levels of professional baseball.

The Haymakers' Climb Back to the Big Show (1873–1878)

Eighteen seventies America underwent a number of significant economic shocks that undermined popular confidence and left its mark on individual and civil prosperity. The Panic of 1873, which was triggered by a post–Civil War speculation bubble, led to a deep depression that lasted over a quarter of a century. Another major economic dislocation in 1873 was the passage of the Fourth Coinage Act (1873), which so depressed the price of silver that, in effect, the country was put on a gold standard. As the decade drew to a close, the Great Railroad Strike (1877) further delayed economic stability and recovery. Troy was not immune from the effects of these events, and there was little economic support for baseball in this period. However, if baseball did not flourish in Troy after the demise of the NA, it did survive and continue to be played, including in the first years of professional minor league baseball (1877–1878).

The National League was founded in 1876 and was flailing about in 1877 and 1878 with only six league teams. Such a damaging event as the 1877 Louisville gambling scandal was nearly fatal to the young National League. Former Haymaker players Bill Craver and Mike McGeary were implicated in the scandal. McGeary was suspended for the 1878 season, but he returned the next season to play major league baseball until 1884 when he completed a solid eleven-year major league career with a .276 batting average and .858 fielding average, mostly as an infielder. The NL also suffered uneven popular support due to its 50-cent admission fee that put the games out of reach for many immigrant and working class potential customers. Further, the NL's strict prohibitions on liquor sales and the lack of Sunday baseball further depressed gate receipts.

Organized top-level baseball began play in 1877 with a competitor for National League supremacy, the International Association (IA). Based on a proposal from baseball pioneer and entrepreneur Albert Spalding to hinder player movement, which was increasing player salaries, the League Alliance (LA) was also founded in 1877 as a protective measure to prevent raiding of member rosters as the competition for players rose exponentially with the creation of the IA. The LA was composed of 28 teams from Ludlow, Colorado, to Winona, Minnesota, and Albany, New York. The Troy Haymakers fielded a team in 1877 that included former NA stars Steve King and Clipper Flynn as well as teenager Fatty Briody, who was a Lansingburgh native as were all of the players on the roster in the first incarnation of the Haymakers.[52]

During the 1877 season, the Troy Haymakers took on all comers, including black touring clubs, and were often forced to reschedule events at the least minute due to the lack of any effective organization of the League Alliance:

> The game of base ball played on the Haymaker Grounds' yesterday between the Mutuals (colored) of Washington and the Haymakers, resulted in the usual victory for the latter by a score of 16 to 5. Though the visitors played a fair game, they are no match for the Haymakers, who are constantly improving, and should arrange a series of games with some of the crack clubs of the country. A match had been announced between the Crickets of Binghamton and the Haymakers, to come off on Friday, but a

THREE. *The National Association and Independent Baseball*

telegram was received yesterday stating that the eastern tour had been abandoned by the former, and they would therefore be unable to keep their engagement with the Lansingburgh boys. The public will, however, be given a good game on that day. Probably the South Adams club will be sent for to play here.[53]

The 1877 Haymakers had a natural rival in the A.M. Nolan Baseball Club of Albany, and their games were among the most hotly contested games of the year both on and off the field. Both clubs were recognized as superior baseball teams and vied for local primacy:

> Yesterday afternoon one of the most interesting games of base ball ever played in this vicinity took place at Albany between the Nolans of that city and the Haymakers of Lansingburgh. Each club had won a victory over the other by scores of 2 to 0 [a Nolans victory] and 3 to 0 [a Troy victory], and, in this third game, great interest was centered, in so much as it was practically the "rubber" between the two organizations, and a contest which would demonstrate to the public the champion club of this section of the state. Of course, the friends of the Haymakers were not over sanguine of the success of their favorites, as they were obliged to play upon strange grounds and the presence of a crowd of people which would naturally side with the Albanians. That the game agreeably surprised their admirers and at the same time practically demonstrated the fact that they *could* play ball, might be inferred from the result.
>
> At 3:30 o'clock game was called, with an assembly of upwards of 600 people on the grounds. In every respect the Haymakers outplayed their formidable opponents, and at the commencement of the ninth inning the game stood 1 to 0 in their favor. The excitement was intense, and up to that time there had been little or no batting done at all, when a palpable error on the part of the umpire, Mr. McAllister of Albany, gave one of the Nolans second base. A previous wrong decision in the same inning, alike favorable to the Albany club, was rather too much for the Lansingburgh boys to complacently abide by, and the policy of discontinuing playing was freely discussed by the latter. Finally, it was decided that the game should be played out, though all unprejudiced witnesses of the contest admit the unfairness of the umpire. Mr. McAllister expressed on the difficulty which had arisen, though he declared his belief that his decisions were impartial, and that he was perfectly unbiased in rendering them. Nevertheless they were certainly unjust.
>
> The Nolans in the beginning of the ninth inning had scored one run, which tied them with the Haymakers, and when the latter went to bat the excitement of the Trojans can be imagined. "Sangree" secured his base, worked around to third, and on a base hit by Caperoon reached the home plate. This decided the game in the favor of the Haymakers. A "sky-

scraper" by Steve King permitted Caperoon to score his run before the ball was returned to the in-field, and with the next striker the game ended.

The playing of the Lansingburgh nine was remarkably good, Briordy [Briody], Caperoon, and "Sangaree" covering themselves with glory—though each member of the club did his share in gaining the well-earned victory. Briordy was hurt several times during the game by foul tips, and though his hands were badly bruised, he pluckily stood behind the bat and did all that a catcher could do.

The game was thus won by the Haymakers 5 to 1. The Nolans certainly anticipated an easy triumph, but this third contest should settle the question of superiority between these two rival clubs. Another game has been arranged between the Lansingburgh nine and the Nolans.[54]

Just two days later, at Vail's Lot in Lansingburgh, the Nolans and Haymakers again faced off. As hard fought and contentious as the previous three games, the contest ended in a disputed and rancorous forfeit in favor of the home club with 1,000 fans in attendance in a game that lasted two and a half hours with 30 minutes being devoted to a first inning brouhaha:

The umpire, Thomas Rankin, who seemed to act with the utmost impartiality, decided that Drack of the Haymakers had not been put out by McCaffery, second baseman of the Nolans, while the former was running to second base. The decision was so close that it would have been fair enough to have been acceptable had it been in favor of either side; but as soon as the umpire decided it "not out," several of the Nolans uttered exclamations of dissatisfaction. An angry squabble ensued, winding up with the withdrawal of the Nolans from the field, and a declaration of the game in the favor of the Haymakers by a score of nine to nothing. The crowd flocked around the gate demanding the return of their admission money, and finally the Nolans agreed to play out the game as it stood, with H. McCormick as umpire. His decisions were fair, but no more than Mr. Rankin's.

The game was skillfully played with few errors, few base hits, and but one run, which was credited to the Nolans, in the sixth inning, the total score standing one to nothing in their favor. Clark, centre field for the Nolans, was struck over the eye during the sixth inning and badly bruised. A magnificent game was marred by the Nolans' growling in the field and by unseemly displays of partisan feeling by spectators of both sides.

We are informed by an officer of the Haymaker club, since writing the above, that the game yesterday was won by the Lansingburgh nine by a score of 9 to 0, and the contest which followed the "squabble" was simply an exhibition game to satisfy the spectators, who had paid their admission fee and wanted to see ball playing therefor [sic]. As the games now stand between the clubs, the Haymakers have won three and the Nolans one.[55]

THREE. *The National Association and Independent Baseball*

Within a few days of their disputed forfeit win over their local rivals, the Haymakers were brought back to earth by a thorough thrashing at the hands of the Auburn, New York, Auburnians, 17–0. Troy hurler Caperoon was clobbered surrendering 16 total based hits in just five innings as the team suffered a "Waterloo defeat." Yet hope sprang eternal for both the reporter(s) and his readers and attention was quickly placed on the next game: "The Auburn nine is composed of very gentlemanly players, who certainly demonstrated their superiority over the Haymakers in ball playing. An interesting game is anticipated this afternoon between the latter and the Fall Rivers, when, the boys say, they will retrieve their fortunes. With their friends we can say we hope so."[56]

The year had been successful for the Troy Haymakers, who parlayed a few aging stars—Clipper Flynn and Steve King—and a host of young (teenage) talent—including local favorites Fatty Briody and Pat McManus—into a winning baseball team with a bright future in the professional game:

> Yesterday afternoon the Haymakers played a game of baseball upon their own grounds—the last of the season—with the Nolans of Albany. Caperoon, the regular pitcher of the Lansingburgh nine, did not play, and it was generally supposed that the local team would suffer defeat. Foley, however, knew that he was capable of doing more effective work in that position than the North Adams man, and the general playing of the Haymakers, both at the bat and in the field, showed that they were greatly superior to their opponents. The latter were not permitted to score a single run, while the Lansingburghers managed to pass ten men over the home plate. Surely this score of 10 to 0 should satisfy the visitors that our boys can outplay them at base ball.
>
> This too is an excellent game for the latter, and they should now feel perfectly contented to retire from the field and congratulate themselves upon their record during the past season. Their friends are not a little proud of their efforts when the fact is taken into consideration that the members of the nine are hard-working mechanics and receive no compensation for their services at base ball playing. An enterprise is talked of which, if carried out, would give Troy a first class professional nine, capable of coping with the best clubs in the country.[57]

The 1878 season began with a roster of relative unknowns: "Haymakers (Troy N.Y.): F.C. Dungon, J. Butler, T. Morris, E. Farley, J.P. Connors, W. Diach, J. Taylor, and M. Lawler."[58] The club had a solid season on the baseball diamond, including a rain-shortened (five innings) home shutout of the Rochester Flour Citys in early August.[59]

As was the custom of the Haymaker management from its earliest days, 1878 saw Troy opportunistically signing players throughout the season to strengthen the club. For example, when the nearby Pittsfield club disbanded in late August, Troy jumped at the chance of adding the Pittsfield catcher Quilty to its roster. On September 26, 1878, with the ultimate goal of improving its roster and fielding a team in the National League, Troy signed shortstop Ed Caskin (Rochester) and outfielder Al Hall (London (Ontario) for the 1879 baseball season. Reflecting on the volatile nature of player-management relations, voiding and violation of contracts, and ever-changing rosters in the nineteenth century, the 1878 Utica Utes in their first year of organized baseball sought to recruit the talented Caskin for the last week of the 1878 season: "The Haymakers have disbanded for the season. How would it do to secure Caskin to play with the Uticas until the 15th? It would not interfere with his arrangements to play in Troy next season."[60]

In further attempts to improve their image on and off the diamond, the Haymakers cut ties with the problematic Bill Craver—"At a meeting of the directors, Monday, Craver asked for his release and it was granted. If reports are true he should have been summarily dismissed and not suffered to resign"—and changed their team name to signal a break from their past and the long-held negative public image it inspired: "Troy expects to have a first class base ball nine next season. It will probably be a league affair, and will be called the "Troy City Club," and not the Haymakers; hence, it will be strictly speaking, a Troy organization. Already about $3,000 have been [raised] as a nucleus for the organization of the nine, and some of the players of the current Haymaker have signified their willingness to engage for next season."[61]

In 1878, the Troy Haymakers were essentially an independent club. The team was a member of the loosely organized 13-team New York State Baseball Association and also had a 1–1 record in the IA. However, The Haymakers most significant action of 1878 occurred after the playing season was long over.

On December 5, 1878, the major league baseball owners met in Cleveland to consider rules and equipment changes for the upcoming

THREE. *The National Association and Independent Baseball*

season: "The National League of Professional Base-Ball Players [added] several amendments to the playing rules were adopted, the most important of which was the dispensing with foul-bound catches.... A lengthily and excited discussion took place over the adoption of a uniform ball to be used by all the League clubs, which resulted in the choice of the Spalding ball."[62] One week later, the NL clubs faced a much more significant issue: the application of the Troy Baseball Association for entry into the NL.

On December 12, 1878, the Haymakers petitioned to enter the National League and were accepted even though the city did not meet the league minimum for home-city population, which was 75,000.[63] As with almost every major event in Haymaker baseball history, Troy's entrance into the National League was not without contention and controversy:

> The entry into the National League of the [Troy] Trojans [known officially as the Troy Citys and unofficially as the Haymakers] was greeted with enthusiasm by its supporters, but it was not without controversy. Part of the Trojans' financial success stemmed from their games with their neighbors across the Hudson River in Albany. Troy requested the inclusion of the Albany ball club into the National League, a request which was denied because scheduling problems which would result from a nine-team league. Additionally, the National League's territorial rights rule prevented more than one team per city and no games between cities fewer than five miles apart. [Troy and Albany are separated by 4.75 miles.] This rule prevented Troy and Albany from playing exhibition games against each other. Eventually, the Trojans settled for an amendment of the territory rule, reducing the gap from five miles to four and allowing them to play exhibition games against their Capital District neighbors.
>
> Troy's acquiescence to the territorial rights amendment also had an indirect side effect which they had not counted on: it kept Albany from joining the National League. The Syracuse Stars, which had entered the league with Troy, closed shop after the 1879 season. To replace the defunct Syracuse club, the Albany and Worcester teams both applied for National League membership, Because Worcester's population was less than 75,000, a league vote, in accordance with National League rules, had to be unanimous. The league's sentiment favored Worcester; [Troy] still wanting Albany's entry into the league, announced that they would veto Worcester. The National League, with the Trojan-influenced territory rule amendment still fresh in their memory, decided to include people living with a city's four-mile radius as part of its population. With the new rule clarification,

The Haymakers, Unions and Trojans of Troy, New York

Worcester had more than 75,000 residents, eliminating the need for the unanimous vote. The league voted to accept Worcester, and the Albany ball club was relegated to playing non-league exhibition games against their Troy neighbors.[64]

Troy was shepherded into the National League by Chicagoan William Hulbert, who served as a champion of Troy professional baseball until his death before the 1882 National League season.

William Hulbert was a successful grocer and commodities trader who was elected secretary of the Chicago White Stockings in 1874, the year Chicago re-entered the National Association after a two-year hiatus in which the club regrouped after being devastated by the Great Chicago Fire. Hulbert set about improving his roster in 1875. After another mediocre season on the playing field that year, Hulbert assembled in the off-season the nucleus of a championship team with such star players as Adrian Anson, Ross Barnes, Cal McVey, Deacon White, and, most significantly, Albert Spalding, who was also to manage the 1876 Chicago club. Hulbert saw clearly that the National Association was a failing institution with rampant player violation of contracts, unruly spectator behavior, and yearly declines in fan attendance that was fueled by the popular belief that the game was controlled by gambling interests. Hulbert reasoned that baseball could only survive as a business if it were radically reorganized and integrity restored in the eyes of the public. Thus, William Hulbert with the moral authority of Cincinnati baseball pioneer Harry Wright and the media support of Editor Lewis Meachem of the *Chicago Tribune* founded the National League (NL) in 1876.[65]

However, Hulbert's founding was not entirely altruistic and served his own business interests. As secretary of the White Stockings, he signed players from competing clubs prior to the 1876 season in clear violation of the NA's own league rules. In essence, Hulbert reorganized professional baseball before the NA could bring action against Chicago. However self-interested his motives, William Hulbert's assessment of the major problems of the NA was clear-sighted in addressing baseball's problems that needed immediate action: "rumors of game fixing," "rowdiness on the field and in the stands," "mounting debts," and "competitive imbalance."[66]

Hulbert's NL constitution wrested control of the game from the

THREE. *The National Association and Independent Baseball*

players and made owners the dominant force in order to maintain long-term team and financial stability, thus making baseball a more attractive prospect for future investors and management:

> Hulbert appealed to the owners, businessmen all, by using some simple economic logic. If the businessmen ran the teams and the players concentrated on playing ball, each party could concentrate on doing what they did best and everyone would be better off. The geographic exclusivity he [Hulbert] promised to each club appealed to the owners as well. Establishing the NL as the premier professional league with entry strictly controlled by the monopolists themselves appealed to their pocketbooks. If the new league was recognized as the premier assemblage of baseball talent then it would be able to attract a greater percentage of the better players, and with no equals to bid them away; it would lower the payroll burden, leaving a larger percentage of the revenues for the owners[67]

While still running his own Chicago White Stockings, William Hulbert became the NL's second president after the uninterested Morgan Bulkeley's resignation. The Chicagoan served from 1876 to his death in 1882. As chief executive officer of the NL and as an involved club president, there was no financial matter that was too unimportant for his purview: "[After the 1876 season, the owners] fixed the rate of 15 cents per person as the gate share for visiting teams in league contests, fixed umpire salaries at $5 a game, and required that each player make a $30 deposit on his uniform, launder and repair it at his own expense, and pay fifty cents per day for room and board while on road trips." High salaries were the bane of owners in the first years of the NL with Hulbert among the first and the loudest of the voices asserting the need to reduce player salaries. He was a strong advocate of the implementation of the reserve (or "Buffalo") clause prior to the 1880 season.[68]

Hulbert worked tirelessly and decisively to restore baseball's tarnished reputation. He quickly eliminated those elements of professional baseball that he believed offended the sensibility of the average citizen whom he desired as spectator: Sunday baseball, alcohol sales, and gambling.

Hulbert also would not tolerate player malfeasance. He banished four Louisville Grays players after the 1877 season for supposed game fixing; he also banished other players for alcohol abuse. Hulbert was just as rigorous with ownership. He expelled the Cincinnati Red Stockings after the 1880 season because they would not agree to abide by the rewritten NL constitution that denied the leasing of a ball club's playing grounds for Sunday baseball and for alcohol sales at such games. Hulbert's high-handedness and sanctimony with regard to his treatment of Cincinnati led to that club's management becoming a major player in the creation, in 1882, of the American Association, which would pose the first serious challenge to the primacy of the NL.

More important to the Troy baseball narrative, Hulbert expelled the New York and Philadelphia franchises after the 1876 season for not completing their season schedules by refusing to take late season road trips to the western NL cities. He was so outraged by such open contempt for a key tenet of the league that he ran the NL as a six-team league in 1877 and 1878.[69]

After the 1878 season, the National League found itself in dire straits. The financial resources needed to start-up and to maintain a franchise were high. Fan perception of the sport as a tainted, corrupt business was underscored by the recent player scandals, by individual club ownership's disregard for league regulations, and by negative newspaper reporting. All of these elements alienated potential investors in the sport. When the high cost of tickets and the no Sunday baseball and drinking prohibitions were factored into the equation, the national pastime was in serious jeopardy. Prior to the 1879 NL season, Troy was an attractive alternative to some larger municipalities: It was in close proximity to state capital Albany, possessed a strong economic and industrial base, and had a long history of playing and supporting baseball from the Civil War forward.[70]

In 1879, Hulbert accepted the application of the Troy Trojans to compete in a completely revamped eight-team NL, disregarding his own regulation that league franchises must have a population base of 75,000 inhabitants. Whether his influence was due to necessity, to his continued animus toward New York and Philadelphia, or to knowledge and acceptance of the Collar City's long involvement with the national pastime; Hulbert supported Troy baseball until his untimely death before the 1882 NL season. Hulbert helped save baseball on the national level and set the business of baseball on firm financial ground (at the expense of the players) for a century. He also enabled Troy to compete at the highest level of baseball during the Upstate New York's city's halcyon days.

THREE. *The National Association and Independent Baseball*

In 1878, Troy was also the site where a number of the Worcester Red Stockings made the decision to desert their team. The Worcester Baseball Association made it clear to the public that it did not release the players. When the International Association dissolved at the end of the year, Worcester in 1879 fielded a team (Grays) in the newly established minor league National Association. It was from the rebellious act of the Massachusetts players in 1878 that the Troy and Worcester baseball franchises became linked in the minds of the public and the baseball press. They remained so until 1882 when both clubs were forced out of the National League.[71]

Four

National Leaguers at the Gates of Troy

1879

Eighteen seventy-nine began with major rules changes that moved the baseball play much closer to the sport we know today. Pitching was altered by having every pitch thrown called either a ball, strike or a foul, with nine balls earning a base on balls. Pitchers were liable for fines for hitting batters, and they could not turn their back completely during delivery of a pitch. Batting orders were regulated by having the first hitter in an inning be the one scheduled to follow the last hitter in the preceding inning. (Previously, the leadoff hitter was sometimes determined by the way the previous inning had ended; if the third out came on the bases, the first batter in the following inning might be the one scheduled to follow that runner in the line-up—even if his at-bat had led to a force out on the bases.) Most important, one-bounce catches—fair or foul—would no longer be good for an out.

The 1879 enthusiastic and sunny pre-season national forecast underscored the growing hold baseball had on the American public:

> With the brightening business prospects of the present year the base-ball fraternity looks forward to the season of 1879 with sanguine hopes of a far more successful season's play than they have had in past years. As far as the game is concerned it is asserted that since professional ball-playing was established no season has promised as much in the way of honest ball-playing.
>
> There will be two races for the association pennants this season, one by eight clubs for the [National] League pennant and the other by nine clubs for the National [Association] trophy. The former include representative teams from Cincinnati, Chicago, Cleveland, and Buffalo in the West, and from Boston, Providence, Troy, and Syracuse in the East. The latter com-

FOUR. *National Leaguers at the Gates of Troy*

prise club teams from New Hampshire, Massachusetts, New York, and the District of Columbia, the cities represented being Manchester, Springfield, Holyoke, Worcester, New Bedford, Albany, Washington, and Utica.

The eight teams of the [National] League cannot be said to open the season equal in strength to last year's teams. This season special interest will attach to the struggle between the Boston and Providence teams, captained respectively by George and Harry Wright, and the personal rivalry between the brothers will make things decidedly lively both in Providence and Boston.

That there will be a close fight for the pennant between Boston, Providence, and Cincinnati there is not the least doubt; and as there is but little choice as regards the strength of the teams the issue promises to be doubtful up to the last month of the season.

Another thing that will impart interest to the [National] League campaign of 1879 is the fact that the crack International clubs of 1878—the Buffalos and the Stars of Syracuse—have entered the League to try to win the pennant of 1879.[1]

The news report continues, listing the proposed starting team lineups of both the NL and the NA [which had been the IA in 1878, before losing the London, Ontario, Tecumsehs], including the club batting and fielding averages of the new rosters. Troy players hit for .250 and fielded at .823. The club rosters included such past and future Troy players as the NL's Force, Hankinson, Dickerson, McGeary, and Ward; and the NA's Allison, Higham, Gillespie, Dorgan, Cogswell, Connor, Goldsmith, Briody, Roseman, Ferguson, Pike, and Cassidy.

Troy entered the National League with the Syracuse Stars, and both teams filled their rosters with former International Association players. The starting Troy Trojan lineup (with their former club(s) in parentheses) for 1879 is as follows:

1B* Aaron Clapp (Hornellsville, New York)
2B Thorny Hawkes (Manchester, New Hampshire)
SS Ed Caskin (Rochester, New York)
3B Herm Doscher (London, Ontario)
LF Jake Evans (New Bedford, Massachusetts)
CF Al Hall (London, Ontario)
RF Tom Mansell (Syracuse, New York)

* (Dan Brouthers of the Wappingers Falls, New York, Actives [amateur club]) split duty with Clapp

The Haymakers, Unions and Trojans of Troy, New York

C Charlie Reilly (New Bedford, Massachusetts)
P George Washington Bradley (New Bedford, Massachusetts)

The overhauled Troy roster also had new uniforms in its debut season in the National League: light corduroy pants with red silk cords, scarlet stockings, and a gray flannel shirt trimmed in red with a "T.C." across the chest. The Troy Citys began play at the refurbished Putnam Grounds at the intersection of Peoples Avenue and 15th Street.

The 1879 Troy ball club had high expectations and what turned out to be false bravado before their first National League game: "On Tuesday night the Albanys will start on an eastern trip. This looks very much as if they are afraid of meeting the Troy Citys this spring. Their [Troy] present condition appears to be too formidable to the Albanys. The gage of battle has been offered the latter, but they refused to accept. Are they afraid of defeat?" Reality soon set in for the Troy baseball community.

While the Troy community was supportive of its major league franchise, on the actual field of play the Trojans were a dismal failure, finishing in eighth (and last) place with a 19–56 record that proved the gamblers correct in their early season assessment of the 1879 NL clubs: "The bookmakers at St. Louis thus rank the eight clubs entered for the League Championship = Boston and Cincinnati even, with the odds 6-1 on either of them; the Providence team third; Chicago fourth; with Buffalo, Syracuse, Troy, and Cleveland on even terms for the other places."

By early May, NL newspapers were consigning the Troy Trojans to the cellar: "It looks as though the Troy Citys are to be the dummy against which the rest of the League will practice all summer." Troy newspapers agreed that the Troy Citys were "outclassed" and felt that the team's roster did not have the established talent necessary for a successful run at the NL pennant. In 1879, the NL was home to such diamond stars as George Wright, James O'Rourke, John Montgomery Ward, and former NA Troy Haymaker Mike McGeary. Lesser luminaries included Ed Cogswell, John Morrill, Davy Force, Cal McVey and Ezra Sutton. One of the most popular of such talented NL all-stars was Troy native and favorite son, Mike Kelly: "Michael J. Kelly—'the only Kel'—likewise known when he was sold by Chicago to Boston as 'the $10,000 beauty.' [Eighteen seventy-nine Cincinnati Red Stockings third baseman] Kelly was a truly wonderful ball-

Four. National Leaguers at the Gates of Troy

player—a great hitter, a fine fielder in any position, a fast and scientific base-runner and perhaps the trickiest ball-player that ever faced a pitcher."[2]

Prior to the opening of the 1879 NL season, with the league facing financial pressures with rising costs in transportation and on-the-road housing, teams posted the number of miles each club would travel during the 1879 season: "The following are to be computed to be the number of miles to be traveled by the different clubs in the League during the coming season: Boston, 5,100; Providence, 5,600; Troy, 5,700; [Syracuse] Stars, 4,600; Cleveland, 5,600; Buffalo, 4,700; Cincinnati, 6,100; Chicago, 6,700."[3]

An early season exhibition loss to the neighboring Albanys at Troy was an early indication of what was to be an inauspicious season for the Trojans. Albany provided Troy with needed money games and the Trojans were reluctant to give up such contests. Within ten days of their NL debut, the Troy club tested league regulations regarding such in-season exhibitions, violating the spirit, if not the letter, of this league rule:

> The seeming inconsistency of the Troy Citys in not playing yesterday [April 23,1879] is explained by the fact that they were telegraphed by President Hulbert of the League that they had no right to play. The [*Troy*] *Whig* insists that the Troys have as much right to play the Albany clubs, as the Bostons have to play the Harvards, and the Buffalos the Essex clubs, and adds: 'The phase this matter has taken is much regretted by the managers of both clubs. It was a double advantage for the Troy Citys as it was not only a pecuniary benefit to them, but it gave them excellent practice prior to their encountering the stronger nines of the League. The managers of the two clubs have found a way to obviate this difficulty and to-morrow afternoon the [Albany] Capital Citys play here with eight of their regular nine with the active Shoupe of the Troy City, thus making the nine a picked one, and escaping the rule. A very exhibition of ball playing is anticipated, and no doubt every one [sic] at the game will depart from its grounds with entire satisfaction, as they did on Tuesday last.'"

The dissatisfaction with Hulbert's ruling regarding his decision to prevent Troy from playing exhibition games against its geographical rival Albany was not confined to the local Troy newspapers and the comparison with the favored Boston Red Stockings and Harvard College was again referred to in arguing for the Troy Citys' position: "Why the Troys cannot play an Albany club while the Bostons are allowed to play the non-local Harvard club of Cambridge is a puzzle. The Harvard club is no more a local team than is the Albany club, and if it is against League rules for the Troys to play the Capital City team, it is certainly so in the case of the Boston and Harvard."[4]

The Trojans began their initial season in the NL by losing their first seven games of a twelve game road trip. In keeping with their checkered history, Troy had a player banned from the league before the club played its first home game. Trojan First baseman Alex McKinnon rotated to the International Association's Rochester Hop Bitters over a contract dispute: "At a meeting of the Troy City club on Friday last, McKinnon was expelled from the league for breach of contract. He signed articles with the Troy Citys, and accepted an advance of seventy-five dollars on his first month's salary of $300, and then refused to join the nine. Whether the expulsion will disqualify him from membership in the National Association remains to be seen."[5]

In keeping with their history of signing strong defensive catchers, the Troy Citys inked Bill Holbert, who became a mainstay of the Trojans for their entire NL run. He was a sure-handed fielder and a student of the game who despite his offensive deficiencies knew how to win. Early in the 1879 season, Holbert made his biggest error by agreeing to umpire a local contest.

On Memorial Day in 1879, Trojan catcher Bill Holbert experienced a hellacious verbal attack while serving as the umpire of a hard-fought 4–3 victory by the Capital Citys of Albany over the Washington Nationals: "Holbert went down to the 'sand banks' yesterday to umpire the National-Albany game. His decisions were very fair, but did not suit the Albany crowd, who yelled and blamed, and he refused to umpire any longer [after the third inning]. When last seen he was giving his 'experience' at the Greenbush Depot." Even those spectators who agreed that Holbert was a disaster as an arbiter believed that he was treated poorly by the Albany crowd: "Holbert did umpire poorly and unfairly, but for all that, it is to be regretted that the audience should have showed their displeasure the way they did."[6]

Bill Holbert was much more successful behind the plate as a catcher than he was as an arbiter. He was always known as a heady player as is evident in the following anecdote about his throwing in an amateur tilt after his major league playing days were over:

Four. *National Leaguers at the Gates of Troy*

Holbert remained with Troy until it dropped out of the National League, when he went with the Metropolitan team of the American Association. During the exciting Amateur League games in this city [Troy] in 1889 "Billy" turned up one day as the catcher of the Citizens' Corps team. His throwing arm was not strong enough to line them down to second, but he retained his old-time accuracy, and when a runner started to steal second "Billy" threw down and hit the umpire in the back, thus compelling the base-runner to return to first. The same thing happened several times more in the course of the game, and then the indicator man began to realize that he was being made a target of, so he kept one eye on "Billy" instead of turning squarely around and watching the play at second base. This put a stop to the veteran catcher's clever manueuvre [sic], but the game was almost over anyway, and it did not make much difference. Holbert admitted that he could not have thrown as far as second base if his life depended on it.[7]

While compiling only a .208 batting average over a twelve-year career, Bill Holbert was a canny backstop who was known as an excellent handler of pitchers. He played for Troy during the club's entire NL tenure. Holbert's tutelage of young catcher Buck Ewing, who joined the Trojans in 1880, is perhaps his most lasting contribution to the national game in the Collar City.

The Troy Trojans had their moments of glory on the diamond in 1879, but all-too-frequently they suffered defeat due to one poor inning that inevitably undermined their chances of victory. In Cincinnati against the Red Stockings, one poor inning consigned the Troy club to a narrow defeat: "The Trojans allowed the pork packers to scoop seven in the second innings. This gave them the game, as the playing after that was quite even, but the Trojans kept gaining until at the close they had scored twelve. The Cincinnatis won by a single run, their final score being a baker's dozen."[8]

The Troy Trojans continually tinkered with their roster as the club's loses mounted and the Troy fans became noticeably more vocal. The 1879 season was a star-crossed one for Troy even off the diamond. Even when the club made a strong move—"Bruthers [future Hall of Fame member Dan Brouthers] the new found first baseman of the Troy Citys, is another [Cap] Anson in size"—management did not realize the player's potential and released him before he reached his prime.[9]

The experts were writing off the Troy club two months into the season along with the other new entries in the NL. From the viewpoint of the sporting press, the primary fault for the poor showing of these teams was poor management: "Bad management on the part of the senior club of Cincinnati—presidential interference like that which caused the Chicago Club to fail in 1877 and 1878—and blundering by the management of the junior clubs of Syracuse, Troy and Cleveland have been the cause of the falling off in the play of the strong nines of these four clubs ... may be properly considered out of the race."[10]

At the end of June, however, the Troy Citys began to show a bit of life, defeating the Syracuse Stars in four straight games in which they outscored their opponent, 18–4, including a five-hit shutout of the under-manned Stars by Trojan pitcher George Washington Bradley: "The Stars received another whitewash yesterday, it this time being applied by the Troy Citys. Although the Stars were without the services of Dorgan and Farrell, whose places were supplied by Kelly and Osterhout, an amateur player, there is no excuse for allowing the Trojans to make six runs in one inning [the second]."[11]

Dan Brouthers began his career with the Troy Citys in 1879. He was a quiet, sensitive player who, though not a natural athlete, became a prolific batter. After his release from the Troy Citys roster, he blossomed into one of the leading hitters in the nineteenth century and an eventual Hall of Famer (courtesy of the National Baseball Hall of Fame Library, Cooperstown, New York).

The Western New York papers did not let such play against the weak Trojans go unnoticed: "The Stars of Syracuse played the Troy Citys again yesterday [June 25] and managed to get one run to their opponents' five.

FOUR. *National Leaguers at the Gates of Troy*

The [Syracuse] *Courier* says: 'The Troy Citys were out-fielded.' Perhaps they were, but somehow most of the scores are made now-a-days on the infield. We suggest that the Stars change their name to the Satellites."[12]

The Troy Trojans were a poor fielding club and a 3–8 loss at home to the Buffalo Bisons was indicative of the club's season-long inability to catch the ball: "June 26 [game was] marked by hard hitting by the Buffalos and poor fielding by the Troy Citys.... Errors by Doescher [Doscher] (3B), Clapp (1B) and Reilly (C) gave the Buffalos seven runs." The most ominous aspect of this contest for the Trojans was the very small crowd: "Only 200 people were present." The only positive for the Trojans was that pitcher George Bradley struck out Bisons' right fielder Walker in five consecutive at bats.[13]

In fact, in spite of the Trojans' encouraging June win streak, the Trojans were averaging only 400 fans per home game and the local newspapers were continuing their campaign to write off the season as a lost cause.[14] The Trojan ownership had no recourse except to state that they were firmly committed to making the Troy franchise a successful NL entry: "The Troy papers abuse the home nine unmercifully, but the management insists that it has money enough to keep the club running until the end of the season and that it intends doing it , whether they win or not."[15]

While their home club was also suffering through a poor NL 1879 season, the Syracuse newspapers were among the many league NL cities whose newspaper reports observed that the Trojans were the worst club in the league: "Those who watch the various fortunes of the different League clubs were somewhat surprised when the announcement came over the wire from Buffalo that the Troy Citys, after a hard fight, won a game from the Buffalos by a score of 1 to 0. The Troy Citys have been considered the weakest organization in the League, and even their own friends have acknowledged that there is no chance for them; but the result of yesterday's contest will awaken new interest in their fortunes."

On July 2, 1879, the Syracuse hurler Harry McCormick shut out the visiting Troy Trojans, for the Trojans first such defeat in the NL, by a score of 4–0: "The Stars yesterday settled down to business and played a fine game giving the Troy Citys the first white wash they received this season. In the eighth inning the team kept the Grays on a hunting expedition after the sphere.... A succession of base hits were then made by Mansell, Farrell, Dorgan, Purcell and McGuiness." The Stars were praised for scoring three earned runs and pitcher McCormick for allowing only four base hits and five total bases. It is to be noted that the Syracuse Stars were only marginally more successful than the Trojans in 1879, finishing in seventh place with only three more wins than the cellar-dwelling Troy club.[16]

July was a poor month both on the field and at the gate for the Troy Trojans. Even the elements seemed to work against the club: "The Troy Citys were extremely unfortunate on their Western trip. They played fifteen games, winning only three: three games were prevented by rain, two were played in the morning, necessarily before small audiences, and rain interfered with the attendance in each city visited, except Syracuse and Chicago. Their receipts were diminished by upwards of $1,000 by these misfortunes."[17]

In July, the Troy ball club played some decent baseball, though their fielding was still very shaky: "July 12th—The game between the Troys and Buffalos was one of the best ever played in this city [Buffalo]. The batting was light on both sides. [Troy pitcher] Bradley bothered the Buffalos considerably. An error by Brouthers lost the game for the boys in the twelfth inning."[18] George Bradley pitched a four-hitter but was again let down by his infield defense.

As early as late July, rumors were reported that large markets were angling to replace the struggling franchise in Troy: "We have it from a very reliable source that New York and Philadelphia both expect to be in the [National] league next year with strong teams under honest, trustworthy management. The movement to organize these clubs has already been secretly put upon its feet [*Philadelphia Inquirer*]."[19]

The 1879 Troy Trojans roster was composed in the large part of experienced ball players who never meshed as a team and had down years that did not reflect their careers as a whole. Starting Troy pitcher George Washington Bradley was such a player. He had the first National League no-hitter while pitching for St. Louis on July 15, 1876, but had the worst 1879 pitching win-loss percentage in the league at 13–40 (though he did have a very respectable 2.85 earned run average). In fact, George Bradley was a respected player who served as the Trojan captain

FOUR. *National Leaguers at the Gates of Troy*

in 1879. He had a long, if peripatetic, 11-year major league career playing for 10 teams in four leagues: National Association (1875), National League (1876–1883), American Association (1883, 1886, and 1888), and the Union Association (1884).

In 1876, George Bradley had a 45–19 won-loss record with the St. Louis Brown Stockings with league-leading statistics in shutouts (16) and earned run average (1.23). For the second place 1884 UA Cincinnati Outlaw Reds, Bradley went 25–15 with a 2.71 earned run average. Even with the Trojans in their disastrous debut season in the NL, Bradley had his moments on the mound with three shutouts: May 16 at the Buffalo Bisons (1–0) for the Trojans first major league victory after six early defeats, June 23 at home versus the Syracuse Stars (6–0), and July 24 at Cleveland (2–0). The shutout in Cleveland was the Trojans only victory in a 19 game stretch.

Adding to his longevity on the diamond, Bradley, beginning with his rookie season, was also a serviceable utility shortstop and outfielder with a .229 lifetime batting average.

Although George Bradley was a key performer for the 1879 Troy Trojans, the club took some of the pressure off their pitcher by relieving him of some of his managerial responsibilities: "Caskins has been substituted for Bradley as Captain of the Troy Citys."[20]

Pitching was a major problem for the 1879 Trojans that continued to plague the club throughout most of the season: "P. A. Mc Manus who afterward became Assistant District Attorney of Rensselaer County and [is now] a prominent New York lawyer [took up Troy' mound duties]. 'Paddy,' as he was always called, had pitched to the Manhattan College nine, but the National League was a trifle too fast to him." Only at the end of the year did the Troy Citys find a permanent solution to their pitching woes:

> Dan Brouthers who had pitched during his amateur years in Wappinger Falls took a turn on the mound to little purpose: "...that Brouthers one day at Providence tried to be Bradley's understudy. His debut in the box was not a success, as seventeen hits were off his delivery, and the Grays won by a score of 16 to 6." Gardner and Salisbury were given tryouts but were only somewhat successful. Finally, in August of 1879, Troy finally signed a winning battery: "...late in the season, secured a battery that was a real crackerjack. It was composed of Fred Goldsmith, who had pitched the previous

year for the [London, Ontario] Tecumsehs, and Holbert, who had caught with the Syracuse Stars. Goldsmith remained with Troy only until the end of the season [though he was one of the five players Troy placed on its reserve list in the first year of this new regulation], for "Pop" Anson, even then famous for judging the caliber of a young player, picked out as a wonder and signed him for the Chicago.... Holbert stayed with the Trojans for the rest of his major league career.[21]

With dwindling financial resources and a disgruntled fan base, Troy continued to make significant changes in the team as the loses mounted heading into August, including releasing starting left fielder Mansell and replacing the manager: "Manager Phillips, of the Troy Citys, has been released from further control, by the directors of the club.... The Troy Citys entertain high hopes of bettering their record, under the management of Bob Ferguson. It is said that they expect to engage several new players."[22]

Troy, however, had difficulty in drawing players to commit to such a poor team. For example, Monahan from the Dubuque (IA) baseball club that had folded a few weeks previously was supposed to play third after a roster spot was opened with the release of Mansell. There is no record of this player ever having donned a Trojan uniform. By mid-August, the 1879 Troy Trojans, both on the field and in the front office, were the laughingstock of the NL: "The fight for last place must be between Troy and Cleveland, and [recently appointed Troy manager] Ferguson is not going to be left out in the cold in this struggle." The Trojan management did not escape the satiric jibes of the local newspapers:

> At Troy, yesterday, it was rumored that the board of directors of the Troy Citys had been released. This gave the home nine nerve enough to bat for four runs in the first inning. They might have gone on for thirty-two more, but someone was mean enough to tell that the old board still remained, after the second inning had been played, and they did not score any more. The Trojans can play ball if they do not have more than ten managers. One to each man they can stand, but when the odd fellow is brought they lose, and this is the custom.[23]

One of Bob Ferguson's first moves as Troy Trojan manager was to search for a reliable change pitcher as Bradley's arm began to wear down: "The Troys have laid Bradley off for a time and in Saturday's game, with

Four. National Leaguers at the Gates of Troy

the Providence nine tried Gardner, a Massachusetts pitcher. It was not exactly a satisfactory entertainment as the Grays hit him for twenty-one bases."[24] Bradley stayed in the starting lineup by playing the hot corner: "Bradley has been playing in good style for the Troy Citys." For example, in a 7–2 exhibition game victory against neighboring Albany, "The Troy Citys played well to a man to support the effective hurling of new pitcher Fred Goldsmith with third baseman Bradley flawlessly handling seven chances."[25]

The hitting on the club was not much better than the uneven pitching and fielding with Dan Brouthers leading the team in 39 games with a .274 batting average and four home runs (third in the league and the only circuit blasts hit by the Trojans in 1879). The second leading batter at .267 was Aaron Clapp who shared first base duties with Brouthers. Playing in 70 games, Ed Caskin led the club with an anemic 21 runs batted in.

The only individual player who was an unequivocal bright spot on the 1879 roster was playing captain and infielder Bob Ferguson, who took over as manager in August 1879 and retained that position until Troy left the NL after the 1882 season. Though his 1879 record was only 7–22, Ferguson had a fine eye for talent and was managing four future of Hall of Famers—pitchers Tim Keefe and Mickey Welch, first baseman Roger Connor, and catcher and infielder Buck Ewing—during his Trojans tenure. Ironically, in the 1879 off-season, Ferguson released a fifth future Hall of Famer—Dan Brouthers—primarily because of the fledging slugger's overly sensitive reaction to criticism. This was an error of epic proportions, as Dan Brouthers became one of the most feared hitters in nineteenth-century baseball.[26]

In the mid–1860s, Dan Brouthers' family (originally "Bruder") became coal miners in central New York State near Poughkeepsie, finally settling in Wappingers Falls. As a teenager, Brouthers did manual labor in dye and printing mills as well as pursuing the popular American pastime—baseball.

By the mid–1870s, Poughkeepsie had four baseball teams and Wappingers Falls had three.

Brouthers played with the semi-pro Wappingers Falls Actives in 1876–1877. In his formative years, he was a poor hitter and fielder but a somewhat successful hurler. He became the starting Actives hurler in 1877 when a freak accident occurred in July of 1877. Brouthers collided with Harlem Clipper catcher John Quigley, who hit his forehead; on August 12, 1877, the young backstop died and the local coroner exonerated Brouthers from any responsibility. Shaken, Brouthers quit baseball for the rest of the 1877 season. Reputedly, the Wappingers Falls native was haunted by memories of this incident for his entire life.

Brouthers returned to the mound for the Actives in 1878 when he first showed signs of his future batting prowess. On August 23, 1878, now playing for Stottsville, New York, Brouthers had six hits, including a home run against Hudson. The next day, again versus Hudson, Brouthers had another five hits.

In spring of 1879, Dan Brouthers was playing for the consolidated Troy Haymaker and Hudson club in the New York Association Base Ball League. This Troy ball team played the NL Troy Citys club in an exhibition. The major league Troy club was managed by Horace Phillips, who signed Brouthers immediately after the game to play for the Trojans. Brouthers was now a major league ball player after a brief two-year apprenticeship.

Dan Brouthers' first major league manager was Horace Phillips, who nurtured the shy rookie. If Bob Ferguson had not been hired to replace Phillips in mid-season, Phillips may have been able to keep Brouthers in Troy for the bulk of what became a Hall of Fame career. Phillips was a master of public relations and of building strong financial backing for a number of teams he managed, including teams from Philadelphia, Hornellsville (New York), and Binghamton. However, Phillips was frequently at odds with his ownership over control of the club, and when this crustiness was combined with his volatile nature, Phillips moved on in search of new fields to conquer. He had a direct hand with O. P. Caylor in the formation of the American Association (AA) in 1882 and managed the Pittsburgh franchise from 1882 to 1884 and the NL Pittsburgh franchise from 1885 to 1888. Phillips' volatility worsened and he died in the Philadelphia Hospital for the Insane a few years after he left baseball.[27]

In many ways, Horace Phillips was the polar opposite of Bob Ferguson, who replaced him as manager of the Troy Trojans in August of

FOUR. *National Leaguers at the Gates of Troy*

1879. Phillips knew little of the game of baseball and left most of the strategic decisions to his captain George Washington Bradley. Phillips would manage from the grandstand and functioned more as a general manger would today.

Bob Ferguson was a very good, intelligent player-manager whose fiery leadership and win-at-all-costs attitude marked his managerial style. From Ferguson's Troy debut on the bench and as the club's starting third baseman, Dan Brouthers played erratically with the fiery manager in the dugout. Even on his infrequent pitching starts, Brouthers performed miserably under Ferguson's tutelage, including giving up 17 hits in an August 15, 1879, loss to Boston, 0–16. The big first baseman did not respond well to Ferguson's authoritarian behavior and *ad hominem* attacks. He was dropped twice by the Trojans, first at the end of the 1879 season and then after a brief recall in early 1880. Brouthers resurfaced in Baltimore, which was an NA minor league club (and where his old manager Phillips was running the ball club). He then joined with Buck Ewing, who had created a semi-pro club that would play in Troy when the NL Trojans were on the road.

In a few games between the Troy teams, Brouthers again played poorly in Ferguson's presence. He was ignored by the Trojan manager while Ewing was offered a contract to play for Troy in 1881.[28]

Once he was released from the oppressive influence of his nemesis Ferguson, Brouthers became a power hitting star, being the first player to win back-to-back batting titles in 1882–1883 and hitting a remarkable .342 over a nineteen year career in the major leagues. He had a career slugging percentage of .519, including six of his seven slugging crowns coming consecutively from 1881 to 1886. Even his fielding greatly improved after he escaped from Troy with the big first baseman compiling a .971 percentage over his long career.

Bob Ferguson may have a keen judge of talent; however, his blind spot with regard to the potential of Dan Brouthers seems to call into question his dictatorial managerial style and his disdain for his self-effacing, sensitive first baseman.[29]

One factor that may mitigate Ferguson's blind spot regarding Dan Brouthers was the fact that the young slugger was not a natural athlete and had little aptitude for the game other than when he was in the batter's box. For example, over a decade into his major league career, an anecdote from 1890 demonstrates to what degree Brouthers was inept when asked to play the preferred "scientific" baseball of the nineteenth century:

> Brouthers was a natural slugger but not a natural ball-player. Indeed, he was such a big, lumbering, clumsy fellow that the wonder is that he ever got to be fast enough in fielding to be utilized, even though the batting was [that of a] heavy hitter. Brouthers was a slugger and nothing more. Of the fine points of batting he knew little or nothing, and he could never learn to bunt. Eleven years afterward, when he was playing with the Boston Players' League team, he made one bunt that has been handed down in baseball history.
>
> It was a close game and runs were exceedingly scarce. Finally Boston managed to get a runner on first base, and it was Brouthers' turn at bat. As he started for the plate he was ordered by Hugh Duffy, the Boston captain, to bunt. "Why I can't bunt, Hughey," declared Brouthers, who was anxious to hit it out. "Well, you've got to bunt this time," returned Duffy, "if you don't it will cost you ten dollars, for we've got to get this run in, and to do it you'll have to sacrifice this man to second. Then it'll be up to me to bring him home." Brouthers grumbled, but he knew that there was no chance of persuading Duffy to change his mind. So the big fellow picked up the flat bat that was used for bunting those days and lumbered up to the plate. He tried to bunt the first ball pitched but only hit the air, and it was the same on the second trial. Brouthers looked pleadingly in Duffy's direction, but the latter showed [no response].
>
> This time he [Brouthers] met the ball, but Dan's taps were a little different from the ordinary kind, and the sphere, instead of dropping a few feet in front of the plate, went sailing to the right field fence and finally cleared that obstacle. As Dan trotted around the bases and scored Boston's second run he looked decidedly sheepish, and as he confronted Duffy his embarrassment increased. "Honestly, Hughey," said he, "I tried my best to bunt." "Oh, that was a good bunt," returned the little Boston captain, "I really think you are improving in bunting, Dan."[30]

Bob Ferguson was a jack-of-all-trades for the 1879 Troy Citys, and his influence in that disastrous year, whether it is predominantly positive or not, is questionable. What is undisputable about Bob Ferguson, however, is the originality of his nickname, "Death to Flying Things." Bob Ferguson was a heady player often credited as the first National Leaguer to employ the hidden ball trick and a pioneer in the use of defensive shifts on certain batters. Ferguson's first victim was the most feted player of the era, Cap Anson, early in the 1876 season. He also would routinely

FOUR. *National Leaguers at the Gates of Troy*

drop catchable pop flies before the institution of the infield fly rule. Ferguson was also the polar opposite of the Trojan field manager he replaced in 1879—the reserved Horace Phillips; the fiery Ferguson was "quick-tempered, impulsive, and impatient."[31] He was also not above influencing talent on other clubs to play for him. For instance, he "discovered" three Irish-Americans playing for the Holyoke, Massachusetts, Shamrocks who became Troy mainstays: Mickey Welch, Roger Conner, and Pete Gillespie.[32]

Bob "Death to Flying Things" Ferguson was the epitome of the baseball Renaissance man. A solid baseball player on many highly competitive nineteenth-century clubs, he would later become a manager, scout, National Association president, and well-respected umpire. Ferguson was the player-manager for the Troy NL franchise for three and a half of its four seasons (courtesy of the National Baseball Hall of Fame Library, Cooperstown, New York).

Bob Ferguson was a baseball lifer. He played and was involved in various facets of the game for twenty-seven years. More specifically, Ferguson was a true Renaissance man of the national pastime, serving as a player, captain, manager, umpire and (while still an active player) National Association president (1872–1875). Ferguson was the premier third baseman of the 1860s and early 1870s as well as being a heady, versatile player, who was among the first catchers to field the position directly in back of the hitter.

From 1866–1874 (except for 1871 when he played for the New York Mutuals), Ferguson was a valued member of the Brooklyn Atlantics. What is remarkable about the Atlantics club during the mid-late 1860s was the relative stability of the roster.

The Haymakers, Unions and Trojans of Troy, New York

During that period, he played every year with such Brooklyn stalwarts as George Zettlein (P), Dickey Pearce (SS), Joe Start (1B), and Dan McDonald (OF).

Ferguson was also a central player in one of the most memorable games in nineteenth-century baseball. On June 14, 1870, the Cincinnati Red Stockings arrived at the Capitoline Grounds in Brooklyn riding the wave of an 89-game undefeated streak. At the end of nine well-played innings, in which there were only three errors committed between the two teams, the game nearly ended in a 5–5 tie. Atlantics captain and catcher Ferguson was quite willing to settle for the tie. At the urging of sportswriter Henry Chadwick, however, the game continued, with the Reds scoring two runs in the top of the eleventh inning and the Atlantics coming back with three runs in the bottom of the inning for an exciting 8–7 victory. Bob Ferguson was in the thick of the winning rally. The Atlantics' captain has been frequently credited with being the first player to switch-hit; the side from which Ferguson took his swings depended on the game situation. He hit left-handed in the Cincinnati game to keep the ball on the right side of the infield and away from star shortstop George Wright. Ferguson was responsible for the tying run and scored the winning run on two errors on the play by first baseman Charlie Gould.[33]

From 1869 until the early 1880s, Bob Ferguson served most frequently as the captain or manager of the teams with which he was associated. The scrappy player was a key factor on the field during this time. He played the hot corner and catcher during the early part of his career and settled into second base as his career neared its conclusion. He was adept at garnering walks, averaging over 25 bases on ball a season in his three full years with the Trojans and leading the league in 1880. He was a consistent .265 hitter throughout his fourteen year professional career, but he had his moments at the dish. For example, on July 4, 1870, in a game with his homestanding Brooklyn Atlantics versus the very strong Chicago White Stockings club, Ferguson hit three home runs in his first three at-bats with one blast being a grand slam and another being a three-run shot. He also had a triple and scored five runs in that game in a 30–20 Brooklyn win.

As a manager, Bob Ferguson inspired a number of adjectives, both positive and negative, to describe his attitude and behavior on the base-

FOUR. *National Leaguers at the Gates of Troy*

ball diamond: "competitive, authoritative, intelligent, rule-wise, short-tempered and tactless." His dictatorial manner quite possibly cost him at least one championship. In 1874 as manager of the Hartford (CT) Dark Blues, Ferguson had a confrontation with ace hurler Tommy Bond, who was 31–13 for the season. Bond asked for and was granted his release. While Bond's backup Candy Cummings went 16–8 with an earned run average under two, Ferguson's behavior in all probability had a negative impact on his club's second place finish to the powerhouse Chicago White Stockings. It is no surprise that when Ferguson signed with the 1884 New York National League entry, which had a few former players whom he managed while in Troy, he was forced out before managing a game by the players' long and loud objections.[34]

What may strike some as surprising is the late turn his baseball career took when he became one of the most respected umpires in the professional game. Ferguson's philosophy as an umpire was uncomplicated: "The only thing to do is to call things as you see them, and go ahead standing firm by your decisions.... The moment an umpire is driven by the crowd to favor one side or the other, he ought to be called off the field. If a home club or crowd tries to rattle me, it just sets me the other way and they're apt to catch it." He was an arbiter in the National League (1885), the American Association (1887–1889), and the Players League (1890). He had an exceptional knowledge of the rulebook and became the model for the decisive, take-no-prisoners umpire who, nevertheless, had a reputation for fairness and impartiality. Ferguson remained old school to the end by umpiring without a mask and without using a ball-strike indicator.[35]

The *New York Clipper* summed up the 1879 Troy Trojans' season as an unequivocal disaster: "It is generally conceded that the Troy team is n.g.—no good—and will be scalped wherever it goes.... In short, by the time they reach home, all Troy will be so heartedly disgusted that no one will support the organization. Result—bankruptcy and disbandment? What realistic citizen will organize a vigilance committee and lynch each and every player on the Troy nine?" In spite of such negative reporting and weak attendance figures, by the end of August of 1879, Troy had raised half of their proposed goal of $10,000 for fielding a team the following year with Bob Ferguson in full charge of the team.

The Haymakers, Unions and Trojans of Troy, New York

While the 1879 Troy Trojans were a major disappointment to fans and ownership alike, the city did have a number of successful amateur clubs that soothed the pain of Collar City baseball fans who were desperate to support winning baseball. After covering the desultory play of the Trojans, the local sports reporters were happy to provide space for these clubs: "The Troy medical nine that vivisected nine professional brethren from Albany on the Troy City ground on Saturday, will prepare the skeletons next Thursday afternoon, when another game will be played in the capital city."[36]

More important, the Troy Trojans played a series of exhibitions in Troy with the Shamrocks of Holyoke and the "Troy enthusiasts sat up and took notice: 'We want them here in Troy' was the general clamor, and Troy got them—at least five of them—Connor, Dorgan, Gillespie, Harbridge, and Welch."[37]

With Bob Ferguson at the managerial helm from opening day and this influx of new proven players, prospects were much improved for the 1880 Troy Trojans.

1880

On September 29, 1879, baseball's owners instituted the reserve clause, which stated that a certain number of players designated by the club—five for the 1880 season and increasing throughout the decade to 14 players, virtually an entire team, by 1887—were not to be signed by other clubs. The Troy Trojans' first reserve list was composed of Jake Evans (OF), John Cassidy (OF), Ed Caskin (SS) and Bob Ferguson (2B and team captain), all of whom played the entire season as Trojan starters. The fifth member on the club's reserve list was Fred Goldsmith (P-1B-OF), who played for the Chicago White Stockings in 1880.[38]

The Reserve Clause signaled the end of baseball as a player-dominated profession and put the reins of power directly into the hands of the owners. The Reserve Clause set off player-ownership battles for nearly a century throughout its inception until its effective elimination in the Peter Seitz free arbitration ruling of December 23, 1975, that allowed Dave McNally and Andy Messersmith to become free agents.

Four. National Leaguers at the Gates of Troy

The balance of power switched back to the players who have fought ownership attempts to create a salary cap and to impose the institution of draconian payroll tax penalties for the past thirty-nine years.[39]

While the baseball club owners of this era are usually presented as rapacious, profit-dominated businessmen of the Gilded Age, they did face some rather daunting financial and social problems as the 1880 season began. Even the usually supportive sporting press began to decry the decline of the national pastime:

> Will any one regret to learn that baseball is on the decline? If so, his grief will be aggravated by the fact that the above mentioned decline is of a hopeless character. Base ball was ruined by bad associations which gradually surrounded it, and hence the season opens with but little promise. The number of clubs is less than at any time during the past five years. In 1878 the national base ball association had 18 clubs competing for the championship. Last year, however, the number of contestants was but nine, while this season opens only with three. Among other unpromising features in this amusement is the destruction of the Brooklyn play-ground by the intersection of streets, while the Williamsburgh play-ground is soon to be divided into building lots. The grounds formerly occupied by the Jersey City club have been to other uses by its proprietors, the Pennsylvania railroad company, and thus the game, at least in this vicinity, is in a shattered condition. There was a time when base ball deserved encouragement as a fine athletic exercise, but it has been so degraded of late years that its decay does not surprise.[40]

Yet despite its many problems and the continued downward spiral in spectator and media support, baseball did not seem to lack for communities, large and small, to lobby for major league franchises.

Worcester made its first appearance in the NL in 1880 and became linked with Troy as a fellow small market Eastern team with major league ambitions and a storied baseball history. While the Trojans had future Hall of Fame members on its roster, none had yet developed into a baseball star of the first magnitude, and none had a debut as impressive as Lee Richmond, who had one of the most dominating rookie seasons in nineteenth-century baseball and was the primary reason Worcester received an invitation to join the NL.

Richmond played only three full major league seasons and had decent numbers: a .250 batting average as a utility outfielder, a 71–91 won-loss record, and a career 2.99 earned run average with the

After defeating a small handful of National League teams in 1879, the Worcester, Massachusetts, Grays were admitted into the National League in 1880. The team was immediately linked with Troy as a small-market club that had a great baseball lineage but an insufficient population base. (Courtesy of the National Baseball Hall of Fame Library, Cooperstown, New York).

FOUR. *National Leaguers at the Gates of Troy*

Worcesters. However, Lee Richmond accomplished many impressive feats on the mound. Moreover his combined college (Brown University) and professional career (Worcester) from 1879 to 1882 led to a major regulatory decision in December of 1879 that prevents athletes to this day from playing professional sports on the pain of losing their remaining college eligibility. Richmond and his catcher Winslow were able to lead Brown to consecutive collegiate championships in 1878 and 1879 because they were grandfathered in with the passing of the "no professionals" policy of 1879.

Eighteen seventy-nine saw Richmond pitch a no-hitter in his professional debut in an exhibition 11–0 win over the Chicago White Stockings, pitch a two-hitter against the NA league-leading Washington Nationals, and pitch a no-hitter against Springfield on July 28, 1879, in a game in which he had four base hits. On June 12, 1880, Lee Richmond pitched the first major league perfect game in a 1–0 victory over Cleveland. This game was only part of an unbelievable pitching streak of 42 consecutive scoreless innings and three shutouts in a one week period. Richmond was instrumental in Worcester's fifth place 1880 finish at 40–43, one game behind the Troy franchise. Richmond's meteoric pitching career was essentially over in 1882 when he went 14–33 and saw his Worcester club along with the Troy Trojans chased from the NL. Richmond continued his studies receiving a medical degree and returning to his native Ohio where he set up a practice but soon changed careers; he became a respected educator for forty years[41]

In 1880, the Troy Trojans finished in fourth place with their best record ever in NL play, 41–42. The year was the major league rookie season for four future Hall of Famers: Mickey Welch (P), Tim Keefe (P), Roger Connor (1B), and Buck Ewing (C-INF). Mickey Welch led the way, going 34–30 in 574 innings (fourth in the NL) with a 2.54 earned run average. Arriving in Troy on August 4, 1880, Tim Keefe only had a 6–6 won-loss record; however, Keefe held hitters to a .199 batting average and had a sparkling 0.86 earned run average, the lowest in major league baseball history. Roger Connor had a monster rookie season, leading the club in triples (8), home runs (3), runs batted in (47) and slugging average (.459).

Connor also hit for his highest batting average as a Haymaker, .332.

The Haymakers, Unions and Trojans of Troy, New York

Only seldom-used Buck Ewing had a subpar rookie season, hitting .178 in 13 games. In a true rarity, hurler Welch tied Pete Gillespie for the team lead in doubles (20).[42]

The undisputable most valuable (and best) player for the 1880 Troy Citys was Roger Connor.

Roger Connor was one of the most popular and respected baseball players of the nineteenth century. He garnered the most triples in the century (233) and the second most bases on balls (1002); he also was fourth in doubles (441) and runs scored (1620). He was a multi-faceted batter leading the NL in nearly every traditional hitting category: games played (1884 and 1892–1893), hits (1885), times on base (1885), doubles (1892) triples (1882 and 1886), home runs (1890), extra base hits (1882, 1889, 1892), runs batted in (1889), walks (1888), batting average (1885), on-base percentage (1885), slugging percentage (1889–1890), and total bases (1885). However, Roger Connor is remembered today, if he is remembered at all, as the game's first true power hitter, leading the major league in career home runs with 138, which remained the record until it was broken

Roger Connor was the premier slugger of the nineteenth century, holding the career home run crown until it was broken by Babe Ruth. At first a poor-fielding third baseman, he was later moved to first base, where he would establish himself as one of the more sure-handed defenders of his day. Connor was elected to the Baseball Hall of Fame in 1976 (courtesy of the National Baseball Hall of Fame Library, Cooperstown, New York).

FOUR. *National Leaguers at the Gates of Troy*

by Babe Ruth. Furthermore, his home runs were often prodigious blasts, including the only ball ever hit out of the original Polo Grounds.

Roger Connor helped his club in other ways than with his bat. After a very poor start as a left-handed third baseman when he committed 60 errors in 80 games (.821 fielding percentage) for the 1880 Trojans, Connor was second in the nineteenth century in career fielding as a sure-handed first baseman (.978 as a first baseman and .970 overall). He led the NL first baseman in putouts (1887, 1890, and 1893), assists (1885 and 1890), double plays (1881, 1885, and 1890), and fielding percentage (1887, 1890, 1892, and 1896). Furthermore, though he was a big man at 6-feet-3 and 220 pounds, Connor also averaged 20 steals a season from 1887 to 1896. He also is often credited with the "come-up" slide (today known as the "popup slide").[43]

Roger Connor's baseball career began in 1877 with his playing third base and hitting from the right side for his local semi-pro club, the Waterbury (CT) Monitors. He showed enough promise to be given a two-week tryout as a first baseman with the 1878 IA New Bedford, Massachusetts, Whalers, but was given his release by famed manager Frank Bancroft. On his return to the Waterbury Monitors, Connor blossomed (quickly) as a left-handed batter and (steadily) as a first sacker.

By mid-season, Connor was back in the IA, playing for the Holyoke Shamrocks, for which he was named captain in 1879. Though he was uncomfortable in the position of captain, which he resigned early in the season, Connor did not suffer any discomfort at the plate. Roger Connor hit a robust .367 that year and so impressed Springfield playing manager Bob Ferguson, who was employed by the 1879 Troy Trojans late in their initial season as a NL franchise, that he signed the big power hitter for the 1880 season.

Despite possessing Troy's best ever major league record (41–42) in 1880, the Trojans finished 25.5 games behind the pennant-winning Chicago White Stockings, a perennial power in the 1880s. Winning five championships in the decade, Chicago was led by hitting star and astute field general Adrian Anson (the first major leaguer to garner 3,000 hits), who hit .334 with an NL-leading 74 runs batted in. Cap Anson is generally credited with being the first to employ offensive and defensive signals, use the steal as a major offensive weapon, have fielders back up one another, and rely on a two-man pitching rotation.[44]

The Haymakers, Unions and Trojans of Troy, New York

Roger Connor was not only the best Troy ball player but the city's first media star and its most popular player with the fans. After his admirable season on the diamond, which included major league baseball's first hitting cycle (against Boston pitching ace Tommy Bond, no less) and a two home run game against Chicago fireballer Larry Corcoran on July 17, 1880; newspapers began to notice both Roger Conner's athleticism (he was also a boxer) and his cultured manner. In a postseason brief biography in the October 2, 1880, edition of the *New York Clipper*, Roger Connor was described as "admirably proportioned" and "as fine a specimen of physical development as any in the profession" and "[he] evidently possesses extraordinary powers of endurance." In a similar vein, Connor, who owned a strong tenor voice that he often accompanied on the piano, was praised for his "honorable and affable nature" and for being a "Gentleman of the Diamond."[45]

Judged by his own high standards, Connor in 1881 had a mediocre year (.292 batting average), but he did hit the NL's first grand slam home run off rival Worcester's pitching ace Lee Richmond on September 10, 1881. Eighteen eighty-one was also a memorable year in Connor's personal life. Since the club had no uniform big enough to fit him, he was sent to the shirt factory where a local woman, Angeline Meir, was working as a seamstress. She took his measurements both literally and, apparently, figuratively as well. They married and remained so for 47 years.[46]

In 1882, Troy's last year in the NL, Connor seemed to be one of the few Trojans to take an interest in the play on the field. He hit .330, which was 55 points higher than the next best average on the team.

In 1883, Roger Connor remained in the NL by signing with the New York Gothams. He was joined by his 1882 teammates, the Trojan starting battery of Mickey Welch (P) and Buck Ewing (C). The Gothams owner John B. Day also supported the AA New York Metropolitans franchise, to which he assigned former Trojan pitcher Tim Keefe and catcher Bill Holbert, both of whom were under the tutelage of manager Jim Mutrie. The Mets with little direct help from Day won the 1884 AA pennant. During the 1883–1884 seasons, Roger Connor hit at an all-star level and was again a great run producer. However, in 1884, he had a terrible year in the field playing second base, third base, and center field in an attempt to incorporate a rookie first baseman into the starting lineup.

FOUR. *National Leaguers at the Gates of Troy*

In 1885, Gothams owner Day was determined to have a winning NL club and went to great lengths to stack his roster with the best team his money could buy. Day reassigned Mets manager Mutrie to the Gothams and circumvented the league regulations to sign Mets' ace Tim Keefe. Finally, he signed Jim O'Rourke and John Ward, which gave Day a roster with six future Hall of Fame members. Roger Connor had a career year for New York in 1885; he was in the top five of most hitting categories.

The Giants won back-to-back pennants and championship series against the AA winners in both 1888 and 1889. Connor jumped to the Players League in 1890 where he played for Giants' teammate Buck Ewing's Big Giants. He returned to the 1892 NL Giants and had decent if unspectacular numbers. From 1892 to 1897, Connor began a brief baseball odyssey by playing for the Philadelphia Phillies (after one month playing with the Philadelphia team in the AA, which folded early in the season), the Giants, and the St. Louis Browns, who released him upon his request at mid-season. Connor spent the rest of the 1897 season in the minor leagues, first with the Waterbury (CT) Pirates (Connecticut State League (CSL)) and then with the Falls River (CT) Indians (New England League (NEL).[47]

In 1898, Roger Connor purchased the Waterbury Pirates (renamed the "Rough Riders" that season) and served as the owner-player. He won the CSL pennant in his first full year. Conner remained in these dual roles until 1901 when he sold the club to a local businessman. He signed on for the rest of the 1901 season with the rival New Haven Blues. The following year Conner established the Springfield Ponies that were accepted into the CSL that year and for whom he served in the twin roles of owner-player through the 1903 season when he retired from organized baseball. However, he continued to play for Waterbury semi-pro and amateur teams until 1910 at the age of 53. He was elected by the Veterans Committee of the Baseball Hall of Fame for inclusion in the Cooperstown class of 1976.[48]

Future Hall of Famers Mickey Welch and Tim Keefe also made their NL debuts with Troy. Welch made 65 appearances on the mound, winning 34 games and losing 30, while Keefe got into 12 games, going 6–6. A third Trojan pitcher that year was former star Terry Larkin, who averaged 29 wins and 54 decisions in the previous three years with Hartford and Chicago. He came to Troy suffering from a sore arm and went 0–5 with an 8.76 ERA. The overmatched Larkin gave up 83 hits in 39 innings with 10 walks and five strikeouts. After his release by Troy, Larkin never played another game of major league baseball.

Mickey Welch was the epitome of the pitcher who lacked that great dominating fastball and won his games with guile and off-speed pitches. Mickey Welch (born Michael Walsh) began his professional baseball career in Poughkeepsie, New York, in 1877 and then played the next year with the Auburn, New York, baseball club. In 1879, he signed on with the Holyoke Shamrocks and went 23–14 while playing with future teammate and fellow Hall of Famer Roger Connor. Holyoke in the mid-nineteenth century had 25 paper mills in which many Irish immigrants found employment.

Ironically, Bob Ferguson, who was to be his 1880 manager with the Trojans, became aware of Welch when the latter pitched against his Springfield club in 1879. The hotheaded manager complained loud and long that Welch's junkball pitches were illegal because the hurler was releasing the ball above his waist. The Irishman's own self-assessment reveals how he was able to succeed on the diamond for some many years: "I was a little fellow and I had to learn to use my head. I studied the hitters and I knew how to pitch to all of them, and I worked hard to perfect my control. I had a pretty good fast ball, but I depended chiefly on a change of pace and an assortment of curve balls."[49]

Sharing mound duties with Tim Keefe in 1881, Mickey Welch remained the ace of the staff with a 21–18 won-loss percentage and a 2.67 earned run average. The following year amidst the pressure of trying to maintain an economically professional ball club in Troy, Welch's stats fell to 14–16 and his earned run average ballooned to 3.46.

With the demise of the Trojan franchise prior to the 1883 season, Welch signed on with the New York Gothams (soon to become the "New York Giants") in 1883 and pitched at an all-star level for most of his nine-year tenure with the team. He had a career year in 1885 with a 44–11 won-loss record and the lowest earned run average of his career (1.66). He led NL pitchers that season in win-loss percentage (.800) and was second in total wins and earned run average. He was also second in the

FOUR. *National Leaguers at the Gates of Troy*

league in hits allowed per nine innings (6.85). He was a member of the NL pennant-winning Giants in 1888 and 1889. He pitched in both years' World Series, which resulted in Giants victories over the American Association's St. Louis Brown Stockings (1888) and the Brooklyn Bridegrooms (1889).[50] Again, a former Troy Citys player helped lead the New York Giants to championships in the 1880s.

Mickey Welch's career with the New York Giants did not end on a positive note. Even though on October 22, 1885, he helped John Ward organize his response to the implementation of maximum (and minimum) player salaries with the creation of the Brotherhood of Professional Base Ball Players, he did not jump to the 1890 Players League but stayed in New York with the Giants and inked a three-year contract for the most basic of reasons:

> The [salary] figure suited the leader of the [Players League] movement, but the financial men would only guarantee me my salary for 1890. Some time ago Mr. Day [owner of the New York Giants] made me a big offer, and said that he would sign a three years' contract, he to assume all risks. I am in the business for dollars and sense, and, as the offer of the old League was the better one, I risked it.[51]

Hall of Famer Mickey Welch led the Trojan staff from 1880 to 1882. He dazzled opponents with a series of off-speed pitches and great control. After leaving Troy, he went on to pitch for the New York Giants, where he became one of the early members of baseball's 300 Win Club (courtesy of the National baseball Hall of Fame Library, Cooperstown, New York).

The Haymakers, Unions and Trojans of Troy, New York

After a solid 17–14 season in 1890, Welch pitched ineffectively for the Giants, going 5–9 in 1891 and the early months of 1892 before being demoted to the now minor league Troy Trojans to finish out his three-year contract.[52] On his death in July of 1941, Mickey Welch received a long newspaper tribute regarding his baseball career that described in depth his long career in organized baseball and a few of his many accomplishments, including his 17-game consecutive winning streak in 1885 and his striking out of the first nine batters in an August game with the 1884 Cleveland Blues.[53]

Mickey Welch achieved a number of impressive career and individual game accomplishments. He pitched in 13 major league seasons and was the third 300-game winner. Welch had 40 career shutouts and 10 1–0 wins; he completed the first 105 games of his career. Furthermore, in the first half of his career, he was a respectable utility outfielder with 492 career hits, 93 doubles, and a .292 lifetime batting average. Welch even had two complete game victories over the Buffalo Bisons on July, 4, 1881.[54] In 1973, Smiling Mickey Welch was voted into the Hall of Fame by the Veterans Committee.

The 1880 Troy Trojans saw the arrival of another rookie pitcher who would become a Hall of Fame member. Joining the club in August as a change pitcher for the overworked Mickey Welch, Tim Keefe was already a noted pitcher in the Capital District area. During the early months of the season with the Albany NA entry, he fashioned a lackluster 7–9 record but had an eye-catching 1.87 earned run average. After the Albany team disbanded on July 21, 1880, Keefe finished the Trojan season with a 6–6 won-loss record; once again he had an unbelievable stretch on the mound, setting the all-time single season NL earned run average with a minuscule 0.86. Tim Keefe went on to have a brilliant pitching career with 342 lifetime victories and the major league record for consecutive victories in a season with 19 in 1888.

Tim Keefe was born in Cambridge, Massachusetts, and began his professional career in 1878. He played for seven minor league clubs in Massachusetts and New York in three years, including a short span in 1879 with the New Bedford, Massachusetts, NA team that was managed at the time by Jim Mutrie, who was to play a large part in Keefe's future baseball career.

FOUR. *National Leaguers at the Gates of Troy*

After his breakout season in 1880, Tim Keefe hoped to cash in on his success on the diamond but was instead one of the Trojans' reserved players for the 1881 and 1882 seasons and had no recourse but to accept Troy's offer(s) since he was unable to offer his services to other clubs. Keefe's frequent unpleasant contract negotiations, his threats to hold out unless his salary demands were met, and his displeasure with the effect the reserve clause had on depressing major league salaries were factors in his involvement with the Brotherhood of Professional Base Ball Players (1885) and the Players League (PL) (1890).

From 1883 to 1891 with the exception of his 1890 defection to the PL where he was managed by Buck Ewing, Tim Keefe's manager was Jim Mutrie, who fashioned a nine-year record of 658–419 (.607). Under Mutrie's guidance, Keefe led the New York Metropolitans to New York's first major league pennant and was instrumental in the NL New York Giants' first world championships in 1888 and 1889.

Future Hall of Famer Tim Keefe joined the 1880 Trojan staff as a change pitcher for an overworked Mickey Welch. Debuting as a major leaguer in August, Keefe would pitch twelve games (105 innings) for Troy and set the all-time record for lowest season ERA at 0.86. He and Welch pitched for the Trojans through 1882 and then formed a formidable duo for the Giants from 1885 to 1889 (courtesy of the National Baseball Hall of Fame Library, Cooperstown, New York).

The Haymakers, Unions and Trojans of Troy, New York

Tim Keefe was an NL veteran and steadying influence on the 1885 New York Giants, who had five other future Hall of Fame members on the roster: Roger Connor, Buck Ewing, Jim O'Rourke, John Ward, and Tim Welch. Keefe had his greatest year in 1886 when he led the NL in wins (42), complete games (62) and innings pitched (535). Perhaps his best year was the championship year of 1888 when he led the league in wins (35), winning percentage (.745), earned run average (1.74), shutouts (8), and strikeouts (335). The 1888 season also saw Tim Keefe achieve his amazing 19-game consecutive win streak and collect four wins against the AA St. Louis Brown Stockings in the championship series. During his great run with the New York clubs, he also served as the secretary/treasurer of the Brotherhood prior to jumping to the PL New York Giants in 1890.

As with his pitching partner Mickey Welch, Tim Keefe depended for much of his success on the mound on guile, bluster, and sleight of hand. Until 1887 when a rule change demanded that the pitcher face the batter and keep both feet on the ground, Keefe employed a twisting run-up in the pitching box that was similar to the deception a spin bowler in cricket would employ.[55] Keefe's main strength was in his motion that upset the batter's timing: "His real effectiveness lay in his change of pace. He could pitch a speedy ball with the same preliminary movements as he used with a slow cut-curve; consequently the batsman never knew just what kind of a ball to expect when he [Keefe] was pitching."

In a summary analysis of the Troy Trojans' 1880 season, the consensus view of the club's improvement was due to the late season acquisition of Keefe: "'Tim' Keefe was wonderfully effective in the old style of underhand pitching and he was also one of the most graceful twirlers ever seen on the diamond. He had all the big batsmen of the league guessing, and helped materially in the brace that Troy made late in the season—a brace that finally landed them in fourth place."

In a self-assessment of what led to his success as a pitcher, Keefe revealed that "[the] change of pace for pitchers was important in those days. It was, as now, largely a case of outguessing the batter." Finally, Keefe gave much of the credit for his success to his catcher Buck Ewing, "[who] knew how to steady a pitcher, knew all the points of the batsman in the league and used those points to great advantage. He was always

FOUR. *National Leaguers at the Gates of Troy*

constantly up to the tricks of the game and never forgot a weakness of his opponents."[56]

After an ineffective two-game appearance in the 1889 NL championship series, Keefe, after the Brotherhood announced in November the formation of the Players League for the 1890 season, signed with the New York entry in the new league. Keefe's involvement with the Players League was deep-rooted and extended beyond the playing field. His sporting goods company had contracts to provide the league ball as well as much of the league's equipment. Keefe re-signed with the NL Giants in 1891 but was ineffective and was released in July when he re-signed with the NL Philadelphia Phillies, who released him in August of 1893.

Tim Keefe was a NL umpire from 1894 to 1896 when he resigned because of the constant "kicking" by the players. He had coached Amherst College for a few years before coaching the Harvard nine from 1892 to 1896 when the school abruptly decided to not rehire him.

Though he was the major league career leader in strikeouts and second in career wins at the time of his retirement, Tim Keefe was perhaps best known for his inspiration and influence on Ernest Thayer's beloved poem, "Casey at the Bat," which the pitcher apparently sparked in an interview with the author in 1887 when the latter was a reporter for the *San Francisco Examiner*. Tim Keefe was finally recognized for his talents on the baseball diamond with his 1964 election to Cooperstown by the Veterans' Committee.[57]

The 1880 Troy Trojans roster had an odd symmetrical occurrence among its utility catching crew. Buck Ewing and Bill Holbert usually shared the catching duties for the 1880 Trojans. However, two players manned the position for one game each with one player playing his first major league game and the other playing his last. For both backstops, this was the only game they ever played for the Trojans.

Charles "Fatty" Briody was a Lansingburgh native, who caught for his hometown Trojans on June 16, 1880, making a less-than-successful debut. He went 0–4 at the plate and had three errors in 10 chances. Briody had a peripatetic eight-year playing career for seven teams in three major leagues. He hit .227 and fielded .901 as a catcher over that time.

The other catcher in question has a much more interesting (and notorious) back-story. On May 25, 1880, Dick Higham played his final major league game. As with Briody, Higham had an unmemorable day, going 1–5 with a putout and two passed balls. English-born, Dick Higham played for 12 major league seasons, hitting a more than respectable .307. He played for his 1880 Troy manager Bob Ferguson earlier in his career when both were with the 1876 NL Hartford Dark Blues, and Higham led that year's club in most offensive categories, including a league-leading 21 doubles.

In spite of his success on the field, Higham was frequently not re-hired because of questions about his intensity and honesty. This suspicion was apparently borne out in fact when an investigation instigated by the NL Detroit Wolverines turned up written evidence that Higham allegedly established a coded expression that signaled gamblers when to bet on Detroit. Higham was dismissed as an NL umpire on June 22, 1882, and banished from baseball two days later. Dick Higham was the first and only major league umpire to receive a lifetime disqualification.[58]

The Troy Trojans began the 1880 season with positive signs that they would no longer be the doormats of the NL. The outlook for Troy was sunny prior to the NL's opening day: ""The Troy Citys made a very favorable impression yesterday [April 15, 1880]" as they defeated the Dalys, 10–0.

The starting battery was new and predicted to be a winning combination: "Welsh [Welch] and Harbridge promise to make a good team. The latter is a plucky catcher and the former has a very effective delivery, peculiarly deceiving to a batsman on account of the various curves he resorts to." The Trojans played all comers during their pre-season training, which they employed to get players in shape and to search for an effective change hurler: "The Troy Citys will play the Union College nine to-morrow, when Larkin (who yesterday played first base for the visiting Dalys) will pitch, Holbert catch, and Ferguson will play second base. A good game may be expected." Troy's sporting press was not shy about giving Manager Ferguson advice on how to prepare the club for the upcoming season: "An excellent picked nine could be made up of for the Troy Citys to practice with, which could include three of the Troy players and such others as Doscher, Briody, Diack [Diach], and Taylor. Try it once, Capt. Ferguson."

FOUR. *National Leaguers at the Gates of Troy*

The April 15, 1880, exhibition game was closely contested until the Trojans broke open the game in the last two innings:

> The opening game of the Troy Citys yesterday afternoon was well attended considering the weather, and those who were present witnessed a fine exhibition. The Dalys of West Troy [Watervliet], with whom the Trojans played, constitute a pretty strong amateur club, and the first six innings were very closely contested, the score standing 1–0 in favor of the Troys. In the seventh inning the Troys by tremendous batting added five runs to the score and tallied four more in the ninth, retiring their opponents in each successive inning with a blinder. Three times the Dalys succeeded in getting a man on third base, but on each occasion Welch, who pitched for the Troys, succeeded in putting the last man out on strikes before a run could be obtained. The Troys played well throughout the game, making very few errors. Cassidy guarded second base, Connors [Connor] acted as captain, and Ferguson umpired.[59]

The Troy Trojans continued to play impressive early season baseball. On April 20, 1880, Troy pitcher Mickey Welch no-hit a strong Union College (Schenectady, NY) nine: "The Troy Citys and Union college clubs played a fine game yesterday afternoon, the college boys making a number of surprisingly brilliant plays. The high wind prevented effective batting, which amounts for the small score by the Trojans. The Unions were unable to secure a single base hit, and their solitary run was obtained on a bad throw by Harbridge (C) and a fumble by Cogswell (1B). Cassidy played second base remarkably well." Roger Connor led the Trojans with a double and a single.[60]

On April 29, 1880, the Troy Trojans in preparation for their NL opening day game, suffered a blow to their pride and to the team's hopes for a winning season, in a 1–3 loss to the their arch-rival, the light-hitting NA Albany, New York, baseball club:

> The Troys and Albanys played a most remarkable game of ball at Albany yesterday—one of the most remarkable on record—and its particular feature was the defeat of the Trojans. It had been conceded, even by the Albanians, that the Trojans were the superior club, and in view of this voluntary concession, and the overwhelming defeats the Albanys suffered on their eastward trip, the Troy Citys supposed they had an easy victory. But for once they were mistaken, and the close of an exceedingly well-played game saw the Troys with only one tally to three for the Albanys. A strong southeast wind, increasing at time to almost hurricane velocity, caused frequent temporary cessations of the contest. This, with occasional

dashes of rain, rendered ball playing decidedly unpleasant, besides interfering in a great measure with the heavy batting of the visiting club. The game was called at 3:05 o'clock, with H. Doscher as umpire and the Troys at the bat.

Cogswell was retired on a foul fly, Gillespie reached first on eight balls, but was put out in attempting to steal second, Ferguson and [?] made hits, and both were left by the retirement of Connor. Morrissey led off for the Albanys with a two base hit to left, and finally scored on a wild pitch and a passed ball, after which the side was quickly retired. In the second Caskins [Caskin] was given first by Dorgan's error, and Dickerson sent him home on a two base hit over the left fielder's head. Larkin followed with a single and Dickerson was put out on the home plate, which he recklessly attempted to reach from second on Larkin's hit. Holbert made first on a force hit, upon which Larkin was retired while imitating Dickerson, and Coggswell [sic] closed the inning on an out at first. The Albanys were retired in one, two, three order in this inning, Cassidy making a difficult catch from [former Troy Haymaker] Pike's bat, being compelled to jump over the right field fence into the crowd in order to get the ball. The Trojans made two hits in the third inning, but no runs were scored. Morrissey secured another double for Albany and reached third, where he was finally left. In the fourth inning Caskins, Dickerson, and Larkin led off with hits for the Troys, and the bases were filled before a man was put out. But, strange to say, no run was scored, for Holbert and Cogswell forced Caskins and Dickerson out on the home plate, and Gillespie was retired at first. In the seventh inning Say made a two base hit, eventually scoring an earned run, and in the eighth inning Morrissey tallied again for Albany on two single hits and errors of Connor and Caskins.

This ended the run getting, for notwithstanding that the Troys made hits in every inning except the fifth, it was impossible for anyone to tally. Four of the Troys were put out on the home plate, and the Albanys made two double plays, the Trojans securing one. The game was lost by poor base running at the start. If good judgment had been exercised in this particular, the contest would have been easily won. The Troys held their opponents too cheaply, and paid the usual penalty. The Albanys played a strong fielding game, but were weak at the bat, securing however enough hits to win. The attendance was about 1,000, more than one-third of the persons present being Trojans.[61]

In another ironic twist of fate, the winning pitcher for the Albany club in the April pre-season victory was Tim Keefe, who later in the season began his major league career with the Troy Citys as a change pitcher for regular hurler Mickey Welch.

The Trojans gained a measure of respect the following day with a

FOUR. *National Leaguers at the Gates of Troy*

6–3 victory over Albany. The Troy club was led by winning pitcher Mickey Welch, who had seven strikeouts and allowed six hits. Trojans Dickerson and Ferguson led the hitting with two hits apiece.[62]

The 1880 Trojans who had a more stable and talented roster than they did in their first season in the NL were able to work on the finer points of the game, including experimenting on finding the most effective batting order:

> *The Chicago Times*, in an article written in the interest of the holders of score cards at League match games, says that "there is little or nothing in the batting order," arguing that the changing of the order is a matter of no importance. Now, it appears to be quite the reverse. An order is made out for the first match of the a season, and the progress of the game shows that the wrong men follow each other in the order, and at once it becomes desirable to change it. In other games which follow, too, experience shows that more change in the batting order is needed. If it happens that a batter who seldom makes more than a single base follows a still weaker batsman then a change becomes necessary as to make a heavy batter follow a weak batter or a poor base runner. All those things require study, and it is only after a month or two of trials that the correct order can be arrived at, and even then changes may occur which render it necessary for a new order to be made out.[63]

On May 15, 1880, the Trojans defeated the NL Providence Grays, 6–4, in Troy. It was a well-played game with the star of the game the Trojan center fielder: "Dickerson won the game by his brilliant fielding and a three base hit in the seventh inning, which sent men across the plate." However, the most important event of the day occurred after the game.

The Rhode Island club desired to play a makeup game with the Trojans two days later, on the May 17, but Troy refused: "The management of the Providence club [directors] announce their intention of claiming a forfeit game from the Troys because of the refusal of the latter to remain [in Providence] and play them to-day. If the Troys had played in Providence to-day, they would have been unable to reach Troy until 4:15 o'clock and been unable to play a regularly scheduled tilt against the Worcester Ruby Legs."[64]

In keeping with a long-established baseball legacy, nineteenth-century Troy baseball franchises never seemed able to complete a season without some major controversy, often of their own creation, that threatened their professional existence. On May 17, 1880, the Trojans played their longtime geographical and Capital District rival Albany in an exhibition game that they won, 8–7, and that resulted in a financial windfall for both clubs. However, the National League office scheduled a make-up game of an earlier Troy rainout for the same date with the Providence Grays. Troy risked league expulsion for playing such a "money" game; however, NL president William Hulbert again came to the team's defense.

The league office denied the Providence grievance on a technicality: Since May 17, 1880, was originally an off-day for Troy, the club did not, strictly speaking, violate the NL regulation that prohibited clubs from playing a non-league exhibition on a date of a regularly scheduled contest. Troy escaped any sanction or fine. As a result of this controversy, the NL tightened the wording of the regulation regarding the scheduling and the playing of non-league exhibition games.

Troy was frequently in hot water for scheduling exhibition games with their Capital District rivals. As early as April of 1879, the Troy Trojans were being warned against playing exhibition matches with Albany: "Yesterday morning the management of the Troy Citys received a dispatch from President Hulbert, of the [National] League, stating that the Troy Citys had no right to play the [Albany] Capital Citys. It is evident that someone has made a mistake as the rules seem to be very plain on this subject. The only question that can arise is: Are the two Albany clubs local? We would say yes, for it was so understood by Buffalo when the league met at that city. It was understood that the five mile ban that the other league clubs could not play in Albany and that makes the Albany clubs local."[65]

While the Trojans played only .500 baseball for the 1880 season, the club was certainly playing at a major league level as is evidenced in its exhibition games played against National Association clubs. For example, on April 20, 1880, the Troy Citys defeated the visiting NA Baltimore team, 21–1, in an exhibition game that featured Baltimore's one-armed pitcher, Daley:

> There were numerous baseball admirers in Troy who at least predicted a hard struggle for the Troy Citys yesterday. The overwhelming defeat of the

Four. National Leaguers at the Gates of Troy

visitors was therefore a surprise even to the most sanguine supporters of the Troy Citys. The Baltimores were content with playing only seven innings.... Daley was batted out of his position in the fifth inning and Bruthers [Dan Brouthers], who played for Troy the previous year and was unceremoniously dropped from the team by manager Bob Ferguson] took his place with little better success than his predecessor.

Baltimore was effectively handcuffed by winning pitcher Larkin and scored its only run on "pardonable errors" by Caskin and Ferguson. The Baltimore team was equally inept in the field committing 26 errors, including passed balls and wild pitches. Troy's leading hitters were Caskin with a double and 2 singles and Cassidy with a double and single.

Holbert's catching—one passed ball—and throwing earned the observer's special praise. The only unusual play was Troy's Buttercup Dickerson hitting a triple but being called out for not touching one of the bases.[66]

The 1880 Troy Trojans often demonstrated superb baseball skills and team work that would seem to belie their mediocre record. On May 25, 1880, for example, Troy easily defeated a solid visiting Boston Red Caps team:

> About 600 persons witnessed the game yesterday between the Troy Citys and Bostons on the grounds of the former club, and testified by loud applause their delight at the signal victory achieved by the home club over the ex-champions. The score of 8 to 1 was the conclusion of the game marked by especially heavy batting and by much brilliant fielding on the part of the Troys. Welch pitched and Harbridge caught for the home team, and they worked together effectively.
>
> The Bostons broke the uniformity of their cipher row in the fourth inning, and saved themselves from a tediously familiar "shutting out." James O'Rourke scored the lonely run. Having secured first base on a hit, he reached second and third on passed balls, and was brought home by Burdock's baser. The Citys gained a commanding lead in the second inning when, by Connor's three-bagger, a happy bunching of hits by Caskins, Cogsswell [Cogswell] and Ferguson and errors of Burdock and Sutton, four runs were made. In the third inning Connor's heavy hitting, Harbridge's two-baser and Sutton's error made the easy journey of two more Trojans to the home plate. The eighth inning capped the score with two added runs, secured by Gillespie's single, an error of Houck's and Connor's long and surprising hit, to the left centre outfield. Bond was batted for 17 base hits, and 9 were scored on Welch's delivery.
>
> Connor was the hero of the batting. In the third inning the ball, sent thither by his long and surprising hit, cleared the south fence by many a

foot, and Connor made the circuit of the bases. In the second inning the same batsman reached the third base after a stroke which sent the ball full and fair against the fence, and a two-base hit and single completed his unique record [hitting for the cycle] of strong and skillful willow-handling. Gillespie, Welch and Ferguson also swung the bat with noticeable success. On foul hits the Bostons twice sent the sphere over the east fence.

In the field Harbridge made a number of fine foul captures and an excellent double play. Coggswell [Cogswell], by force of habit, never misses a ball, Ferguson and Caskins [Caskin] did admirable work, two rapid and graceful double plays standing in the credit of the trio. Powers caught well for Boston and Foley's base play was good.

The men from Massachusetts were maimed as well as beaten. In endeavoring to capture Connor's far hit in the second inning, John O'Rourke fell over a fence strut and was severely injured about the face and breast, He was led in from the field bleeding from a long and gaping laceration of the cheek and throat. Dr. McLean, who was on the grounds, furnished the necessary surgical attention. Houck was placed in the right field and James O'Rourke took his brother's position. During the progress of the game Powers and Burdock also were temporarily disabled.[67]

After such impressive victories over the best NL clubs, the Trojans seemed to find ways to outplay opponents and still lose the game. In a mid–May game against Providence, the Troy Citys had multiple hits in the game by Cassidy, Gillespie, and Welch with the defensive plaudits going to Caskin, "who played brilliantly," and Dickerson, who "carried off the honors in the out-field." Yet the Trojans lost the game, 5–6, due to "careless base running and erroneous decisions of the umpire."[68]

In late September, Troy lost another close match to Providence, 3–5, again surrendering three runs in the seventh inning which was aided and abetted by Welsh's two walks and Ferguson's dropping a fly ball "to complete the agony."[69]

Even when one allows for the rationalizations of a "homer" Troy reporter, the Troy club was talented but rather undisciplined, demonstrating all the signs of an inexperienced and youthful team.

A month further into the 1880 season, the Trojans were defeated by the "one big inning" syndrome that seemed to dog them in their major league tenure and by an indifferent and passive performance that seemed in direct opposition to the old Haymaker hell-for-bent, battling approach of the early Troy teams:

Four. National Leaguers at the Gates of Troy

The Troys started off most auspiciously in their game with the Chicagos yesterday, obtaining three runs in the first inning, and retiring their opponents for three successive blinders. In the fourth inning, however, unfortunate errors and some hard batting gave the Chicagos four runs, and from that time on the Troys played spiritless and in many respects a careless game. They played without life or energy, and deserved the sound thrashing that they received. During the game a most disgraceful attempt was made by Burns, Chicagos shortstop, to prevent Ferguson from reaching third base. It was noticed by the umpire, however, and he refused to allow the claim of "out," at which Burns slunk back to his position like a whipped cur. About 700 people witnessed the game.[70]

The Cleveland Blues were a nemesis of the Trojans in 1880, defeating Troy seven out of nine games, including five of six tilts in July. Cleveland pitcher Jim McCormick seemed to stymie the Trojan hitters whenever he faced them: "The Troy Citys were unable to hit McCormick of the Clevelands for more than five hits yesterday, and the Clevelands got a like number off Welch, but succeeded in scoring three unearned runs to the Troy Citys one. Connor, the heavy slugger of the Citys, struck out twice. Hanlon made two and Dunlap one of the five hits credited to Cleveland."[71]

Even when McCormick was not on his game, Cleveland would find a way to win against the Troy club: "Cleveland visited Troy yesterday and administered a sound thrashing to the Troy Citys, outbatting and outfielding them, and winning by a score of 9 to 5. The Troys made 21 errors, counting passed balls and wild pitches, while the visitors were credited with 11.[72]

The sports post-game commentary for the July 14, 1880, game between the Providence Grays and the homestanding Trojans focused not only on the results of the game itself but also on the possible collusion between the visiting club and Umpire Daniels and the conflict between the telegraph company and its reporting of Troy baseball games:

> Ward pitched a good game yesterday, [Umpire] Daniels performed some of the most daring feats ever performed on a ball field, and the Troy Citys were defeated.... The umpire called 31 strikes off Ward and only 8 off Welsh [Welch]. There is not so great a difference between the pitchers, and the only inference to be drawn from this showing is that Mr. Daniels acted with unwarranted severity toward Welsh, and with unusual leniency toward Ward....

The Haymakers, Unions and Trojans of Troy, New York

The visitors went to the bat, and succeeded getting a man on first. Welsh noticed that the man was leading off too far for safety, and turned to throw the ball to Coggswell [Cogswell]. The umpire promptly called a balk, and gave the runner his second. Welsh looked at Ferguson in wonderment, and then turned toward Daniels with a mute plea of not guilty. The men from Providence mentally thanked Providence for such an umpire, and the game went on. But a great light had already broken in upon the home nine, and they played throughout the remainder of the contest like men who felt that awful calamity in the shape of a league umpire with a bias had fallen upon them. Nevertheless, they struggled well to keep down their opponents' score, and in view of the fact that all hope of victory had departed they made a very creditable showing in the field.

At bat they were powerless, and for the best of reasons—strikes were called upon them with such reckless rapidity that in sheer desperation they fell to fanning the air when the ball was not 10 feet of the plate. In the seventh inning, they scored their first, second and only runs, Caskins [Caskin] bringing in the pair by a good drive to left field before Daniels had sufficiently collected himself to call the batsman out on strikes. Meanwhile the visitors were having a picnic, each man being permitted to wait until Welsh put the sphere on the club rather than have a base given on balls. The result of this uneven contest—10 men against nine.... It only remains to be said that that while Daniels may be an honest man his performance of yesterday proves him to be the most unjust umpire that ever cast a baleful shadow on the Troy City grounds.

Troy found some consolation in the loss by avoiding a shutout, which in the world of nineteenth-century baseball was to be avoided at all costs: "The Troys narrowly escaped a whitewash yesterday, but Caskins [Caskin] saved the day, still leaving the home team the great unwhitewashed.... Troy have given three [whitewashes and] received none."

The Troy-Providence game also revealed a sore point for nineteenth-century baseball management in their tug-of-war to protect and extend their financial investment:

> The directors of the Troy City club learned recently that the telegraph company is compelled by nearly all league cities to pay for the privilege of placing an instrument on the grounds. Not to be behind in the matter of enterprise the Troy directors notified the manager of the telegraph office here that operator and sounder could no longer work together on the club grounds unless the privilege was paid for in money or by the extension of the franking privilege to official business. The telegraph company refused to comply, and when its representative reached the grounds yesterday he was not permitted to "work the little machine." Thereupon he climbed a

Four. National Leaguers at the Gates of Troy

poll, tapped the wire, and from his commanding position telegraphed to headquarters the result of each inning, thereby winning the first battle for the telegraph in its contest against the directors. It is rumored that this morning a platform is to be built near the top of the convenient pole, and it will be occupied by an operator, who has through the war, whenever a game takes place. This probably accounts for the fact that the Troy City directors purchased to-day a quantity of canvas, which, it is surmised, will be stretched upon a framework to be placed in such a position as to shut out the operator.[73]

The 1880 Troy Trojans were compiling a strong roster composed of young players who were mostly scouted and directly signed by Manager Ferguson. As Troy began a month long road trip on August 10, 1880, a number of promising Trojans were left behind in the Collar City to gain needed experience for future play with the major league club:

The following players have been selected to play amateur games under the auspices of the Troy City Base Ball Association during the absence of the Troy Citys. The new idea is to give Brouthers and Ewing necessary practice; Larkin pitch, Ewing catch, Brouthers first base, Briody second base, Shoupe third base, Ahearn, shortstop, Lecour left field, Harbridge right field, Higham centre field. Tobin and Straub will be released.[74]

On the first part of their August western swing through the NL, the Trojans played winning baseball, buoyed by the improved play of Manager Ferguson and the addition of a superb change pitcher from across the Hudson River in Albany, Tim Keefe:

The Troy Citys won another victory yesterday and the Worcesters lost, which gives the Troys an unquestionable hold on fourth place. The game yesterday was long and uninteresting. The batting was very weak on both sides, and the only redeeming feature of the game was the fine playing of Ferguson. The Troys obtained their three runs on errors by Galvin and Rowe, the batting being done after the side should have been put out.

This Troy victory was Tim Keefe's first game with the Trojans and he pitched a four-hitter. Holbert and Cassidy led the attack with two hits each. The newspaper report also defended Trojan Bob Ferguson as both a manager and player by comparing his on-field production with Cleveland Blues' second baseman Fred Dunlap:

The chronic grumblers who so strenuously urged a short time ago that Mr. Ferguson, Troy's second baseman and manager, was played out—too old

The Haymakers, Unions and Trojans of Troy, New York

for active service and unable to control his men—have changed their minds, and well might they do so. Comparing Mr. Ferguson's record with that of Dunlap's, who is claimed to be the best second baseman in the country, it is found that Ferguson excels him at every front. Dunlap has been 219 times at bat, has made 36 runs, 62 base hits, put out 143, assisted 163, and made 29 errors. Ferguson has been 201 times at bat, made 37 runs and 58 base hits, put out 175, assisted 151, and made 30 errors. Ferguson's batting average is .288, Dunlap's .283. Ferguson's fielding average .918, Dunlap's .910."[75]

On September 2, 1880, in the Windy City, the Troy Trojans split the first regularly scheduled NL double-header in major league baseball history: "The Chicagos and Troy Citys played two games yesterday, one in the morning and the other in the afternoon. The first was won by the Chicagos by a score of 1–0; but in the afternoon the Troy Citys by good play managed to score a victory over their formidable opponents by a score of 5 to 1."[76]

The Trojans often fell far short of their full potential, however. The major concerns of the Trojans' 1880 season were inconsistent fielding and indifferent play, both of which were in evidence in a July 27, 1880, victory (8–6) over the inept and dispirited Buffalo Bisons:

> Miserable muffing characterized the game between the Troy Citys and the Buffalos yesterday, both clubs indulging in about an equal amount of bad playing. The Troy Citys acted as if they thought they had a sure thing, and the Buffalos were apparently convinced from the start that they would be beaten. Nevertheless it was a disgraceful exhibition, unworthy of the name of base ball, especially when played by professional teams, the members of which receive large salaries for their services.
>
> The Troys were minus the services of Caskins [Caskin], who was summoned on Saturday last to the bedside of his dying child, but Larkin took his place and did exceedingly well under the circumstances. The only brilliant play throughout the contest was made by Ferguson, who captured a hot grounder from Latham's bat in the sixth inning, after the ball had bounded over second base, and threw the runner out at first. Welsh [Welch] either lost his head or his skill in the fifth inning, when he gave Latham a base on balls and then permitted Galvin, who struck out every other time he went to the bat, to secure a safe hit, and gave [former Troy Haymaker] Force a two-bagger. Gillespie muffed a fly ball and had a passed grounder. Connor failed to put Force out in the fifth inning when that player was running to third base, and other foolish errors were made through the game which would have done discredit to the junior Troy

Four. National Leaguers at the Gates of Troy

Citys, an organization composed entirely of boys. The errors of the Buffalos were principally made by Easterbrook, who dropped four thrown balls on first base, and is credited with one wild throw. Galvin (P), Latham (SS) and Rowe (C) also made errors which materially assisted the Troy Citys in their run getting.

The Troy supporters took their baseball seriously. The game report for July 28, 1880, is notable for underscoring the code of personal behavior that was expected to be observed by spectators at National League games under the stewardship of the ethically upright (and uptight) league president, William Hulbert:

> In the game yesterday Ferguson was about to catch a ball which had been hit high, when some contemptible wretch at the right of the grand stand tried to disconcert the player by making a sound very like the braying of a jackass. The dastardly attempt was unsuccessful, but the person or thing guilty of it is none the less deserving of punishment. The directors should see to it that an officer be stationed at the point named, and that he arrest for disorderly conduct the first loafer who shall repeat the offense of yesterday. Judge Donohue is a lover of the national game, and he will not fail to do his duty if the defender is ever arraigned in police court. Our word for it, the prisoner will make s long home run to the penitentiary.[77]

As the 1880 season wore down, the Troy Trojans played out the string as reflected in a series of games of uneven and uninspired play. In a battle with the Massachusetts club for fourth place in mid–September, Troy lost a home game to the visiting Worcesters, 2–6, who "batted Welch just hard enough to win legitimately" with an umpire's decision (once again) called into question by the Troy sporting press: "The umpire gave them one run in the third inning by an erroneous decision at home plate. In the sixth inning the Troys made a double play which [Umpire] Doscher would not give, and after that the Worcesters scored two more runs undeservedly." The listless Trojans made two runs, neither one earned."[78]

On their season-ending road trip to the eastern clubs, the Troy Trojans suffered their worst loss of their NL season in a game against their small-city rival, the Worcester Grays, in a game that was a [literal] laugher:

> *The Worcester Spy* provided the following description of the 17 to 2 game recently played by the Troys in that city:
> After the Troy strikers had been retired in one, two, three order, Stovey

opened for the Worcesters with a base hit, and then the fun began, reaching its height in the fourth and seventh inning. The ball was driven into, over and through the infielders, outfielders were kept almost constantly in motion, and the ball was kept agitated so vigorously by the home nine that demoralization instead of Bob Ferguson was soon the conqueror of the Trojans.

The Worcesters ran the bases freely and almost recklessly, but they were seldom in danger of being caught, and the danger was usually diverted by a wretched muff or wicked throw. All hands were in the scrape, and Capt. Bob had to actually squat right down on the ball field and laugh at the wretched exhibition his giants were making. The fun was almost continuous, and the Worcesters improved the opportunity to improve their batting averages, and gave Welsh [Welch] about the worst pounding he has received this year.

Every one of the Worcesters hit the ball hard, tried to lose it in fact, and Stovey nearly succeeded, getting two home runs, a two-baser, and single in five times at bat. Although the fielding of the Trojans was wretched, every man being charged with one or more errors, the Worcesters earned six runs and hit Welsh safely in every inning save the eighth.

The first signs of a rattle among the visitors appeared in the first inning, when, with one out and the bases full, Wood struck out; Ewing attempted a double play by dropping the ball, but held it a bit too long, and, amid the general shouting which followed, threw it over first base way out into the centre field, allowing two runners to cross the plate. In the fourth inning the entire Worcester nine took a hand at the bat, and scored five runs, and in the ninth 12 men practiced on Welsh for six runs. Stovey's batting was terrific while Richmond reached first base every time he went to bat without making a safe hit. Stovey also played a fine game at first, and Whitney did some as fine base running as has been seen on the local grounds this season. Richmond's pitching was very effective, only three base hits, one of them a scratch, being made on him.[79]

Whenever the Troy Trojans managed to win a late-season game in 1880, as they did 7–6 over the woeful Boston Red Caps, there was not much to say about the lackluster Trojans as the end of the season loomed. The entirety of the game report, which was accompanied by a complete box score, was the following: "The Troy City club won a creditable victory over the Bostons yesterday."[80] It appeared to be crystal clear that the Troy Trojans 1880 NL season was over and that all who followed the club were relieved that it was so.

The 1880 Troy Trojans seemed to regain their equilibrium and played winning baseball in a post NL-season, self-proclaimed New York

Four. National Leaguers at the Gates of Troy

State championship against the first year New York Metropolitans, who just the month previously had moved into the Polo Grounds. In a game against the one-armed pitcher Hugh Daley, the Trojans won, 4–2, as Welch seemed to have sufficiently recovered from the pasting he received a few weeks earlier by the Worcester NL franchise:

> The Troy Citys played a very creditable game of ball at New York yesterday, considering that changes were made which permitted Connor to play first base. Ewing guarded third, and both these positions were filled very satisfactorily.
>
> The first game of the series for the New York state championship between the Troy club and the Metropolitans of this city [New York], drew fully 1,000 spectators to the Polo grounds yesterday afternoon. The game was splendidly contested throughout, and although resulting in favor of the visitors, reflects no discredit upon the home club, who played a magnificent uphill game, and would have come off victorious had it not been for several telling errors made at critical parts of the game.
>
> Daily [Daley], the one-armed pitcher, who is exceedingly sensitive, taking offense at a remark made by an outsider, withdrew from the field and refused to pitch any longer. Schenck, the third baseman of the Jersey City club, who is also a good pitcher, was substituted and the playing was resumed after a delay of about ten minutes. The Metropolitans scored their first run in the sixth inning. Clinton hit a high fly ball to Caskins [Caskin] (SS), who dropped it, because of the sunlight in his eyes. Much mirth was occasioned in the fourth inning by the nonchalance with which Scheneck caught a hard line ball from Evans. Everybody laughed and even the ball players applauded.[81]

With Roger Connor and Buck Ewing playing new positions, Bill Holbert firmly ensconced behind the plate, and the Tim Keefe and Mickey Welch tandem prepared to share the pitching duties, the prospects for the 1881 season looked very promising for the Troy Trojans. However, there was much doubt in the Collar City that there would be a next year for the Troy Citys. Again, the reason for such a cloudy future for the club was money:

> Every club in the [National] league lost money during the past season except Chicago, and in every city except Chicago the matter of sustaining a club for 1881 was thoroughly canvassed before it was to go on. In Boston the club has been steadily losing money for a number of years, and the association is now upwards of $25,000 behind. The present Providence organization has been three years in the league, and the only year it did not run short was 1879, when it won the championship. This year the defi-

ciency was about $3,500. The Buffalo club has lost for two years, and the present season would have ended its existence if not had not been for a change in management and an almost entirely new list of subscribers. The Cincinnati and Cleveland clubs are also behind, while the Chicago club is about $12,000 ahead.

In Troy the club started with a debt of $1,800 and a stock subscription of about $4,000. Deducting the debt the actual subscription amounted to only $2,200, and the expenditures have exceeded that sum by about $1,000, making the cost of the club over and above receipts, say $3,500. This is of course a much better showing than was made in 1879, when the club was behind some $8,000, and there is no particular cause for discouragement.

The season was disastrous to the Troys in many respects, notably on the last western trip, and it is believed with a good club next year the expense would be considerably reduced. There appears to be enthusiasm enough in the city, and money enough, too, for that matter, but a failure heretofore to attend meetings called for an interchange of views has to some extent discouraged the present board of directors, and they have not yet decided what to do. A meeting of the friends of base ball will be held tonight at the city clerk's office in the city hall. Its object will be to decide whether or not there shall be a club in Troy next year. The league meeting will be held in Rochester on Monday, and if decisive action be not taken to-night no delegate will be sent to Rochester. Therefore it behooves all who desire to see Troy represented in the league next year to be in attendance.

It surprised no one in 1880 (and few would be surprised today) that the players' supposed greed and high salaries were at the heart of the owners' implementation of the reserve clause the previous fall and of their desire to set limits on players' remuneration:

> High salaries, if continued with the league teams, will kill professional base ball in this country in one more season. It has been demonstrated that [clubs] cannot afford to pay from $14,000 to $12,000 annually for players, and it is probable at the approaching league meeting that a strong effort will be made to secure a reduction of salaries, and the establishment of a uniform basis for paying base ballists.[82]

The battle line was drawn that would determine player-management relationships throughout the turbulent 1880s.

Five

The Fall of the Trojans

1881

The Trojans seemed to regress in 1881 when they finished in fifth place with a 39–45 win-loss percentage. The club led the league in fielding with a .917 team average and all starters except John Cassidy and the pitching staff of Mickey Welch and Tim Keefe had fielding percentages above .900. Welch and Keefe seemed to have some adjustment problems with the new 50-foot pitching distance. Welch remained the ace of the staff with a 2.54 earned run average and a 21–18 won-loss record in 1,104 innings while Keefe went 18–27 with a 3.24 ERA in 1,206 innings. Both hurlers completed every game they started in 1881. However, the Trojans were a very mediocre hitting team (.248) with no team member hitting above .300 and only first baseman Roger Connor distinguishing himself at the plate. Connor led the club with a .292 batting average and also had the team high of doubles (17), triples (6), home runs (2), and runs batted in (35).[1]

One Troy Trojan player who did have something of a breakout year in 1881 was William "Buck" Ewing. Though he hit only .250 in 1881, the 21-year-old did have 68 hits in 67 games with 14 doubles, seven triples, and 25 runs batted in. While Ewing did go on to hit a respectable .303 for his 18-year major league career and was acknowledged to be one of the NL's best base runners, he was perhaps best known as a heady, innovative player and team leader. As a catcher he stood close to the batter, gave hand signals to the pitcher, set up the defensive alignment, and threw out base runners from a crouch.

Ewing had to overcome a number of physical disadvantages in his early career as a catcher. He had no chest protector for first three years on the job and no catcher's mitt for eight years. He never used a padded face mask or shin guards. Equally important, Ewing had to adapt to four changes in pitching distance and in his last three years as a catcher he was receiving overhand throws from 50 feet.

Ewing possessed an iron will to win and was known as both a first-rate complainer of umpire's calls and an authoritarian field manager in the mode of his first major league manager Bob Ferguson. His career was summed up as follows: "[Buck Ewing had] a well-rounded reputation as a peerless handler of pitchers, a daring base stealer, an innovator in the field ... and a better than average hitter..."[2] Perhaps Buck Ewing's greatest attribute on the diamond was his versatility. He and native-born Trojan and fellow Hall of Fame member Mike "King" Kelly are the only major league players to have played at least 25 games each at all nine baseball positions. Finally, Ewing was a baserunning threat who on more than occasion led his team in steals and who still holds the career (354), season (53, in 1888), and the single-game (three, in 1888) record for steals in a game by a catcher.[3]

Often described as the nineteenth century's best all-around catcher, and one of its best base runners, Buck Ewing began his major league career with Troy in 1880. Along with Welch and and Connor, he was moved to John B. Day's New York Giants, which would replace Troy in the National League in 1883. As one of only two major league players (the other is Troy native and fellow Hall of Fame member Mike Kelly) to play at least 25 games at all nine positions, he was also versatile (courtesy of the National Baseball Hall of Fame Library, Cooperstown, New York).

FIVE. *The Fall of the Trojans*

Ewing played 13 games for the 1880 Troy Trojans after signing with the club in September. He had been playing for Rochester in the NA before that club folded. He was managed at Rochester by Horace Phillips, the former manager of the Troy Trojans in 1879.

Buck Ewing's improvement at the plate was a slow and steady process through the 1881–1882 seasons with the Trojans from .178 to .271 with steady increases in extra base hits. However, from the start of his career, Ewing was a positive presence on the base paths and a strong defensive player (with the exception of four games in the outfield in 1880 where he made three errors in seven chances) from the very outset of his career. In 1881, he even filled in admirably for an injured Ed Caskin at shortstop.

In 1881, while Buck Ewing's career was on the ascension, Troy's days as a NL franchise appeared to be numbered. By mid–July, the Trojans were mired in fourth place and were a very poor road team that drew only hundreds of paying fans at home and had lost media support with the club labelled as "Ferguson's Sluggards." By the end of August, players were owed back salary and the team was $3,000 in debt. The team's increasing debt and lack of financial stability undermined the Trojans' ability to compete not only during the 1881 season but had a direct impact on the club's future chances for success. For example, with no money to attract star replacement players for their 1882 season, Troy had no alternative except to bring up rookies and promote them. In 1882, Fred Pfeffer played shortstop and hit at .228 clip but did lead the league in fielding. Chief Roseman broke in that season and was a serviceable starting outfielder.

Adding to the early season malaise were significant injuries to Ewing and his teammates Roger Connor, Mickey Welch, and Bob Ferguson. With attendance continuing to nosedive, the Trojans had to accept funds from the other NL owners to keep the Troy franchise functioning. With Troy's ability to stay afloat financially in serious jeopardy, Trojan players and playing captain Ferguson began being scouted and wooed by other clubs more than ready to sign them when the franchise went under. Upon his return from the injured list, Buck Ewing was given the lead-off spot in the Trojan lineup, a spot he filled for most of the rest of what was to be a Hall of Fame career.[4]

Controversy seemed to swirl around Buck Ewing both on and off the diamond. The young player was notorious for his cleverness in negotiating contracts and angling for the best financial conditions in his contracts. As a result, he was christened with the "Bread and Butter Ewing" sobriquet for his publicly-perceived selfish behavior. When the Trojans disbanded in 1882, Ewing headed to the New York Gothams (also named the "Maroons" for their white and magenta uniforms) with his former Troy teammates, Roger Connor, Pete Gillespie, Mickey Welch, Frank Hankinson, Ed Caskin, and Mike Dorgan[5]

Buck Ewing became a star with the NL New York franchise, for which he played from 1883 to 1892 with the exception of 1890, when he played for and managed the PL's New York entry. While Ewing had his moments at the plate, including leading the NL in home runs with 10 in 1884 and in triples with 20 in 1885, he was most appropriately recognized as a very strong defensive player, frequently in the top three of catchers in games played, putouts, assists, double plays, and fielding average. He was at his best in the Giant championship years of 1888–1889. In the latter season, Buck Ewing led the NL in all the major fielding categories except for fielding average, in which he placed second at .937.[6]

Buck Ewing was a multi-talented and brainy baseball player who was lauded by the entire baseball community, especially among the sporting press, as deserving of the highest praise:

> Of Ewing there is so much to be said that it is difficult to know how to say it in a limited space. His only real rivals among the catchers of the day were Kelly and "Charley" Bennett, and in many respects "Buck" had a little on this capable pair. His throwing to bases was worth going miles to see. When he sent the ball down to second it seemed to travel on an absolutely straight line and land in the baseman's hands at just the place where he needed it to tag the runner. "Buck" also had a trick of snapping the ball down to first to catch the unwary base-runner, and he did this so successfully that opponents grew cautious and stuck to the bags as though glued there. Ewing was also a fine hitter, and, what was better, a "pinch hitter," and he knew all the subtle points of the game. If a runner were coming home from third on a fly to the outfield it was not by accident that Ewing's mask, hurriedly snatched from his head, would fall exactly on the base line at just the point where it ought not to be for the runner to slide safely.

Perhaps the best indicator of Ewing's great skill lies in the number of respected contemporaries who proclaimed him to the best catcher in

FIVE. *The Fall of the Trojans*

baseball history: John McGraw, Connie Mack, Clark Griffith, Frank Bancroft, John Montgomery Ward, Tim Keefe, Jim O'Rourke, O. P. Caylor (baseball manager and editor of *The Sporting News* and *New York Herald*), Tim Murnane (former player and journalist), and his New York Giants manager, Jim Mutrie[7]

Weather played havoc with the Haymakers' late season 1881 schedule and the uncharacteristic meteorological happenings early that fall served as an apt metaphor for the Trojans' lost season and their uncertain NL future. On September 26, 1881, in a game played at Haymaker Grounds on Center Island before 2,000 fans, the National League pennant-winning Chicago White Stockings lost to the home-standing Troy Trojans, 8–1. While the gate of 2,000 fans was the largest paid attendance for the Troy franchise in 1881, the final attendance figure was limited by an intense heat wave that prevented 1,000 potential game attendees from making it to the much-anticipated game because the street car horses were unable to be employed.[8]

Trojans might be excused for thinking that Armageddon was at hand with the abrupt shift in the weather on the following day.[9] On September 27, 1881, in the last game of a three contest series played at Haymaker Grounds in what has been variously described as a "steady downpour" and a "driving rainstorm," the National League pennant-winning Chicago White Stockings defeated the Trojans in the final home game of the season, 10–7. The game was played to completion and the attendance was an all-time major league record low of twelve (or fewer).[10] The September 27 game was a disaster from a number of different perspectives, both on and off the diamond, including the impossible playing conditions, uniforms, and an unnecessary major public confrontation between the Chicago manager and his pitcher:

> The twelfth game and last of the series between the Troy and Chicago clubs was played yesterday in a drenching rain storm. Less than a dozen persons paid admission to the grounds. If the contest was not decided yesterday it would not have been played this season so [Troy captain] Ferguson concluded to play. Many of the ball tossers, not expecting to play, did not bring their suits, and when the order was finally given, there was great scrambling for something suitable to wear. Some of the ball tossers appeared on the diamond in very mixed suits. [Troy outfielder Gillespie's] combination of lavender gray, navy blue, white and red stockings, and pea-

gray hat was ludicrous in the extreme. It was impossible for any good ball playing to be done. The ball was so slippery and the ground so muddy that the game was nothing but a farce. In the second inning the Troys by good hitting assisted by the most laughable errors on the part of Dalrymple, Goldsmith, Flint, and Burns, scored six runs. In the next inning another was recorded by the home team, and until the seventh inning it looked as victory would perch upon the banner of the Trojans. At that point however, Nichols of the Chicagos made a base hit and for five minutes the lavender grays pounded the ball all over the diamond until six runs had been scored. In the next inning, with but one man out and three on bases, there was a chance for the home team, but they did not improve it.

[Chicago pitcher] Goldsmith was sent from the field by Capt. Anson in the sixth inning, being replaced by Williams, whom the Trojans did not seem to be able to hit. There promised to be a lively time for awhile [sic]. Goldsmith complained of a sprained foot and Anson doubted him. Certainly he was sending the balls in so nicely that the Trojans hit where they chose. Anson intimated that Goldsmith was a liar and the latter "sasses" the captain. "I fine you $50" said Anson. "Fine and be _____" said Goldsmith. "I fine you $150 and suspend you for the season" was the quick reply. It is understood that the matter was amicably adjusted after the game.[11]

The violent natural phenomena of the last 1881 Troy homestand were a harbinger for an equally disastrous off-season in which National League president William A. Hulbert, champion and stalwart defender of Troy baseball, died on April 10, 1882. With no league support, player unrest, political inaction with regard to transportation and facility needs, and the continued national and local economic downturn(s), Troy's days playing at the highest level of professional baseball were severely threatened as the Troy Citys looked forward with trepidation to the 1882 National League season.

Just prior to these two bizarre "weather" games with the Chicago White Stockings in late September, the Trojans were playing sound baseball with clutch hitting and timely fielding as evidenced in a 4–1 exhibition victory in New York City: "About 3,000 people went to the Polo Grounds yesterday to witness the contest between the Metropolitan Base Ball Club and the Troy League Club. The game was won by the Troy men by superior batting and fielding." Troy's left side of the infield had a rough day defensively with Cassidy (SS) and Hawkins (3B) evenly splitting six errors. Both Cassidy and Ewing (C) had two hits each.[12] A more typical result

FIVE. *The Fall of the Trojans*

of the good field, no hit 1881 Trojans took place in Troy on September 28, 1881, in a 4–2 victory over the Detroit Wolverines in which Troy had only one hit and one error to Detroit's four hits but seven errors.[13]

September of 1881 also provided a major league first that went unmentioned in the newspapers of the day: "In Albany yesterday [September 10, 1881] the Troys defeated the Worcesters in a very interesting game, which was well contested on both sides. The hitting of both teams was strong." Troy won the game 8–7 and had nine hits and 12 errors while Worcester had eleven hits and five errors. What was not mentioned was that Roger Connor hit the National League's first grand slam home run. The Trojan batting star did so in dramatic fashion in the bottom of the ninth inning by hitting his circuit blast to overcome a 3-run Worcester lead.[14]

The 1881 Trojans continued their mastery over the New York Metropolitans, with whom they played a number of exhibition matches. On July 28, 1881, before 2,000 persons at the Polo Grounds, Tim Welch pitched a two-hit shutout of the New York club. The Troy club scored a run in the first inning:

> Connors [Connor] followed and secured a base hit and stole second base cleverly. Next came Holbert who made first base on a hit, also sending in Connors. The next batter was Ewing, who was thrown off by Brady at the bat.... In the seventh inning Hankinson was at the bat. He made a base hit to left field. Welsh [Welch] followed and knocked a fly, which was caught by [former Trojan] Roseman. The next man was Cassidy, who secured a base on a hit to right field, which sent Hankinson to third. Connors came next and while he was at the bat the ball was thrown by Farrow (RF) over Brady's (2B) head to prevent Cassidy from stealing second base, thus sending in Hankinson on a wild throw. Cassidy, however, was caught while trying to steal third base.

The game was effectively over at the end of the seventh inning. Welch's stellar hurling was supported by Conner's three hits and two hits each by Evans and Hankinson.

On August 18, 1881, at the Polo Grounds, the Trojans defeated the Metropolitans again in a closely fought contest. The major issue was an old (but apparently unresolved one) for the Troy club: The game was played with a lively ball that suited the Troy Citys free-swinging style that was a guaranteed crowd-pleaser:

The Haymakers, Unions and Trojans of Troy, New York

> The contrast between the game of baseball played yesterday at the Polo Ground and that of the previous day [August 17, 1881] was almost as great as the difference between moonlight and sunshine. Wednesday's game between the Metropolitans and Albanys was dull and uninteresting, although the score was at the model figure of 1-0. Yesterday, however the game between the Metropolitans and the Troys was at much larger figures, the score standing at 7 to 4, and it is seldom that a livelier or more interesting game is played. The batting and fielding were all that could be desired, the balls being hit hard and the fielding very good. It is a lively ball game where the batting is heavy enough to please the public. At that of Wednesday the ball was so dead that it was with great difficulty it was sent beyond the infield. Owing to the threatening conditions of the weather there was not over a thousand spectators assembled at the Polo Ground yesterday, but those who did venture out were well repaid for their trip, as a most excellent game was played.

The Trojans pounded out 12 hits, with Holbert leading the way with three hits and Gillespie, Ewing, and Hankinson each collecting two base knocks.[15]

While the Troy Trojans had many memorable moments in 1881, the team lacked consistency and focus, winning two fewer NL games than the previous year. The Trojans were firmly ensconced in last place by early August and the club's slide continued with a record of seven wins and seventeen loses against their eastern foes with most of these defeats occurring on an extended road trip. The high point of August was a 7-6 victory against the homestanding Worcester ball club.[16]

The Troy Trojans' last twelve games of the year were a microcosm of the club's strengths and weaknesses as a subpar NL entry. The Trojans went 5-6-1 during this streak and had impressive wins in an easy victory over the league champion Chicago White Stockings, a drubbing of the Buffalo Bisons, and a shutout off of the Cleveland Blues.

On September 14, 1881, the homestanding Trojans defeated the Cleveland Blues, 8-0, with Tim Keefe whitewashing the Blues, who put up little resistance in what amounted to a yawner for the few fans in attendance: "A small assemblage yesterday witnessed the dullest game of ball played in Troy this season. The Trojans defeated the Cleveland team in a contest that was notable for the multitude of errors and for the wretched play of the visitors. Of the eight runs scored but one was earned. The play of the home team in the field was good, and they were

FIVE. The Fall of the Trojans

fairly good at the bat. Keefe pitched an excellent game. The Buckeye Blues received nine blinders."

The Trojans scoring opportunities were a combination of a few well-placed hits among many Cleveland blunders:

> The Trojans scored three unearned runs in the third inning. Evans reached first on Taylor's muff, stole second and touched the home plate on Hankinson's safe hit. "Hank" reached second on Keefe's daisy cutter, and both were advanced a base on Dunlap's fumble of Cassidy's hit. Hankinson came home on Taylor's muff of Conner's fly, and Cassidy scored on Gillespie's sacrifice hit. In the sixth, Holbert, after getting his base on balls, got home on Clapp's wild throw to second and Schaeffer's muff of Ewing's fly. In the next inning Keefe hit the sphere for three bases and scored on Phillips' fumble of Conner's hot grounder. Conner was advanced to second by Ferguson, and after each gets a base on a passed ball by Clapp, both tallied on Gillespie's clean hit to centre. The only earned run was scored in the eighth, when Ewing knocked two bases out of the ball, reached third on Evans sacrifice hit and [came] home on Hankinson's pretty grounder to left centre.

The Cleveland Blues "played without any life" and Dunlap's hitting was described as "lame." In fact, the entire Blues team was lackluster, garnering only three hits off Keefe and committing nine errors in the field. Keefe added two hits, as did Hankinson, whose play was praised but characterized as too little too late: "Hankinson is playing in fine form now, but it is rather late in the season. He will not play ball next year."

The most significant observation made in the notes to the box score of this game was the talk concerning the creation of a rival league in 1882—the American Association—which did come to fruition: "A movement is on foot to form a new base ball league for next season, which shall charge but 25 cents admission to all games. Mr. Phillips, manager of the Philadelphia Athletic Club, reports the movement meeting with great favor in St. Louis, Pittsburgh, Louisville, and Cincinnati and other western cities."[17]

As was often the case in the contemporary Troy newspapers, the umpires were blamed for the Troy-Cleveland tie game (6–6) of September 15, 1881, and for the loss to the Blues on September 16, 1881 (7–10): The Clevelands snatched the drawn game from the home team yesterday mainly by errors of the umpire, who was troubled with 'obliquity of vision,' in the first inning when he gave the Buckeyes two bases on flagrant decisions, for which he got what he richly deserved, a sound hissing."

According to the game-day reporter, the September 16, 1881, game evidenced even more of an umpiring fiasco that helped Cleveland establish a large lead: "The Forest Citys, along with the umpire Doscher, tallied five runs in the first inning. In the fifth the visitors scored three more on good hits, assisted by Conner's fumble of McCormick's hot grounder. In the eighth the blue legs tallied one more by two hits and an error by Ewing." The Trojans mounted a feverish rally that fell short of what proved to be the Blues' insurmountable lead: "The Trojans played one of the prettiest up-hill games ever seen on the diamond.... In the eighth and ninth innings, the boys made a great rally, in which they tallied five runs by some of the strongest hitting seen on the grounds this season. Ferguson made a clean home run, almost knocking the ball into the river, but unfortunately there were none on base at the time."

The game summary also stressed that both pitchers—Tim Keefe and Cleveland's the Only Nolan—were ineffectual at best with both hurlers "being pounded around the diamond." The Trojans Holbert and Gillespie "played a great game" and the defense was recognized for completing four double plays[18]

On September 19, 1881, a preliminary evaluation of the baseball season was made that revealed a potential pitfall for the Trojans continued presence in the National League. Trojan Captain Bob Ferguson was acknowledged as a high-performing but selfish player: "Ferguson leads the batting average of the Troy club. Conner and Caskins [Caskin] follow in the order named ... Ferguson and Cassidy played to save their records in Friday's game [vs the Blues]. The business was altogether overdone and reflected no credit on the ball tossers." However, the most important assessment of the Troy ball club was the dwindling attendance that occurred as the 1881 season wore on:

> Two weeks from to-day the base ball season of 1881 will be over. It has been very successful in all respects, and every club in the league has made money with the exception of Worcester and Providence. The Troy nine did well from a financial standpoint early in the season, but their disastrous defeats in the eastern series caused a large falling off in attendance at the

FIVE. *The Fall of the Trojans*

games. Since the club's arrival home they have played well, but the number of spectators at the games is very small. Chicago has won the pennant. Providence is second in the race, followed by Buffalo and Troy.[19]

The carping against the umpiring continued following a 4–10 loss by the Trojans at home to the Buffalo Bisons, a team that Troy most frequently handled with ease. The ace Bison starting pitcher Jim Galvin umpired the game and the Troy media believed he acted in collusion with his teammates to insure a Buffalo victory:

> The Buffalo club, nobly assisted by the umpire, won its third victory from the Trojans yesterday. In the first innings the Bisons "got on" to their inveterate enemy, Welch, and pounded him for five singles. On these, assisted by [shortstop] Ewing's error and the umpire's unfair ruling, six runs were scored by the visitors. The game was a farce. Whenever Galvin at a critical juncture saw a chance to "kill" a Trojan he did so, and not only this, but he allowed his own club to do pretty much as they liked. Brouthers started home on a fly out to Gillespie before the latter caught it, and although [catcher] Holbert called the bisonic [sic] umpire's attention to the matter, the giant was allowed to score. Galvin was hissed several times and jeered throughout the game. It may be pertinent to add that he was prompted to most of his decisions by signals from Rowe and Purcell, respectively catcher and pitcher for the Buffalo club. The Trojans with the exception of Ewing, played a good game, Holbert notably so [with four base hits]. The fine play of [former Troy Haymaker] Force at second for the visitors was frequently applauded.

In a desperate fight for fourth place in the NL, Troy needed two wins against both Chicago and Detroit in their last games of the year. At the same time, Buffalo was making its interest in Bob Ferguson as a player known as rumors continued about Troy's and Worcester's imminent demise and unlikely continued presence in the league. *The Boston Herald* baseball reporter addressed this issue in unambiguous terms:

> Worcester and Troy will probably remain in the league next year, though there is evidence on the part of the other league clubs that they should draw out and give place to New York and Philadelphia, both of which places are ready to jump in. As long as the two former clubs desire to stay and fulfill all of their obligations, they can do so, or at least that is the policy laid down by President Hulbert, and it is a correct one.[20]

Even on the late-season days that the Trojans did play well, the club seemed to have just enough untimely lapses that would lead to a close defeat. On September 23, 1881, the Trojans lost 2–3 to the champion Chicago White Stockings as former Trojan Fred Goldsmith outdueled Troy's Tim Keefe: "The Troys, through their failure to hit safely at critical points, and more directly through the muff of an easy fly by Ewing [who seemed to be playing out of position at shortstop], lost a game to Chicago yesterday."

The game account revealed the closeness of the match and the inability of the Trojans to get the timely hit:

> The opening inning for Troy revealed concern. Connors [Connor] reached first on a baser, second on Burns' fumble of Ferguson's hit, and home on Gillespie's safe drive to right field. Connors expired at the plate in attempting to score on Gillespie's hit. In the second inning Chicago tied the score by a mere chance. Burns hit to right field, and before Evans could regain the ball it had rolled under the gate in the south fence, Burns being credited with a home run. Ewing led off with a two bagger in the second inning, but was left at third. The run-getting was not resumed until the eighth inning, both sides playing a beautiful game. Then Gore gained first on Ewing's disastrous muff of an easy fly and scored on Kelly's hit for three bases, Kelly's coming in on Anson's long fly to Cassidy which was caught. Troy made a determined attempt to tie the score, but without success. Cassidy tallied on his baser, a passed ball and Ferguson's two bagger, and the contest ended three to two in the champion's favor, Ferguson being left at second and the ninth inning ending without substantial results. In nearly every inning Troy had men left on base, when a safe hit would have brought victory. Keefe pitched a fine game, and the fielding of the Troys was first class. Welch, the Troy pitcher, umpired satisfactorily.[21]

The Trojans played the New York Metropolitans in a Saturday game before ending their 1881 season with a split with Chicago in the extreme weather games in Troy and with losing two of three contests to the visiting Detroit Wolverines. All aspects of the Troy Trojan's season were mediocre as was their fifth place finish 17 games behind league-leading Chicago.

On September 19, 1881, the death of President James Garfield two months after his assassination heightened the nation's dark mood as the event undermined people's confidence in their public institutions and cast a pall over the national mood. As a result, public trust in professional sports was further eroded with the continual revelations about gambling

FIVE. *The Fall of the Trojans*

in baseball and other competitive professional sports such as wrestling, race walking, and bicycling. Sports management would often engage in circular reasoning and claim that there was little they could do to police gambling since "...there is no law to prevent it [gambling], as it [sports betting] is not considered as such in a legal sense." The "people generally know them [the aforementioned pro sports] to be gamblers' devices for swindling by false scores and false pretenses as to prizes paid."[22]

To counteract such negative public distrust of professional sports, the National League held a post–1881 season meeting at Saratoga, New York, on September 29 in which the owners took a strong stance to not sign black listed players and to continue (and, in fact, expand) the reserve list. All eight National League clubs were represented at the meeting,

Though the 1881 and 1882 Troy Trojans had four future Hall of Fame members on its roster, the NL team finished below .500 in each of those two seasons, the franchise's last in the major leagues (courtesy of the National Baseball Hall of Fame Library, Cooperstown, New York).

which was chaired by Chicago's W. A. Hulbert with Troy's D. H. Deforest as secretary: "A resolution was adopted not to hire or to play against any other club which employs or presents as player, manager, or umpire certain players who are on a black list for dissipated habits and insubordination. It was not thought best to make the black list public for the present, at least. A certain number of players were named."[23] Though NL management acted to clean up the sport and to regain public trust in their business, there was no transparency in the decision making, which set a precedent for future league actions.

1882

In order to increase fan interest in light of the creation of a rival baseball league—the American Association—which was located in large metropolitan areas, the National League over-reacted in its desire to increase NL attendance and began its 1882 season with a new set of uniform requirements that was a confusing and laughable fiasco. Each club would wear a distinct team color, for example, the Trojans would wear green shirts, socks, and belts. However, all teams' caps were color-coded by position:

Pitcher = light blue
Catcher = scarlet
First Base = scarlet and white
Second Base = orange and blue
Shortstop = maroon
Third Base = blue and white
Left Field = white
Center Field = red and black
Right Field = gray
Substitutes = green

The uniform experiment was abandoned by mid–June.

The American Association (AA), however, was an undeniable threat to the NL because it offered spectators a lower ticket price and the ability to attend Sunday baseball games and to consume alcoholic beverages. As for players, the AA not only offered the reality of higher

Five. The Fall of the Trojans

salaries but other desirable player perks, such as the team purchasing team uniforms and not charging players a fifty cent surcharge when the team was on the road. More important, some teams would pay the players in full before the season actually began.[24]

The 1882 hot stove league began with mixed news for Trojan fans. Almost the entire 1881 roster, which had played below the expectations of professional observers and club devotees alike had been signed for the upcoming season, including all the core players: "The new team for this year has not as yet been fully made up, but the following players have been engaged: Holbert, Ewing, Welsh [Welch], Keefe, Connors [Connor], Pfeffer, Ferguson, Gillespie, and Cassidy."

The more important off-season team revelation was that the always cash-starved Trojans would be playing their NL schedule in a new, as yet undesignated ball park: "A part of the grounds formerly occupied by the Troy Baseball nine has been sold, and management will have to seek a new place to play for next season."[25] The Troy Trojans remained in a shaky financial position during the winter of 1881–1882. They attempted to buttress the spirits of both players and fans by placing public-relations blurbs in New York papers that were far from the reality of the club, including the following fight of pure fantasy: "The Troy Baseball Club have secured some millionaire backers and a free ball ground."[26]

The Troy Trojans Base Ball Club was not the only local entity that was facing economic peril. The city of Troy itself was also undergoing desperate financial straits in light of the beginning of a deep recession at the end of the railroad construction boom; equally important, the railroad crisis led to a sharp decline in related industries such as iron and steel. Troy continued to slide from a position of industrial strength with the local economy suffering a devastating hit in the national stock market crash and bank-run on gold that culminated in the Panic of 1893.

On the field, the Trojans started well with a 16–13 record by mid–June that saw the club in third place. Troy was a strong hitting club and overcame any defensive lapses by their superior batting. For example, in an early May exhibition against the League Alliance New York Metropolitans (who were to be a member of the AA in 1883), the Trojans simply out-slugged their opponents "at the Polo Grounds yesterday [May 9] in the presence of about 2,000 spectators. The Trojans indulged in some very heavy batting, as they 'pounded' Doyle for 18 singles and a total of 24 base hits ... Ewing, Connor, Ferguson, Roseman, Smith, Gillespie ... wielded the 'ash' most successfully ... and Ewing carried off the honors for the best work in the field." Buck Ewing was also the winning pitcher and Roger Conner the batting star in a 15–10 Troy victory in the 105-minute contest. The New York newspapers saw the same game as less of a decisive Troy victory and more of a see-saw battle between high-scoring teams:

> The game opened with the representatives of Troy at the bat, who by some very heavy batting, gained a strong lead in the first inning by scoring 4 runs. The lead taken by the Trojans, however, did not have the effect of disheartening the "Mets" in the least, as they made 1 run in their half of the first inning, disposed of the league men in the second inning without giving sweet melodies [?] soon headed the list [to give] them an opportunity to increase their lead, and in the last half of the inning punished the delivery of Ewing in fine style and took the lead by making 5 runs, which swelled their total to 6. After this neither side succeeded in making a run until the fifth inning, when the Troy once more took the lead by scoring 3 runs. The visitors held the lead until the finish, although the home team rallied in the seventh inning and made four additional runs.[27]

Early in the 1882 season, the Troy Trojans were playing sound, winning baseball; the prospects for the year looked promising: "The Troy nine have been playing remarkably fine games of late. And in consequence have crept from the bottom of the list up to third position, which they now hold. They are steadily gaining on the leaders."[28]

On June 6, 1882, the Cleveland Blues visited the Collar City with the home team winning a 1–0 pitching duel: "Science in the pitcher's box was the chief feature of the contest between the Troys and the Clevelands yesterday afternoon. McCormick was puzzling throughout the game, and Welch equally effective after the first inning, when Glasscock and Phillips each hit for a base, but by sharp fielding were prevented from scoring." Troy scored a tainted run in the eighth inning and held off the Blues with great pitching and defense:

> While the sphere-dealer for the visitors pitched finely his brilliant record was marred by an error that cost them the game. It was in the eighth inning that the misplay was made, and when indications pointed to a struggle of unusual length. Roseman was the first striker, and batted the ball to the centre field fence, taking two bases. Pfeffer's sacrifice hit gave

Five. The Fall of the Trojans

Roseman third. With two out Welch stepped to the plate and fanned the air twice. Spectators were expecting "three strikes and out," when McCormick delivered a widely curved ball, which passed [former Trojan] Briody, and Roseman, cap in hand, tallied the only and winning run. McCormick was so chagrined at his own recklessness that he gave Welch his base on balls, but Ewing's fly was seized by Doscher and the inning ended. Cleveland's chances origatened [sic] in the ninth inning when Schaeffer made a two base hit after a duo of blue stockings had been put out. Richmond foolishly sent the leather to Pfeffer, who gracefully retired the side.

Cleveland's defense was highly praised, with the high point of the contest being a fifth inning triple play:

> The Ohio tossers played a pretty fielding game, and a lucky opportunity for display in that line in the fifth inning lessened Troy's hope of a victory. Roseman had reached third on singles by himself and Pfeffer. Holbert, the third striker, shot a hot fly to McCormick. The ball glanced from his hands into Glasssnock's, and Holbert sat down. Pfeffer and Roseman had run too far from their bases, and quick fielding sealed their fate. It was a timely triple play, and was loudly applauded.

The game day report ends with an assessment of a few gamers who caught the reporter's eyes:

> Cassidy, who played with the Troys for the first time in a league game this season, was not serviceable at the bat—in fact none of those regarded as the hard hitters of the team was capable of solving the tricky curves. Ewing received an injury to his finger, from which the blood gushed, in the first inning, but pluckily caught the game out. Briody of Lansingburgh surprised his friends by the manner in which he received McCormick's swiftly pitched balls.

In the notes following the day's box score, both Pfeffer and Ferguson were praised for their fielding. More important, it was reported that McCormick was questionable as tomorrow's starting pitcher: "McCormick's hand was severely hurt by the hot ball on which a triple play was made yesterday, and Bradley, formerly of the Troy club, will pitch to-day."[29]

On the following day, with McCormick making a quick recovery and taking the mound in a clear-cut, rather routine 7–2 victory for the Cleveland Blues, the reporter ironically framed his game narrative with an incident in which a Scottish terrier had a hand in all of Troy's runs:

The Haymakers, Unions and Trojans of Troy, New York

A little innocent Scot[s] terrier lay beneath the seats to the east of the diamond on Troy's grounds yesterday afternoon, figuring how many more base hits nine ancient maidens would have made than the feeble willow-wielders of the home team. This was in the seventh inning of the contest with the Clevelanders, and he of the shaggy coat was evidently impressed by the probability of Troy's first whitewash of the season. Roseman rudely broke in upon the harmless canine's solitude by hitting for a base. Pfeffer sent the ball to Glasscock, whose inability to stop it allowed the sphere to bound into left field. While the throng shouted the dog said not a word. Muldoon grasped the ball and threw it in the direction of the third base. It passed over the latter, however, and dropped directly in front of the wondering terrier. The temptation was too great. With a bark of delight the "purp" [sic] seized the ball with his teeth and tenaciously clung to it until Roseman and Pfeffer crossed the home plate. Doscher sought to convince the dog that it would be proper for him to drop the leather, but the argument had no effect until the runs were scored. Thus Troy was saved its first whitewash.

The terrier's assist was the high point of the day's action for the Trojans, as the reporter duly notes: "As to the playing of the green stockings [the Trojans], it was mainly defective both in the field and at the bat. McCormick pitched with as much as effect as on the previous day, while Welch was batted at will.... Ewing did not render as good support as usual, but aside from nine errors made by the Troy [3 by Ewing and 2 each by Cassidy, Holbert, and Ferguson] the hard hitting would have won the game for the visitors."

The recap of the game also noted that [first baseman] Smith of Troy split a finger in the third inning but continued to play. Cleveland's Doscher had three hits and three teammates two each among the Blues' 13 hits. A final ironic note was that the game was umpired by George Bradley, the former Troy Trojan who was the Blues' scheduled pitcher.

As was to be expected, the notes on the game focused on the terrier's hand in the only Trojan runs: "A purse for that dog would be in order" and "An admirer of the Clevelands said in *The Argus* said that it was a dog 'goned [sic] shame.'" The local *Albany Express*, however, observed something potentially ominous in Troy's on-field behavior: "The Clevelands fielded beautifully, while the Troys on several occasions appeared to be completely demoralized."[30]

On June 8, 1882, in the makeup of an earlier rainout, Troy's hitting

FIVE. *The Fall of the Trojans*

woes continued as Cleveland again defeated the local club, 4–1, in a rain-soaked contest. What made the defeat especially painful was that it was at the hands of former Troy Citys twirler George Bradley, who spun a masterful two-hitter against his former team:

> In the concluding game of the first Troy-Cleveland series yesterday the home team was credited with a total of two hits. With this sublime record, further explanation of the Troy's defeat is almost unnecessary. Bradley was the Cleveland's pitcher, and up to the seventh inning delivered the sphere so effectively, despite the rain which fell almost during the entire contest and rendered the ball slippery, that Ewing was the only batsman that knocked it outside of the diamond. Seven of Troy's tremendous hitters considered themselves fortunate in sending the ball as far as Bradley, who fielded them out at first on each occasion.

Troy narrowly avoided a shutout by squeezing across a run in the late innings:

> Conner began the seventh inning by hitting safely. He was the second Trojan to live to see the first bag. Smith followed with a single and Conner gained second. Cassidy hit to Dunlap (2B) and while the latter was assisting Phillips (1B) in a double play Smith scored just an instant before the side was retired.

The game was notable for Trojan pitcher Tim Keefe's eight strikeouts and the Blues' first baseman Phillips' 20 putouts. But in the three Cleveland games with the Troy Citys, the major story of the entire series was the local club's near non-existent hitting: "Troy's weak hitting was monotonous and marred the effect of an otherwise well-played game.... Where are Troy's big batters? In the three Cleveland games the home team's total of hits was only 12." Again, the Trojans heart and spirit were called into question, this time by the *Argus*: "The Troys are what may be called a systematic nine, playing brilliantly with the surroundings favorable, but easily dispirited and making a poor showing in an uphill fight."[31]

On June 9 and 10, 1882, after their futility at the bat against the Blues, the Trojans welcomed the visiting Buffalo club. Troy batters seemed to have no trouble hitting the Bisons' starting ace Jim Galvin: "The Buffalos accommodatingly presented Galvin as their pitcher yesterday, and the Troys renewed [their] old friendship with his peculiar delivery. Welch, whom the Bisons fear as greatly as the Troys favor

Galvin, curved the leather for the home nine and, as in past seasons, puzzled the gray stockings."

In the second inning, Buffalo scored a run but, more important, [former Troy Haymaker] Davy Force suffered a serious injury. After Deacon White drew a walk and advanced to second and third on a passed ball and wild pitch, he scored on Foley's sacrifice fly to right fielder Conner. Then "little Force stepped to the bat, and a swiftly pitched ball struck him on the right arm, which swelled rapidly and left him unfit for play. After a delay of 15 minutes [center fielder] Dolan was substituted." The Trojans winning lead came in the fifth inning with a typical nineteenth-century five-run rally full of walks, miscues, and timely hits:

> Holbert went to his base on balls, to second on the failure of Galvin's attempted double play, which put Ewing on first, and to the plate with Ewing on Conner's timely second-bagger. Conner touched third on a passed ball, and scored on Smith's single. Ferguson forced out Smith, and settled on second on [third baseman] O'Rourke's low throw of Welch's grounder. The misplay gave Welch his base. Each was advanced by Roseman's sacrifice, and Pfeffer's hit brought them home.

Smith was the hitting star of the game while Troy's opportune double plays were praised: "Smith excelled with the ash, making four hits [all singles] out of five at the bat. Two opportune double plays by Ewing (3b), Ferguson (2B) and Smith (1B) left several of the Buffalos on the bases." Finally, Trojan pitcher Tim Keefe's umpiring was praised—"Keefe can umpire as well as he can pitch. His decisions in yesterday's game were unquestioned"—as was Welch's steady pitching—"'Welch of the Troys, and a terror last season to the Buffalos, has a lame arm,' says the *Buffalo Courier*. 'Welch's arm was improved yesterday.'"[32]

On the following day, Troy routed the Bisons by a score of 17–4 with the club compiling 18 hits and 32 total bases. The unexpected blowout was due primarily to a major problem of 1880s organized baseball—small rosters with few pitchers, which left teams nearly defenseless when injuries struck:

> The Buffalos experimented with an amateur pitcher named Burke from the Meteca club of Attleboro, Mass., in the game ... Saturday. Twelve hits with a total of 20 were credited to the home team in the first four innings, and the ambitious hopeful was sent to the right field, where he behaved to better advantage. Purcell then [agreed] to deliver the sphere, and [did so] with

Five. The Fall of the Trojans

encouraging success for the succeeding three innings. In the eighth, however, his curves were also mastered to the tune of 12 totals, including a clean home run by Ewing who knocked the ball under the seats at the centre field fence. Eleven Troys went to the bat in this inning and by tremendous hitting and loose play of the Bisons eight runs were tallied.

Six Trojans had two or more base hits in the game: Ewing, Connor, Smith, and Roseman had three each while Keefe and Holbert two apiece. Ex-Trojan Dan Brouthers led the Bisons with two doubles. Keefe was "hit hard" with three of his four runs allowed being earned and Ewing's fielding, as was often the case, was described as "wonderful." The game day reported found the game "tedious, although the remarkable hitting was interesting."

With the new pitching distance changed from 45 to 50 feet for the 1881 season, Trojan pitchers Mickey Welch and Tim Keefe became less effective and a change pitcher was sought to lighten the burden on the team's aces. In 1882, Jim Egan, a .200 hitter and utility center fielder, was enlisted to pitch. In 100 innings and in twelve starts, Egan went 4–6 with a 4.14 earned run average. He often relieved light-hitting (.187 batting average) starting center fielder Bill Harbridge, who also was a utility catcher and first baseman that season. Harbridge was one of those shooting stars who seemed to prosper when first breaking in with Troy in the manner of Count Gedney in 1880. A lifetime .247 hitter in nine major league seasons, Harbridge hit .370 in his rookie year in 1880, collecting ten hits in nine games.

The Troy Trojans found themselves "safely in third place" in the NL and stretched their record to 16–12 before taking to the road on a 3–9 losing road trip. At mid-season, the Trojans were sixth in hits and runs scored and second in the number of errors committed. The Troy Trojans found themselves solidly in seventh place after a 7–17 month. The New York media were lobbying for the New York Metropolitans to replace the woeful Worcester team. Could cries for the removal of the floundering Troy franchise be far behind?[33]

A series of injuries and some very untimely errors led to the Capital District press christening the team "Ferguson's Fumblers." As early as July 7, 1882, there were rumors that Troy would lose its NL franchise due to a demoralized roster of tardy players whose performance, especially with regard to reckless base running, could be charitably called "indifferent." Even straight-shooter Roger Conner while having another superb year at the plate was very erratic in the field, bouncing around the diamond from third base to center field to first base due, in part, to suffering a separated shoulder in mid-season.

A major topic of baseball conversation at mid-season of 1882 that further undermined public trust in professional baseball was the expulsion of NL umpire Dick Higham for "alleged crooked work." The argument was made that the sport too readily believed in the "reformation" of "dishonest" players. Some recalled recently deceased former NL president Hulbert, who had believed "there was no trusting such fellows." If faith in the honesty of baseball is undermined for potential supporters of teams, "stock company clubs may as well as give up their business."[34]

The 1882 Trojans club continued its slide throughout August and September, apparently beleaguered by the constant rumors of the demise of the franchise, which led to even more distracted and inconsistent play. In one 16-game stretch, the Trojans lost 14 and tied two games with most of the defeats coming against the western NL clubs of Chicago, Detroit, and Cleveland.

Desperate for something to cheer about in the waning months of the 1882 season, Troy fans were treated to an exciting, extra-inning, come-back affair against the Detroit Wolverines that was atypical of the club's play late in the 1882 season:

> A more exciting game than that of yesterday between Troy and Detroit has never been played on the home grounds. When all hope of victory for the Troy team had been abandoned the tables were unexpectedly turned, and the uncertainties of base ball were again surprisingly demonstrated. Keefe was detailed to the pitcher's box, and for the third time this week successfully puzzled the opposing batsmen. Weldman dealt the sphere for the visitors, and had he been properly supported by the result would have been different. Wood opened the contest with a three-base hit, and Hanlon's long fly, which Roseman captured, allowed the former to score. Troy made matters interesting in the fourth inning, when Harbridger's [Harbridge] baser, Foster's error and Roseman's double tied the game. Trott's single, a passed ball, Ewing's muff and a sacrifice hit gave the Wolverines a lead of one in the fifth inning, and in the seventh they increased it by two runs on Knight's baser and Trott's double, Ewing's error and an out.
>
> Nothing short of sheer good luck could now save the Troys, and it came in the ninth inning. Ferguson batted safely, and reached third on Rose-

FIVE. *The Fall of the Trojans*

man's single, the latter making second, and both men displaying good tact in base running. Pfeffer, who heretofore had been fanning the air and knocking easy balls to the infield, registered a timely baser, and Ferguson and Roseman tallied. Pfeffer started for second as Holbert drove the sphere to [3B] Bennett. While the latter was fielding Holbert out at first Pfeffer dashed for third. Powell threw wildly to the baseman and Pfeffer ran in, tying the game amid deafening cheers.

In the tenth inning Weldman reached third on Ewing's third error, but fortunately was left. Gillespie gained the same bag in the eleventh and also remained there. The Detroits were retired in regular order in the twelfth. The Troy's trick at the bat settled all argument. With two out Ewing rapped for a base. The ball went between [RF] Knight's legs and Ewing made third. Connor hit wickedly, and [2B] Foster failing to stop the sphere Ewing came to the plate with the winning run, thus ending the game.

To say the enthusiasm of the 410 spectators was intense would be putting it mildly. Hats filled and shrieks rent the air. The fielding was sharp, particularly that of the greens [Troy], all of whose errors were registered against [3B] Ewing. [Outfielders] Harbridge, Roseman, and Hanlon were frequently applauded for difficult catches. It was a grand victory.[35]

A more typical late season result for the Troy Citys was a September defeat in Buffalo by the Bisons, 4–9, a loss attributable to Tim Keefe's poor pitching. The sporting press (again) mocked the uninspired play of the Trojans with only Connor receiving any plaudits. The attendance was again poor, and even die-hard Troy supporters seemed eager to see the end of the 1882 season:

> Ferguson's so-called ball players must be anti-monopolists. They do not want to monopolize even the right to seventh place. The Buffalos, who have usually fallen as easy prey to the Troys, defeated the green-legged Trojans yesterday. It was through no fault of the visitors' fielding that this result was brought about, as the contest was won by the Bisons' superior batting. Keefe received [one] of the hardest drubbings of the season, twenty-three total hits [twenty-three total bases on eighteen base hits] being registered from his delivery. Connor sent in three of Troy's four tallies, and pounded Galvin for a home run, a triple and a single. The Buffalos were perfect in their field work. The attendance was 508.[36]

The press was a bit more forgiving as the 1882 season ended with the star pitching duo of Keefe and Welch clearly exhausted and seemingly in decline. The Troy Trojans team, both on the road and at home, continued to see attendance plummet: "Troy out batted Boston yesterday, but errors by [catcher] Holbert and fickle pitching by Welch lost the game to the visitors. Three men were given their base on balls by Welch and all reached the plate.... The bean-eaters had on their fielding clothes, and not one misplay was charged to them."[37]

The Troy Trojans in 1882 finished in seventh place with a 35–48 win-loss record, finishing above only the hapless Worcester Ruby Legs (also known that season as the "Brown Stockings").

In fact, Troy, which lost ten out of seventeen games to Worcester in 1881, re-established its dominance over its small-market rival in 1882. On May 1, 1882, Troy defeated Worcester, 10–4, in their first matchup of the new season, then followed up with a 4–0 win the next day behind the shutout pitching of Tim Keefe and three hits, including a triple, and three runs scored by Roger Connor. On May 26, 1882, at Troy before 800 fans, the Trojans defeated the Ruby Legs, 9–5, with Buck Ewing garnering three hits, including a triple. Troy continued its mastery over Worcester in three July games in Massachusetts, winning 8–4, 11–8, and 8–4, with Keefe winning the first and third games. Hitting star Connor had 14 of Troy's 53 hits in this series. In a September series in Troy, the Trojans again swept the Worcesters with Keefe winning a pitching duel against pitching sensation John Lee Richmond, 4–1 on September 29, 1882. On the following day, in the last major league game for both franchises, Roger Connor again led the batting stars with a home run in a 10–7 Troy win. In its last major league game at Worcester at the Agricultural Fair Grounds (also named Drive Park), the gross receipts for the gate of fewer than 25 fans totaled $3.

The only true bright spot for the 1882 season was Troy's slight upswing after its move from the Haymaker Grounds to the West Troy Grounds (Watervliet); the club went 22–20 at the new park. Because of bad weather and construction overruns, however, the new field cost a hefty $5,000.

In a related matter, Troy's new ballpark may have had some inherent flaws that further depressed fan attendance and further threatened the club's NL survival:

> An important change was made. The [Troy] base ball grounds had been located on what is now Second Avenue, Lansingburgh, between Third and Fourth Streets, but this property was becoming valuable for building lots, and it was decided to remove to new grounds across the river in Watervliet. Francis N. Mann, Jr., had become President of the club, he having

FIVE. The Fall of the Trojans

succeeded A. L. Hotchkin, who had been Gardner Earl's successor. The new grounds were on what is now Nineteenth Street, diagonally opposite the railroad station, and it was there that Troy teams played baseball for a dozen years. The grounds themselves were excellent and the turf diamond was one of the best in the country, but the location was not a fortunate one. There was no street car service to and fro, and patrons had to rely on the belt line locals, running on that side of the river only every hour. This fact, together with the slump, in the playing of the Troy team—Troy finished next to last that year—resulted in the patronage diminishing almost to the vanishing point. The gentlemen who had been behind the team were all good sportsmen, and they were willing to spend their money to provide the best baseball in Troy, but the team had never been a real winner, and patience had finally ceased to be a virtue.[38]

The irony of the Trojans' meager home attendance was the fact that the club was a decent draw on the road as is evidenced in a weekend series in Philadelphia in late August against the American Association Quakers: "Costly errors by the Troys and superior batting by the Philadelphia team bought victory to the latter in the Quaker city Saturday. Twelve times did the willow strike effectively at Welsh's [Welch] delivery while the home team's pitcher was hit safely on eight occasions. Ewing behind the plate recorded two errors, and Holbert at short, Cassidy at third, Pfeffer at second, and Connor at first one each. Pfeffer with two doubles led at the bat." The big story of the weekend was not this 6–4 Philadelphia victory but the 7,000 fans who attended the weekend series.[39]

The last major league game played in Troy was on August 26, 1882, and it was anti-climactic with the local club getting only two hits in a 0–3 loss to the Cleveland Blues before ending the season with a nineteen game road trip.

By late September, Troy newspapers were reporting that other NL clubs were seeking to sign Trojan ball players to improve their rosters after the raids by the American Association: "A tempting inducement of $2,000 apiece has been said to have been offered to four of the Trojan nine, but in each instance the offer failed."[40] On September 23, 1882, Troy supposedly "resigned" from the NL:

Baseball admirers were surprised this morning [September 23, 1882] by an Associated press dispatch from Philadelphia stating that the executive committee of the league [National League] had accepted the resignation of the Troys and Worcesters, in accordance with the desire of the league that membership should consist only of cities large enough to ensure paying patronage. None were more surprised than the directors of the Troys.[41]

On September 25, the NL owners voted 6–2 in violation of their own by-laws to remove Troy and Worcester from the league and replace them with big market clubs in New York and Philadelphia. The stated reason for the vote to expel the small market clubs was "indifferent play of the players" but was actually due to "market factors" and "financial reasons."[42]

Troy did not take the NL's decision to oust the Trojans without a fight. On September 26, 1882, Troy applied for entry into the AA and threatened to file a $5,000 lawsuit against the NL to recoup what the club spent on the West Troy Ballpark. Furthermore, the Trojans took a public position that they were innocent of any wrongdoing:

> A director of the Troy baseball club denies the truth of the Philadelphia dispatch that the club resigned at the league meeting at Philadelphia on Friday. He said a resolution was adopted expelling the club after December 2, against the protests of its representatives. The directors of the Troy club say they have been at great expense this year in laying out new grounds, and that, according to the constitution of the league, no club can be expelled unless it has violated the league rules. At the meeting the representatives of all the other clubs admitted that the Troy club had violated no rule. The directors declare that if the league insists upon the expulsion a suit for heavy damages will be begun by the Troy club. In the meantime the remaining games of the season will be played by Troy, and as many of Troy's players as possible will be retained for next year.
>
> [Worcester's representative also weighed in on the fateful happenings of the baseball meetings at Philadelphia]: The Worcester and Troy clubs did not resign, but a resolution was adopted declaring that these clubs not be represented in the association next season. The vote stood 6 to 2, the Troy and Worcester Clubs voting in the negative. The resolution was offered by Thompson, of the Detroit Club, who has been the prime mover in the scheme to change the membership of the League, and who recently made a personal canvas of the six clubs voting in the affirmative to secure concerted action at the meeting. The reason given for the turning out of the Worcester and Troy Clubs was that the patronage in either of these cities was not large enough to give the visiting clubs a share of the gate money sufficient to pay their expenses, and that as New York and Philadelphia were anxious to be admitted it was simply a question of business whether two non-paying cities should be continued in the co-partnership when two

FIVE. *The Fall of the Trojans*

paying cities could be secured to take their places. The representatives of the Troy and Worcester nines made a vigorous resistance to this carrying out of the plan of the other clubs, but were powerless.[43]

Troy's resignation was explained in the local papers as the result of insufficient funding, which had been the primary problem for Troy's six-year tenure—1871–1872 and 1879–1882—in major league baseball:

> Several representatives from other league cities admitted to Mr. Hotchkin that the attempt to throw out Troy was rash, but added that the matter had gone so far it would be impolitic to retract the step taken. The entire league than assured Mr. Hotchkin if he would present the resignation that each of the clubs would agree, if a local team for next season was organized to play in Troy to play two to four games with it on the West Troy grounds. Mr. Hotchkin telegraphed the proposal to Troy, and a conference was held in this city. Troy's resignation was presented and accepted.
>
> A strong club composed of local and other players will be formed for next season. It is expected that at least thirty-two exhibition games with league clubs will be played here, and other clubs, including the Metropolitans, will also visit this city. The Troy club has a five years' lease of the new grounds in West Troy, and by the arrangement explained, loss to the stockholders will doubtless be averted.
>
> It was intimated to Mr. Hotchkin that should Troy so desire to join the league again it would be given preference. It is not likely Troy will make such a request in some years. This city entered the league in 1878, since when $50,000 have been paid in salaries to players. Five thousand dollars have been expended in improving grounds, and with other outlays it is estimated that with Troy's four years' connection with the league $75,000 would not more than cover the expense of the sport. The receipts fell considerably below that amount. More than a hundred "tossers" have been engaged and have played in Troy during its league membership.[44]

In the December 6, 1882, NL meetings in Providence, Rhode Island, Troy refused to accept the owners' decision and would not resign in favor of metropolitan clubs in New York (Gothams) and Philadelphia (Phillies). As has been previously noted, a deal was ultimately brokered in which both Troy and Worcester would resign if the remaining NL teams would play two to four exhibition games at the new West Troy Grounds in Troy and in Worcester; this promise was never followed up on by the NL clubs. Troy and Worcester were also assured that they would be given first preference in later applications to the NL. It is this last concession to both Troy and Worcester that has never been rescinded that serves as the basis for the consensus belief that both cities are honorary members of the National League to this day.[45]

> The report of the National League meeting in Providence on December 7, 1882, contained a number of routine matters [that] were dealt with, such as, a strict regulation expulsing any players revolving, the increasing of team series to fourteen games, allowing pitchers to release the ball at any point below the shoulder, the reinstatement of ten blacklisted players (including former Troy players Lip Pike, Buttercup Dickerson, and Ed Caskin), the adoption of the Spalding ball, and the simple statement: "New York and Philadelphia were admitted in place of Troy and Worcester."

The reaction of Troy baseball fans to its home team's dismissal from the NL is encapsulated in an 1882 report that simply states that that "Trojans never felt they were fairly treated by the National League."[46]

In taking a long view of the 1882 Trojan season, it is surprising and seemingly against all logic, that the Troy Trojans were playing winning baseball at mid-season of the 1882 NL season. The Boston Red Stockings visited the Collar City on July 26, 1882, and came away with a narrow, 5–3 victory:

> Matthews went into the pitchers' box for Boston yesterday, and was too much for the Troys, whose short hits and easy flies were sadly in contrast with their spirited batting while Whitney curved the ball. Eagan [Egan] pitched his first game for Troy since Detroit's last visit to this city, and showed marked improvement in control of the ball and of fielding. He was not hit to marked effect and had his support been as his pitching Troy would be rejoicing in its sixth consecutive victory.
> For the third time the Bostons lost the toss, and went to bat first. Hornung hit safely, and stole second. Hobart's fumble gave Deasley first. The latter started for second, and the ball following him Hornung made for the plate, which Connor assisted him in securing by throwing over Ewing's head. In the fifth inning Matthews obtained second on a drive that was plainly a foul, with all respect to the umpire's decision to the contrary. This was the starter for three runs. Hornung and Deasley rapping for singles and Ewing and Eagan erring in the field. The visitors made doubly sure of their victory in the ninth inning, when basers by Burdock and Wise, a sacrifice by Hotaling and a fumble by Eagan scored a run. The side was retired with the bases full.
> It was not until the sixth inning that a safe hit was credited to Troy. Then Ewing batted for a base, and with Eagan, who had gained first on Sutton's error, tallied on Morrill's overthrow to third, after the latter had retired Connor on a foul fly. Cassidy then made a terrific lunge at the ball,

FIVE. *The Fall of the Trojans*

and sent it bounding beneath the seats at the south fence. Cassidy made a commendable effort to score a home run, but unfortunately was retired as he slid for the plate. Gillespie knocked three bags out of the ball in the seventh inning, and came in on Burdock's drop of Roseman's fly. Hotaling thought to shut off Gillespie and threw wildly to Deasley, Roseman reaching third. Pfeffer's fly was captured by Hornung, who by magnificent juggling held Roseman at third and prevented the score from being tied. [Deasley's fielding was praised as was the play of Troy's Ferguson and Pfeffer.][47]

Yet Troy would often revert to its listless and uninterested manner in games of significance. The possibility of the NA New York Mets replacing either Worcester or Troy was aided by two second half loses by the Trojans to the up-and-coming Metropolitans. On July 10, 1882, the New York club decisively defeated the National League club, 9–3, appearing to be the superior team in all respects:

The representative team of Troy was taken into camp by the Metropolitan nine on the Polo Grounds yesterday afternoon in the presence of 1,500 spectators. The batting was even on both sides, each side gaining 11 singles, with a total of 17 base hits. The League players were unable to bunch their hits, while the local team made the majority of hits in the second and fifth innings which, of course, did better service than the scattering ones of the Troys. The fielding of the home team was far superior to that of the visitors and their playing altogether [sic] was in every respect better than that of the Troy men.... Pfeffer the shortstop of the Trojans, made some beautiful throws to first base, and also was the receiver of plaudits. Welch, Brady, Hankinson, and Smith wielded the ash most successfully, the former [Welch] making a clean home run in the third inning.[48]

On August 6, 1882, The New York Mets again defeated the Trojans, 5–2, at the Polo Grounds with a crowd of 3,000 in attendance. The New York club was playing winning baseball and was making a push for future entry into the NL with their defeat of four of five major league clubs during the week. The Trojans were held to seven scattered hits and one earned run.[49]

On June 3, 1882, in an earlier game against the New York Metropolitans at the Polo Grounds, Pete Gillespie, a starting outfielder and one of the few bright spots on the Trojans roster, suffered a serious injury when playing center field. He had a collision with left fielder Cassidy, who suffered only minor injuries. Gillespie was sent back to Troy the following day, and the medical report was at least promising: "Dr. McLean, an eminent surgeon, who has charge of the case, says he does not consider Gillespie's wound dangerous, and that his skull is not fractured."[50]

The near-debilitating injury suffered by Trojan center fielder Pete Gillespie mirrors the rocky 1882 season (and brief NL history) of the Troy Citys: moments of on-field success, even brilliance, amid a steady decline in the fortunes of the franchise (and the player).

Pete Gillespie began his amateur baseball career with his hometown Carbondale, Pennsylvania, Alerts in 1874 and in 1875 when the Alerts merged with the Carbondale Lackawanna(s). He advanced throughout the ranks of organized baseball in 1878 playing with the International Association's Lynn and Worcester, both in Massachusetts; the following year he was a prominent member of the 1879 Holyoke Shamrocks of the National Association. Gillespie along with Shamrocks' teammates Mickey Welch and Roger Connor joined the NL Troy Trojans in 1880.

Beginning with his NL rookie season, Pete Gillespie was among the best fielding outfielders in the game. He led the in fielding average in 1885 (.942) and was second in both 1880 (.905), and 1881 (.933). He was also first in

Troy Trojan Pete Gillespie was a solid baseball player in all aspects of the game, shining especially as a star outfielder. His quick rise to fame and tragic, abrupt decline mirror the fortunes of Troy as a major league city (courtesy of the National Baseball Hall of Fame Library, Cooperstown, New York).

Five. The Fall of the Trojans

outfield putouts in 1880 (185) and second in the league in this category in both 1882 (188) and 1883 (216). Further, Gillespie led the league in outfield double plays in 1883 (6) and was second in 1880 (5). Moreover, the Irishman was a reliable hitter with a .276 career average.

Gillespie had an impressive year at the plate in 1883 when he and a number of former Trojan teammates were signed by John Day to play for the new NL entry in New York. (It has been alleged that prior to joining the new NL New York entry, O.P. Caylor had firm commitments from ex–Trojans Ewing, Welch, and Gillespie to play for his 1883 AA Cincinnati team; however, all three players played for the New York club that season.) Named as the first New York Gothams team captain, Gillespie hit .314 with 23 doubles, 13 triples, and 62 runs batted in, all of which were personal highs in his eight-year professional career.

Pete Gillespie was popular with the fans and a key player in the recently (popularly) renamed 1885 New York Giants spectacular season that fell just short of a NL pennant. The club was first in the league in earned run average, fielding percentage, and batting average.

However, by 1887, Pete Gillespie's major league career was over. Always engaged in contentious discussions with management during his salary negotiations, Gillespie engaged in many disagreements and holdouts with his team's ownership. He wound up with the IA Troy Trojans in 1888 but was released by early June; he then crossed the Hudson and played for the IA Albany Governors but was again let go by late July. Both Capital District teams were disasters on the field finishing 50.5 (Troy) and 59 (Albany) games behind the pennant winning Syracuse Stars.

In contrast to his professionalism and sportsmanship of just a few years prior, Pete Gillespie became a cantankerous alcohol abuser who caused embarrassing public scenes, including one notorious event that involved an inebriated woman and an equally impaired Chief Roseman, with whom he shared a starting outfield position with the 1882 Troy Trojans. The abrupt and rather sad conclusion of his career did nothing to obscure the fact that Gillespie was a slick fielding and valued hitter during the 1880s.[51]

Further, Pete Gillespie's brief baseball career is emblematic of the arc of the Troy Trojans' tenure in the National League: a young ball player unexpectedly appears on the scene; plays with talent and enthusiasm, winning the respect of baseball professionals and the adulation of Collar City supporters; and then suffers a sharp, ignominious decline that consigns him to the forgotten pages of history. This has been the fate of Troy's major league franchises, and, if the analogy is not overly analyzed, the fate of Troy, New York, as an American city of national importance in the nineteenth century.

As early as late October of 1882, the Trojans were in the process of disbanding with, for example, Ferguson and Cassidy playing for the Providence Grays in a series of money games with the New York Metropolitans and with Buck Ewing's signing of a large 1883 contract with the New York Gothams that dominated Troy's sports reports: "It is said the terms on which Ewing of the Troy base ball club signed in New York for next year were $1,200 cash down and $2,000 in contract, making his salary $3,200. This is probably the largest sum ever offered a ball player."[52]

The era of the small market clubs on the major league baseball level was a thing of the past. There was no longer even a lingering doubt among any of baseball's stake holders that baseball was "an established business."[53] Money, as always, was king, and the prospects of professional baseball in Troy beyond the 1882 season were dismal:

> The outlook for a base ball club in Troy next season is not encouraging. Within the past few days the players of the home team have become lukewarm and their expressions of love for the ball club, and it has been rumored that at least six of them had signed with other clubs for the next season. The directors were at sea as to the future.
> Last evening they met at the store of C. H. Dauchy and were joined by players Keefe, Ewing, Welch, Roseman, Gillespie, and Connor. President Hotchkin interrogated the players as to their intentions. Three said they had not at any time [thought] of signing; two "didn't know," and one would sign if the others did. It was evident at this point that the directors had been "left" by the boys. Warm words were exchanged between President Hotchkin and Ewing, whom he charged with deserting the club and signing with the Metropolitans of New York. Ewing emphatically denied the accusation, and said he had not signed with any club whatever. The meeting finally broke up without any definite conclusions being arrived at by the directors.
> President Hotchkin said to a reporter: "See how these men have treated us. It is shameful. They have hung back for two or three weeks and asked

FIVE. The Fall of the Trojans

time for consideration. We have been 'played for a lot of suckers.' I have not a doubt but that the men have all signed for next year. Ewing will probably go to New York."

There is no question that the directors of the Troy club have been eating considerable "taffy" manufactured by Ferguson, Ewing and Co. The players were told that if Troy had a nine next year the club would play in the [National] league without doubt; but all inducements offered by the directors could not gain the consent of the assembled ball-tossers to sign the contracts so temptingly displayed on the president's desk. Previous to the meeting of the directors of the Troy club last night, the opinion expressed was that Connor was the squarest man in the home nine, and was worth about $1,200—or less. Connor is not averse to staying in Troy, but he wants a "bar'l [sic]." President Hotchkin feels very sore over the action of the "big six," and the other directors were emphatic in speech when they refer to last night's meeting. The opinion is generally expressed that no league team will be organized in Troy for next season.[54]

Troy has been without a major league baseball franchise for 132 years.

Six

A Minor League City on the Hudson

On February 17, 1883, in a "Harmony Conference," professional baseball declared a moratorium on a brief period of clubs raiding rival teams' player rosters with the Tripartite Agreement (also referred to as the National Agreement) among the National League (NL), the American Association (AA) and the Northwestern League (NWL). Teams agreed not to entice players under contract to jump teams and to standardize all signings and player contracts.

Simultaneously team owners increased the number of players on a team's reserve list to eleven. Player minimum salaries were also established with $1,000 for the NL and AA and $750 for the NWL.[1] A new National Agreement was signed in 1885 between the NL and the AA that extended the reserve clause and established maximum ($2,000) and minimum ($1,000) salaries. This unilateral action by management enraged many ballplayers who, with New York Giant John Ward spearheading the movement, established a players' union—the Brotherhood of Professional Base Ball players—within a week of the announcement of this second National Agreement. With management now firmly ensconced as the dominant force in the business, major league baseball, at least on the surface, experienced relative peace and stability until the Players League "War" of 1890.[2]

John B. Day, a New York City tobacco manufacturer and factory owner, founded both the 1883 New York Metropolitans (AA) and the New York Gothams (NL) that were also known as the "Green Stockings." Day purchased the rights to the Troy Trojans' roster of the now unattached players whom he distributed between his two clubs with former Trojans Roger Connor (1B), Ed Caskin (SS), Mickey Welch (P), Buck

Six. A Minor League City on the Hudson

Ewing (INF-C), Pete Gillespie (OF), and Frank Hankinson (3B) going to the NL Gothams; and Tim Keefe (P), Bill Holbert (C), Chief Roseman (OF) and Candy Nelson (SS) heading to the New York Metropolitans (AA).

Day turned over the running of the teams to baseball man Jim Murtrie, who managed the New York Mets in 1883–1884 and won the 1884 AA pennant with Tim Keefe on the mound. A year after he led the AA in games (68—all starts), innings pitched (619), strikeouts (359) with a 2.41 earned run average, Keefe helped win New York's first major league pennant in 1884. Sharing pitching chores with Jack Lynch, with each player winning 37 games, Keefe had a 2.25 earned run average. From 1885 to 1890, Keefe averaged 34 wins a season.[3]

Jim Mutrie managed the New York Gothams, who changed their name to the "Giants" beginning in 1885 and won NL pennants with this club in 1888 and 1889.[4] Mutrie was a baseball lifer who brought New York City its first big league team, its first pennant, and its first world championship. Equally important, he helped to establish baseball on a firm financial basis in the late nineteenth century. He even provided his NL New York franchise with its nickname: In response to an observation that he managed a team of tall men, Mutrie responded, "Yes, and they are giants on the field as well."[5]

Troy continued to play minor league baseball for more than thirty years after their brief turn as a major league city. In 1885, the Trojans joined Saratoga and Kingston, New York, in the Hudson River League (HRL), which folded at the conclusion of its initial campaign.

In the mid–1880s, baseball continued to remain popular in Troy even when the city lacked a professional team. For example, on September 26, 1885, after the HRL folded, Troy defeated its rival Albany 35–17 in a game between commercial travelers from both cities. As in the earliest days of amateur baseball, the losing Albanians "put up the stuff for a banquet to their conquerors." The former Troy Trojans' baseball field in West Troy (Watervliet) was almost in constant use. The grounds were frequently employed to benefit local charities, including late June 1885, when games between the Troy Citizens Corps and the Troy Bachelors Club and between Democratic and Republican alderman were played to raise funds for the "Bartoli Statue Pedestal Fund."[6]

In 1886, Troy was a member of the Hudson State League (HSL) and found themselves on the opposite end of their usually overly aggressive history of luring away star opponents. Troy native Jim Devlin was the Trojans' regular starting pitcher. The club appealed to organized baseball to have the New York Gothams of the NL cease-and-desist from pursuing Devlin: "The President of the Troy club claims protection under the national agreement, and insists that the New Yorks have no right to engage Devlin, his left-handed pitcher."[7] A few months later it was reported that the twenty-year old Jim Devlin was now a member of the Gothams: "It seems that New York stole Devlin, its new left-handed pitcher, from the Troy club. He is a Lansingburgh brush maker and is said to be a very promising man."[8]

Jim Devlin had a very inauspicious rookie season with New York. He played in one game, giving up four earned runs in two innings for an earned run average of 18.00. By the end of September of 1886, Jim Devlin's Gothams career was over: "Devlin has been suspended for listless work in the box on last Saturday."[9]

Jim Devlin appeared in two games the following year with the NL Philadelphia Quakers and 20 games in 1888–1889 for the AA St. Louis Browns before returning to the minor leagues and even playing in Canada and going 2–0 for the London (Ontario) Cockneys in 1897.[10]

The 1886 Troy Trojans were not a success on the diamond, finishing with a 20–33 (.378 winning percentage) that was just a bit better the cellar-dwelling Saratoga Springs, New York, club. The Saratoga team was playing its first season of organized baseball and suffered through a woeful debut season at 12–32 (.273 winning percentage). These clubs played a tight, well-played game (only eight errors total) in Saratoga with the home team the loser, 5–6. The beleaguered clubs were looking forward to better days of increased fan interest: "The Saratoga-Troy baseball game was closely contested yesterday afternoon on the South Broadway grounds. There was a good attendance. The playing of both teams was good and on several occasions during the game the applause was loud and long. The closeness of the game of yesterday will no doubt excite considerable interest to-day."[11]

In November of 1886, it was widely reported that the Troy Trojans would join the International Association (IA) along with Cleveland, Newark, and Jersey City. Both Cleveland and Troy were praised for their past support of organized baseball, but only the Newark Little Giants

Six. A Minor League City on the Hudson

and the Jersey Skeeters actually entered the IA in 1887. The reporter's enthusiasm for Troy as a potential member of IA may have been enhanced by its past baseball history: "Troy, years ago, was the home of the famous Haymakers and for a long while represented in the [National] League. Its people therefore are just now hungry for base ball and anxious to patronize a professional club."[12]

In 1888, Troy finally was awarded a franchise in the International Association, which that year was composed of five teams from New York State and three Canadian teams from Ontario. Troy had a disastrous season on the diamond, finishing seventh with a 28–80 win-loss record and a .259 winning percentage. The Trojans were inept in the field with a season total of 614 errors (an average of just under six errors per game). Trojan pitcher George Haddock set an IA record with twenty consecutive losses. The managing situation for the 1888 Trojans was also chaotic with four men filling the position: Ted Sullivan, Mert Hackett, Pat Dealy, and Percy Werden. The fourth choice for a Troy skipper was also a playing manager and Werden's hitting woes that year (.185 in 46 games) were an aberration in an impressive minor career at the plate (a .341 career batting average in 1,536 games and the 1893 NL lead in triples with 29). Troy left the league at the end of the 1888 season.[13]

In February of 1890, Albany and Troy were being recruited to play in the International League (IL). Abner Powell, manager of the Hamilton club in the IL, visited the Capital District to scout whether the cities in question had either $5,000 to create a stock company or sufficient $25 season book pass subscriptions to make the area economically viable for the IL, which sent Secretary White to help Powell in his review of the matter. The sense was that the entry of both or either Hudson River club was too risky for the IL to invite them to join the league: "The feeling here [Albany] is, however, apathetic, and it is doubtful if they can succeed in arousing much of the old-timed enthusiasm ... Albany [and Troy], like many other small cities, is a good place for a winning nine to do business, but a losing one better disband than try to attract an audience."[14]

As a result, in 1890, Troy with fellow Capital District teams from Albany, Johnstown-Gloversville, and Cobleskill joined the New York State League with the Collar City club winning the league crown that year. This was Troy's only pennant in the city's many-decades long participation in nineteenth-century organized baseball. In late July, Troy signed African American star portsider George Stovey, who had a 1–1 win-loss record for Troy before returning to his Albany and Rensselaer League club at Hoosick Falls. The 1890 season was Stovey's last on an integrated baseball team before being relegated to African American only clubs for the remainder of his career.[15]

Baseball continued to flourish in the Collar City in spite of the innumerable shakeups in league and individual club affiliations that were almost exclusively the result of the precarious financial challenges that franchise owners faced in the economically depressed last decade of the nineteenth century. For example, there was a large crowd for a June 25, 1890, exhibition fundraiser for the Fresh Air Fund between Troy City and the Troy Trojans. The game was not an artistic success with the Trojans losing and garnering only two hits while committing seven errors. Knox led the Troy Citys with a double and a triple and the Trojans' Marquette made two circus catches in center field while also hitting a double. However, the city of Troy was the actual winner with two local teams raising money for a worthwhile cause while enjoying a free concert by the Troy City Band.[16]

In 1891, along with the area Albany Senators, Troy joined the Eastern Association (EA) (which renamed itself the "Eastern League" (EL) in 1892) and remained in the EL until 1894 when continued mediocre play and weak attendance figures forced it to disband and move to Scranton, Pennsylvania, where the local Indians merged with the Troy Washerwomen [the renamed Trojans]. One of the highlights of Troy's EA tenure was on April 16, 1891, in an exhibition game with the strong New York Giants NL entry, a club with six future Hall of Fall members on its roster. The game was exciting with the homestanding Trojans winning in walk-off fashion, 5–4. The local fans were enthusiastically supportive of their new club and the four former Troy Citys players on the Giants roster who starred for the Collar City's 1882 NL franchise:

> Troy, April 16—It so happens that the Eastern League teams which the New Yorks have met so far this season have put up a great article of ball in the first game. In New Haven the game was a tie. In Albany the New Yorks were defeated, while to-day in this city the local team walked away with

Six. A Minor League City on the Hudson

the prize of 5 to 4. It was a grand game all the way through, with few errors on each side. The Troy errors were not costly, while just one of the New Yorks was the cause of defeat. Defeat can also be laid to Umpire Battin, who, in the ninth called Touhy safe at first base when Rusie's throw to Connor caught him a foot off the base.

The Troy team batted the ball harder than the visitors, sizing up John Ewing's [Ewing was 21–8 for the 1891 Giants] curve at the very start. He tried to work a slow ball on them, but it failed to have any effect, as they were looking for such meat. He retired at the end of the fourth inning. Rusie [the twenty-year old went 33–20 for the 1891 Giants and was a future Hall of Fame member] then went in, and the first ball he put through to Buckley went like a flash of lightning and everybody looked on in amazement at the show of speed he exhibited. The sun was out and Amos [Rusie] felt like working.

[With Troy's Touhy and Messitt on base in the bottom of the ninth, Giants second baseman Danny Richardson booted a slow roller and both runners scored to win the match.]

The crowd let itself out to the fullest extent and wildest kind of enthusiasm ensued. For a city of only 65,000 inhabitants, Troy shows more interest in base ball than many of the larger cities. One hears very little else talked here now but the national game. The crowd that saw to-day's game numbered 3,000. The New Yorks, of course, received a roaring ovation when they arrived at the grounds. In fact, they own the city while they are here. Their friends thronged the American Hotel last night to see them. Everybody was inquiring for Roger [Connor], Tim [Keefe], Mickey [Welch] and Buck [Ewing].

In 1891, Troy's organized baseball franchise continued to be snakebit and experienced an unexpected hit to their bottom line: "The grand stand at the Troy base ball grounds was burned last night. Loss about $1,200. The club has secured the Laureate amateur grounds for their games."[17]

The Trojan Trojans were a solid Eastern League franchise that often played on even terms with major league clubs such as the 1893 NL Brooklyn Bridegrooms, who finished in the middle of the NL pack: "As was expected the Troy baseball club gave the Brooklyns quite a run in the games at Eastern Park yesterday afternoon. The visitors [Troy] did well in the field, but could do nothing with the pitching of Haddock, Lovett, and Stein and the few hits made were well scattered. Devlin and Donovan were also successful in the box score."[18] The Devlin mentioned in the game report was the same local boy Jim Devlin who had a decade earlier signed a controversial contract with the New York Gothams leaving his hometown club to play in the National League.

Attendance at Troy Trojan Eastern League games continued to decline in 1894 and forced the club into bankruptcy, which led to disbanding the Trojans in late July: "[Troy] Manager Maloney has decided that he can't lose any more coin in the Laundry Town, which does not appreciate a good team."[19]

However, by April of the following year, Maloney was again managing a Troy entry in a New York State League (NYSL): "The Grounds at West Troy are being placed in condition for use, and the bicycle track is being improved." The newly established Troy club was planning to play Williams College at Williamstown, Massachusetts, on April 27, 1895, to prepare for the opening of the league season.[20]

In 1895 the Troy Trojans played in the New York State League and remained a member of the league in its various iterations until 1916. The Troy Trojans extended run as a member of the NYSL at the beginning of the twentieth century was marked by problems similar to the earlier Troy organizations in the nineteenth century: financial instability, major roster overhauls, uneven fan support, management in-fighting, and the vagaries of early season weather in the Northeast. The basic question of who exactly was running the team was often unclear: "The difficulties of the Troy baseball club are still unsettled. As the matter now stands, W. H. Long of this city [Albany] holds the franchise, the players refuse to play under his proprietorship unless paid back salaries, and William Rabbit of Troy wants to get possession of the franchise. As the matters are now, the indications are that the club will continue for the present on its own hook and under the management of "Hank" Ramsey."[21]

Troy minor league baseball was always a hardscrabble existence as weather, team preparation, and frequent roster deficiencies were a continual problem that undermined local support:

> The Troy baseball team is now complete, except for pitchers, and [Troy manager] Mr. Bacon has arranged with some of the Eastern League teams to take the reserved pitchers which they do not sign to play. The work will begin at once on the grounds in Upper Troy. The preliminary games to be played with the Syracuse and Montreal teams have been declared off, as

Six. A Minor League City on the Hudson

the local team cannot get in shape early enough. The first games will be played with the Schenectady team in this city April 29 and 30 and at Schenectady May 1 and 2.[22]

In order to fill the club's coffers, especially early in a season, the Troy Trojans would take on all comers if there was an opportunity to draw a large crowd. One such money two-game series was with the renowned African American club, the Cuban X-Giants, which played the Trojans at Laureate Field in Lansingburgh and defeated the locals in two, close, high-scoring games.[23]

In 1902, the Troy Trojans had a talented roster led by a skinny home grown hero, future Hall of Fame inductee, Johnny Evers. The rejuvenated Trojans sparked renewed interest in the club and more detailed analysis and commentary by a generally supportive press:

> That the Troy baseball team as now constituted is superior in every respect to the Albany nine was demonstrated by the Trojans' easy victory yesterday afternoon on the Laureate grounds. Goodwin's curves were batted at will, nearly every man making a hit, while the visitors secured only three hits. Aside from two home runs by Smith and the excellent pitching of Partridge, Troy's new pitcher, an Albany man, the contest was devoid of any features and was uninteresting. Smith secured first base four out of five times at the bat, and in the third and fourth innings he knocked the ball into the river. The score was 14 to 5, and had it not been for errors by Evers in the second and seventh innings the visitors might have been shut out.
>
> Raub started to pitch the game, but being rather wild he was sent to the bench in the fifth inning and Partridge finished the game. Only one hit was made off Raub's delivery, but he was too liberal with the bases on ball.
>
> Evers, Troy's first batter, went out at first, and Smith secured his base on [1B] O'Brien's error. He stole second. Smink was given four balls, and he retired in a fast double play by [SS] Cargo and O'Brien on Rafter's infield hit. Troy began scoring in the second inning. Hilley was put out at first, and Shortell stole second after reaching first on [P] Goodwin's error. Marshall was safe on another error of O'Brien, and Shortell by fast base running scored Troy's first run. In the third inning the Trojans became familiar with Goodwin's curves and four runs were tallied. Evers got his base on balls, stole second and crossed the plate on Smith's home run. Smink made a hit to centre field and scored on Rafter's two-bagger. Hilley also knocked the ball into Bernard's territory and Rafter came home. The next three batters were retired.
>
> Evers' error in the second inning was accountable for two runs. Tamsett was sent to first by Raub, and was advanced by Brown's sacrifice. Doherty

was also given his base on balls. With the two men on bases Hess sent a ground ball to Evers, who in his anxiety to make a double play fumbled the ball long enough to allow Hess to reach first base, Tamsett and Doherty in the meantime scoring on the throw to first. Two more Albanians crossed the rubber in the eighth inning. O'Brien went out on a foul to Rafter, and Hess sent a long fly to Smith, Goodwin singled, and Cargo reached the first bag on another error of the shortstop. Both scored on Simmons' three-base hit to left field.

The Albany outfielders were busy until the end of the game. In the second inning Evers knocked the ball over the right field fence, but to the displeasure of the "rooters" the umpire called it a foul. He was then given his base on balls, and later he secured two hits off Goodwin.[24]

The early twentieth-century Troy Trojans were also plagued by boorish attitudes and thuggish behavior of its players and fans that seemed a further extension of the poor behavior that plagued Troy baseball from its earliest days and that was thought to be a major factor in the club's low attendance figures:

> A game of fisticuffs introduced into [?] of ball at Troy Saturday induces the *Times* of that city to observe with much truth and logic that fighting between players on baseball grounds will end the attractiveness of the game to the general public. The management of the Troy baseball club will see the necessity of disciplining players who do not conduct themselves as gentlemen on the baseball diamond and the prompt action taken in recent cases by bringing the matter before the police court encourages the belief that baseball in Troy will be kept from the plug-uglyism which has hurt the game in other years and in other cities. Thus far there have been no such exhibitions in Fulton [NY] county, and for the benefit of local admirers of the game and all concerned, it is to be hoped that there may be none. It is to the credit of the locals that in defeat and victory alike, their deportment has been of the gentlemanly kind.[25]

At the beginning of August in 1903, the Troy Trojans were in second place in the NYSL (42–26, .618) chasing the Schenectady Frog Alleys (48–27, .640) with the battery of left-hander Hooks Wiltsie (21–8 with a 2.53 earned run average) and local catcher Jack Rafter leading the club.[26] However, for the majority of Troy's participation in the NYSL, the Trojans were a second-division team with no star attractions to draw supporters to their games. Even the sporting press seemed to lose interest in the club, and the game reports became desultory and lacking any enthusiasm or energy in support of the Trojans. For example, what follows

Six. A Minor League City on the Hudson

is a game report in full of a close match in the Trojans' later years: "Elmira took the second game from the Trojans at Elmira yesterday, 4 to 2. The Colonels scored two runs in the first inning and Troy evened up in the second on doubles by Poland and Gamwell and a passed ball. In the eighth Calhoun walked, Mr. O'Neill was hit by a pitched ball, and both scored on Philbin's long single."[27]

On July, 31, 1899, the Troy Trojans (who were also referred to as the "Troy Washerwomen" in 1900–1901)[28] replaced the Auburn, New York, Maroons and began an association with a New York State League (NYSL) that lasted until mid-season of 1916 when the last place Trojans (7–26) were sold to the Harrisburg, Pennsylvania, Islanders. The consensus media belief was that the major reason Troy did not support its team at the gate and was the fact that potential spectators were spoiled by Troy's past illustrious baseball history.

Yet in spite of the checkered history of organized baseball in the Collar City, Troy continued to have enthusiastic advocates for professional baseball at the beginning of the twentieth century. Having broken in with the 1902 Troy Trojans as a hundred pound nineteen year old shortstop, Hall of Fame member Johnny Evers never forgot his hometown roots as is indicated by his financial support of the NYSL Troy Trojans:

> John J. Evers, captain of the Boston Nationals, and Lew Wachter of basketball fame, who went to the rescue of the Troy baseball club last summer [1915] and lost several thousands of dollars in order that Troy might be represented by a professional ball club, announced yesterday that they will retain the franchise next summer and will give Troy one of the best baseball clubs it has ever had. Furthermore it was stated that Lew Wachter will continue as manager of the club and that the games of the club will be played at the Laureate Grounds.
>
> The announcement came as welcome news to the Troy baseball fans who were in the dark as to the real status to the Troy club and whether the franchise would be retained in Troy next summer [1916].[29]

Troy has long embraced the winning Haymaker tradition (and myth) of its ballyhooed nineteenth-century glories and simply will not tolerate anything less than first-class baseball. As early as the 1880s, Troy was excoriating the contemporary ball players and pining for the successful and exciting days of yore:

The Haymakers, Unions and Trojans of Troy, New York

The peace of modern Troy is threatened by the wooden horse of a prospective club. But it looks as if the animal would stay within the walls. Those who in previous years furnished the money to support a ball club in Troy, in the days of the finical and gabby Ferguson, do not seem disposed to come forward very rapidly with the funds necessary to materialize the project.

After a while it becomes tedious to men in idleness throughout the winter that they may lose games in the summer. Baseball enthusiasm may be all right in its way, but, as one of the initiated said this morning "It comes high—too high." It is our advice to the persons who propose to invade Troy with a baseball club is to strike out in another direction, for there is nothing on the home-plate for them, unless they really bring a first class organization—something that can beat the Detroits. Then some of the old-time enthusiasm might be revived. Albany is the nearest station to Troy. Let the baseball enthusiasts go there. Troy has no use for a fourth-rate baseball organization. This is a peaceful community, but there are some clubs that it could not restrain from clubbing.[30]

Troy was to be without a professional baseball club until the arrival, in 2002, of the New York–Penn League's Tri-City ValleyCats, who play their games at the Joseph L. Bruno Stadium on the campus of Hudson Valley Community College. The ValleyCats are affiliated with MLB's Houston Astros.[31]

Seven

The Legacy of the Haymakers

Troy has always looked with pride upon its history as an influential presence in the development and support of early amateur and professional baseball and as a major player in the early years of the National League. In 1882, four years after Troy's National League tenure ended with the Trojan team being forced to withdraw from the senior circuit, the Collar City was ready to rejoin the ranks of professional organized baseball with the proposed entry of the Trojans into the International Association in 1888. The essence of the argument for Troy to attempt once more to establish a professional club was its rich baseball (and sports) history and its geographical proximity to a large potential fan base:

Delighted Trojans
Ted Sullivan's Projected Club Meeting with Favor on All Sides
Troy, N.Y., Dec. 14 Editor of *The Sporting Life*

The prospect that we are to have a professional base ball team here next season delights Trojans who have always had a leaning to all kinds of sports, particularly the national game. To my mind, Troy was really the home, the birth-place of baseball in the country. Middle-aged men of to-day recall the time when the Haymakers astonished the natives and by the way, sometime in the near future I will tell the readers of *The Sporting Life* all about that wonderful nine and its costly and unlucky successor. The Haymakers were ball players all the way through. All lovers of the game remember the King boys, Bill Craver, the crack catcher; Zettlein, the lightning pitcher; and all the other fellows who played for blood in the long ago. Craver is a dandy "copper" here now. He catches no more balls, but devotes his time to snaking those who have caught too many of the liquid kind.

"Ted" Sullivan promises to bring a strong nine here next year, and if he does, he will do well. I spoke to "Al" Hatchkin [Hotchkin] about the project the other day, and he said—"If Sullivan brings to Troy a nine that will win and not come day after day within one run or two runs of victory, he will get all the patronage he wants." Hatchkin was the life of the company that controlled the old Troy National League team and gave to the world such players as Ewing, Welch, Keefe, Connor, Gillespie, Brouthers, Roseman, Jake Evans, Harbridge, Dickinson, Pfeffer, and others....

The grounds here are on the west side of the Hudson [Watervliet], within easy reach of both Troy and Albany, and there is no reason in the world why the game should not be profitable with good management. Albany has 90,000 inhabitants, Troy 65,000, Cohoes (two miles above the grounds) 20,000, and the villages, which are really merged into Troy, have a population of 20,000 more. Here are 200,000 within a five mile radius of the grounds, and Troy is a great sporting centre, too. Almost nightly during cold weather we have cock fights, dog fights, prize fights and so on, but in the warm weather we must content ourselves with the Saratoga races and the two big trotting meetings at Island Park, the finest track in the country. To be sure we have amateur baseball clubs galore, and they are good ones, too, the Flyaways being fully competent to hold up their end with many salaried teams, but we want a good professional team—one that we can put our money on and throw up our hands about.

We [Trojans] would rather have a good International League club than an [American] Association aggregation which holds up the tail end. Then, too, a fifty cent tariff [admission fee for AA tickets] would be a decidedly risky experiment.[1]

The many loyal Trojans who embraced the national pastime in the nineteenth century cared little for championship trophies or a place atop the final standings as long as their team reflected the community's competitive nature and defiant personality. Baseball was an essential cultural element in the city's years of industrial prominence and its rapid decline. Twenty-six years after Troy's departure from the National League, Trojans were still avid baseball enthusiasts and looking back with nostalgia at their participation in major league baseball. Trojans also shared a bittersweet view of their baseball history with a thoughtful and measured assessment of those past glory days:

> Among the "regulars" at the [New York] State League baseball games played on the Laureate grounds [North Troy] are many who have been "regulars" for a good many more years than they would perhaps like to admit. Some of them can even go back to the days when the Haymakers were Troy's most conspicuous boosters and were making the city famous as a baseball town, but there are more who date their interest in baseball back to the time when Troy was represented in the National League, and they

SEVEN. *The Legacy of the Haymakers*

still "point with pride" to that period as the halcyon time of baseball in this section and refer to players of that day as the greatest ever. Troy was represented in the National League four years, from 1879 to 1882, inclusive, and while the city did not win a pennant, or, in fact, come close to it, except in 1880, when it finished a good fourth and threw a scare into the older members of the organization, it certainly turned out some wonderfully clever baseball players and provided the city with mighty interesting exhibitions of the national game.[2]

In spite of its early and continued love affair with the national pastime, Troy has a baseball legacy that covers the spectrum from negative to positive. The Lansingburgh Unions club of the 1860s was composed of homegrown talent that late in the decade was successful about 80 percent of the time. Their trip to New York City in 1866 when they beat the Mutuals and repeated this unexpected victory later that summer in Troy, so aggravated and frustrated the defeated Gothamites that they referred to their Capital District opponents as country bumpkins. Thus the "Troy Haymakers" were born via the newspaper coverage and the enthusiasm of the club's loyal followers, who reveled in overturning the dismissive (and, often, highly inappropriate) jibes of their big city baseball brethren.

The Haymakers organization was always under suspicion of duplicity for its less-than-transparent franchise funding and management decision-making. Gamblers were generally thought to support the club, and such undesirables often developed questionable relationships with the players. Troy Haymaker native, player, and sometimes captain, Bill Craver was notorious for his revolving and hippodroming and was eventually banned from major league baseball for his unwillingness to testify in the 1877 NL Louisville game-fixing and gambling scandal. He became a recognizable poster boy and lasting symbol of Troy's reputation as a win-by-any-means and at-all-costs club. Even after Craver's reinstatement to organized professional baseball in 1879 by the International Association, his mere presence on the field was cause for controversy and complaints. Any team for whom Bill Craver suited up for after 1877 was under the threat of a possible forfeit:

> The Albany nine by playing with Craver's Haymakers has made itself amenable to possible expulsion, besides cutting itself of from any game with league nines in September. Craver was expelled from the Louisville

The Haymakers, Unions and Trojans of Troy, New York

Club in 1877 and by the [National] League at the annual meeting. The International Association's Judiciary Committee illegally tried to reinstate him, but the National Association [International Association] has adopted the rule that no player expelled by the [National] League can play in a game with a national club reinstated by the League.³

A follow-up story a week later revealed that Bill Craver was also *persona non grata* with the Troy club: "It appears that the Albany Club has not violated the rules by playing a club in which Craver was employed. The Troy Haymaker club's officials were required to take an oath that Craver was not employed by their club in any capacity before the Albanys would play them."⁴

The Troy Haymakers' were also popularly believed to possess an intimidating, thuggish nature that would insure a Trojan beating of its rivals either on the baseball diamond or off it:

> The Syracuse team prepared to take the Haymakers in hand in case they 'started anything,' and had Andy Kelley and his Seventh ward gang, known as the 'Swamp Angels,' on hand. Jimmie Johnson, the crack second baseman of the Central Cities, who was a brother to Frank Johnson, now living in this city, hit the ball over the fence, winning the game. The Haymakers sized up the 'Swamp Angels' and decided to take the defeat without a kick."⁵

This newspaper account has the ring of the apocryphal, but such created (or greatly inflated) reports played into the Haymakers' wish to be seen as a group of unsophisticated toughs and hard men whose mere appearance at a baseball field would defeat their opponents before the first pitch was thrown.

The team's first major league roster [1871 NA] was multi-ethnic in composition, including many Irish players, a few Cubans, and a Jewish player-manager. Such an ethnically diverse team roster triggered contemporary prejudice(s) against these groups, who were perceived as interlopers and were viewed by businessmen as a threat to the mainstream popularity and economic prosperity of the national pastime.⁶ Such prejudice and backward thinking further heightened Troy's sense of being beleaguered by "outsiders" and further cemented the "us-vs-them" attitude of the Trojans.

The Haymakers' negative public profile does not blacken the many

SEVEN. *The Legacy of the Haymakers*

positive developments Troy players and officials contributed to baseball history. For example, James A. Kern was the first president of the National Association, making him the first such executive to serve as a major league chief official. Troy also participated in the first major league regularly scheduled double-header with the Chicago White Stockings on September 2, 1880. In a player first, Trojan Ben De La Vergne, an accomplished catcher and a strong batter, has been credited in a few sources as the first catcher to wear gloves for the Victory Club of Troy in 1867.[7]

In addition to the many positives that Troy baseball contributed to the early development of the sport, Haymaker die-hard supporters were quite conscious of the team(s)' historical importance and were fiercely loyal to and proud of Troy's preeminence as a "pioneer" baseball club. As early as twenty years after the Troy Trojans' dismissal from the National League in 1882, newspaper reports were mythologizing (and burnishing) the early notorious Haymaker narrative by immortalizing the early diamond stars and cataloguing the current talented players produced by and in the Collar City:

> Since the inception of baseball Troy has been an important factor in the advancement of the game and in the support of the game here in its pioneer days and in the number of players who have gone out from this city and become stars. Troy has contributed much to baseball being the national game. This is called to mind by the number of Trojan ball players who are numbered among the "Top-notchers" [sic] in the National and other major leagues.
> Troy was one of the pioneer baseball towns, and the fame of the original "Haymakers" is an integral part of baseball history. Probably the first players who went out from this city were Billy Craver, the veteran catcher who recently died at his home in this city; William "Clipper" Flynn; "Mart" King, catcher; and William McIntyre [McAtee], shortstop, members of the original "Haymakers" who joined the White Stocking team of Chicago in 1871. After the great Chicago fire the White Stockings came to this city and played a game of ball with the Haymakers before 10,000 persons [grossly inflated attendance figure] on the old grounds, where Cragin Avenue is now located. King was the most noted catcher of his day, a time when masks, chest protectors and big gloves were unknown. "Steve" King, the original left fielder of the old Haymakers, refused an offer of $1,000 from the Chicago club to play one season with them. Up to that time it was the largest sum ever offered for a ball player and caused more comment than

the recent offer of $30,000 which the New York National team is said to have offered [Napoleon] Lajoie, the famous Cleveland second baseman, for a three-year contract.

Of the second edition of Haymakers [the NL Troy Citys/Troy Trojans, 1879–1882], Charles Briody of Lansingburgh became one of the famous catchers of the country. He went from this city to Detroit [actually Cleveland], where he caught for James McCormick, at that time considered the greatest pitcher in the world, and Briody was the only man who could "hold" him. A famous quartette of players, who went from this city when New York purchased the franchise of the Troy National League team, were "Smiling Mickey" Welch and "Tim" Keefe, pitchers; "Buck" Ewing, catcher; and Roger Connor, baseman. These players were all developed in this city.

In 1885 Connor was champion batter of the National League with an average of .371. "Billy" Hulbert [Holbert], while not a native Trojan, made his reputation here as catcher of the Troy National League team. Pitcher Goldsmith developed here and went to Chicago. Haskins [Hankinson] of Lansingburgh, third baseman of the Troy National League team, was prominent in the league for several seasons. "Jakey" Evans, the famous throwing right fielder, was a native Trojan. Dan Brouthers, a popular first baseman, was brought out in this city. He was the champion batter in the National League in 1882, in 1889 with Boston and later with Brooklyn. Mansell, the well-known outfielder, started here and in 1883 went to the St. Louis team of the American Association.[8]

The article concludes with a long catalogue of 1902 players who were participating at some level of organized baseball.

Another source of Haymaker nostalgia was the many in-depth media interviews with former Troy players and executives. For example, NA 1872 Troy Haymaker manager and star starting second baseman Jimmy Wood, who was seeking information about the early Haymaker players he brought to Chicago in an effort to stop the Cincinnati Red Stocking juggernaut reminisced about the early Troy-Chicago *contretemps*:

> He asked for information regarding players of the Haymaker team, including Mart King, William "Clipper" Flynn, Michael "Butcher" McAtee and William Craver, whom Wood took to Chicago about thirty years ago as members of the White Stockings, organized to defeat the Red Stockings of Cincinnati, up to that time unbeatable.

In a subsequent letter, Wood recalls the 1870 Troy-Chicago incident in personal detail:

> When I had accompanied my Chicago team, with the exception of the Lansingburgh players, Tom Foley, who was one of the prime moving spirits

SEVEN. *The Legacy of the Haymakers*

in getting up the Chicagos, came to New York to assist me, for I had been for many days securing the men I wanted.

The advertisement [in the New York newspapers] read in substance that the Chicago people wanted a team to beat the justly celebrated Cincinnati Red Stockings, who had gone through the 1869 season without losing a game and had lost but three in 1870, one to the Atlantics and two to Chicago.

After paying out at least $100 to each of his Trojan players, Wood along with Tom Foley, in a show of good faith and seriousness of intention, paid the Haymakers with their own money as the Chicago team was not yet officially organized. However, The Chicagoans left Troy without any players: "[T]he players were to meet Tom [Foley] at the railroad station the next morning and go with him to Chicago. But they played poker all night and none put in an appearance... [Cherokee] Fisher, who had secured most of the [advance] money, never joined us, but Craver, McAtee, Flynn, and King came to time all right." With a first-class team in tow, Wood "took the team to New Orleans and put the players through a practice [spring training] never known up to that time and the rest you know. We beat the Reds two straight games and they disbanded." As for his brief tenure in Troy where he captained the only major league Collar City club to finish above .500, Jimmy Wood gave this assessment of the 1872 NL franchise: "Later I organized the Troy ball club, which was a fine team, but many were ill and remained so until we disbanded."[9]

I

The question remains why with such a rich baseball history and unquestioned desire for professional sports by the locals did Troy's desire to field a team at the highest levels of the national pastime end so ignominiously in 1882. Just as Troy's abrupt rise to economic and cultural heights in mid-century of the 1800s was due to geographical location, immigration, and technological advancement, so to Troy's equally sudden decline was the result of a number of industrial, scientific, and social changes in an ever-expanding and changing nation.

Beginning as early as 1867 with the deflated price of steel rails and a deflated commodity price index, Troy suffered through a period of unrestrained (and unregulated) growth and financial speculation, especially in the rapid development of a national railway system. The result was the Long Depression (1873–1878) with agriculture being replaced as the leading industry in the country's Gilded Age (1870s-1890s) by manufacturing and investment, the railroad strike of 1877, and a number of major bankruptcies in steel and the railroad industry.

After a period of expansion from 1865 to 1873, when foreign demand for "raw materials, mining, agriculture, infrastructure, railroad development, and technology advancements" was high, a crisis in the American economy arose because of the three C's: *corruption, currency* (which was inflated and no longer conformed to the gold standard) and *capital* (misuse of credit):

> These problems were exacerbated by a technology that was too efficient. The population did not grow sufficiently to purchase the consumer goods and services that were being produced and investors began to pull back from the entrepreneurship of earlier in the century and hedge their bets by reducing costs which led to increases in unemployment and the failure of many small businesses, including a sizable number of baseball clubs. The result was that both the producers and consumers lost confidence in the system, especially as the cozy financial relationships between politicians and capitalists were brought to light. The hardest hit sectors of the economy—Civil War veterans, immigrants, and Southerners—became angry and disillusioned as the trade unions that were a prime source of support of the first two groups mentioned previously, began to decline as the economy floundered. Only when currency reform, railroad regulation, the establishment of local social safety nets for the destitute, increased foreign demand for American goods, and a population spurt did the national economy improve and stabilize. Troy, which had been on the rising swell of industrial growth in mid-century, suffered the fate of other "gritty cities— small, tradition-bound communities that were unwilling to embrace the realities of new technologies and unfettered capitalism and thus lost their influence on the national (and often regional) scene.[10]

II

Allowing for the economic and social conditions that fueled Troy's decline as a national force, the question still remains why baseball has

SEVEN. *The Legacy of the Haymakers*

such a historical and mythological hold on its many fervent supporters in the Collar City. The answer may lie in the nature of the sport itself. Baseball is an important element of the culture of the nineteenth-century business model that redefined the lives of an expanding nation that was undergoing a radical reassessment of work and leisure:

> Indeed baseball has been closely linked to the rise of modern business structures. The integrated organization, work patterns and the kinds of success and failure found in the workplace re-appear on the ball field. Although the outdoor game of baseball may have provided some physical change to the inside worker, it was at a deeper level, as a replication of the work experience, that it flourished. Baseball grew because it called for attitudes that had already been formed by the business environment. Contemporary sports critics have charged athletics with perpetuating attitudes useful for big business. This they undoubtedly do—but only because the attitudes were pre-existing.[11]

The Troy Haymaker legacy of hard work, perseverance and a win-at-all-costs ethic was not an idiosyncratic response of an eccentric populace but rather the defining norm for the nineteenth century.

III

The lasting legacy of the nineteenth-century Troy ball clubs, amateur and professional alike, is multi-faceted. The Troy Haymakers were the ultimate outsiders who had a shady reputation on and off the field that was not entirely unearned. The players and the larger Troy community embraced the team's image, cultivated by the newspapers and those avid supporters, as tough characters who beat the big city teams at their own game. This exaggerated perception of the Haymakers as fighters provided an achievable (and attractive) identity to a newly arrived, (mostly) Irish immigrant population that was searching for an American identity that reflected their worth in an alien environment. The baseball diamond became a proving ground for the democratic ideals of equality of opportunity and accomplishment for those talented individuals willing to risk defeat in a highly competitive, late nineteenth-century society.[12]

The Haymakers, Unions and Trojans of Troy, New York

Joe Bruno Stadium, home of the Tri-Cities ValleyCats. Originally based in Little Falls, New York, and called the Mets, the New York–Penn League's ValleyCats moved to Troy in 2002 (courtesy of the Tri-Cities ValleyCats).

IV

The Collar City celebrated its storied past in the June 1992 dedication of a black gem mist polished granite (from Barre, Vermont) monument in Knickerbocker Park in Lansingburgh very near where the nineteenth-century Troy teams played their earliest games. The monument honors the five Baseball Hall of Fame members who played for the Unions/Haymakers—Dan Brouthers, Mickey Welch, Tim Keefe, Buck Ewing, and Roger Connor—and the two native-born Trojans who are also enshrined in Cooperstown—Johnny Evers and Mike "King" Kelly. A highlight of the festivities was a game played by 1882 rules between a team from Troy and one from Worcester. Behind the shutout pitching of Jack Diamond, Troy again defeated its Massachusetts rival by a score of 2–0 just as it had done previously 110 years earlier in the last National League contest for both cities.[13]

Appendix A: Major Pitching Rules and Regulations Changes, 1863–1893

During the Troy Haymakers salad days, baseball changed its focus from a hitting contest to a more "scientific" game built on pitching, fielding, and speed. Pitching, which began as the means to initiate the action as in contemporary slow-pitch softball, was significantly altered to make the pitcher a position of central importance in the defensive scheme of the game as it remains in contemporary baseball.

In essence, nineteenth-century baseball evolved from a slugging contest to a game of fielding and defense.

- 1863—The pitching distance is 45 feet; the pitcher is required to keep both feet on the ground, thus eliminating the running start. The general direction of the early rules changes regarding pitching were to alter and/or eliminate similarities with the "English game" (cricket).
- 1867—The pitcher's arm must be kept straight and the batter is allowed to call for a low or high pitch.
- 1871—The first pitched ball to a batter is not called by the umpire.
- 1872—The ball size is regulated: 5–5.25 ounces in weight and 9–9.25 inches in circumference.
- 1874—A 6 feet by 6 feet pitcher's box is established.
- 1879—The pitcher had to face the batter and he was required to release a pitch below his waist.
- 1881—The pitching distance is extended to 50 feet.
- 1883—The pitcher must release the ball below his shoulder.
- 1884—All restrictions on pitchers are eliminated
- 1887—The pitching distance is extended to 50.5 feet. The pitcher is

Appendix A

required to face the batter, hold the ball so the umpire can see it, and take only one step in his delivery to the plate.

1893—The pitching distance is extended to its current 60 feet 6 inches. The pitcher's box is replaced by a plate (the pitching rubber). Prior to 1904 when the pitching mound was limited to 15 inches in height, pitchers were supposed to pitch from a flat surface, but this rule was often violated by groundskeepers who sought to give their home team pitchers an edge.

Sources: "Baseball Rule Change Timeline," http://www.baseball-almanac.com/rulechng.shtml; "The Evolution of Baseball Up to 1872," http://protoball.org; and Eric Miklich, "The Pitcher's Area," http://www.19cbaseball.com/field-8.html.

Appendix B: Won-Loss Records for Troy's Major League Seasons

National Association

Year	Games	Wins	Losses	Ties	Win-Loss Percentage	Season Finish
1871	29	13	15	1	.464	6th (9 teams)
1872	25	15	10	0	.600	5th (11 teams)

National League
Troy Citys/Trojans

Year	Games	Wins	Losses	Ties	Win-Loss Percentage	Season Finish
1879	77	19	56	2	.253	8th (8 teams)
1880	83	41	42	0	.494	4th (8 Teams)
1881	85	39	45	1	.464	5th (8 teams)
1882	85	35	48	2	.422	7th (8 teams)

Appendix C: Starting Lineups for Troy's Major League Teams

Troy Haymakers
1871

C	Mike McGeary	
1B	Clipper Flynn	
2B	Bill Craver	
SS	Dickie Flowers	
3B	Steve Bellán	
LF	Steve King	
CF	Tom York	
RF	Lip Pike	
P	John McMullin	

1872

C	Doug Allison	
1B	Bub McAtee	
2B	Jimmy Wood	
SS	Steve Bellán	
3B	Davy Force	
LF	Steve King	
CF	Count Gedney	
RF	Phonney Martin	
P	George Zettlein	

Troy Citys/Trojans
1879

C	Charlie Reilly	
1B	Dan Brouthers and Aaron Clapp	
2B	Thorny Hawkes	
SS	Ed Caskin	

Starting Lineups for Troy's Major League Teams

3B	Herm Doscher and Bob Ferguson
LF	Tom Mansell
CF	Al Hall
RF	Jake Evans
P	George Bradley

1880

C	Buck Ewing
1B	Ed Cogswell
2B	Bob Ferguson
SS	Ed Caskin
3B	Roger Conner
LF	Pete Gillespie
CF	John Cassidy and Buttercup Dickerson
RF	Jake Evans
P	Mickey Welch

1881

C	Buck Ewing and Bill Holbert
1B	Roger Conner
2B	Bob Ferguson
SS	Ed Caskin
3B	Frank Hankinson
LF	Pete Gillespie
CF	John Cassidy
RF	Jake Evans
P	Mickey Welch and Tim Keefe

1882

C	Bill Holbert
1B	Roger Conner
2B	Bob Ferguson
SS	Fred Pfeffer
3B	Buck Ewing
LF	Pete Gillespie
CF	Bill Harbridge
RF	Chief Roseman
P	Tim Keefe and Mickey Welch

201

Chapter Notes

Preface

1. Steven M. Gelber, "Working at Playing: The Culture of the Workplace and the Rise of Baseball," *Journal of Social History*, 16, 4 (Summer 1983), p. 7. Although the Haymakers are often thought of as the most famous of the nineteenth century "country clubs," Gelber points out that such a designation was a total misnomer: "The Haymakers represented an industrial area with a population of more than forty thousand. Of the ten members of the 1867 team on whom there are data, eight were either industrial workers (textiles and brush making) or the sons of an industrial worker. Not one was connected remotely with farming." (6)

Introduction

1. Rich Fyle, "Troy Amateur Baseball League Could Rival Anyone with Competition and Camaraderie," http://www.troyrecord.com/general-rules/20101111/troy-amateur-league (accessed 3/14/2014). Dating from 1931, the Albany Twilight League is the longest continuously active amateur baseball league in the United States and has become a Capital City tradition.
2. Gelber, p. 16.
3. Daniel J. Walkowitz, *Worker City, Company Town: Iron and Cotton-Worker Protest in Troy and Cohoes, New York, 1855–1884* (Urbana: University of Illinois Press, 1978), pp. 6, 8, 13, and 14.
4. The major ethnic group of nineteenth century Troy was Irish. Unskilled immigrants were instrumental in the growth and development of Troy. In the first part of the nineteenth century, Irish immigrants helped to build the Erie Canal and the railroads. During the Irish Potato Famine (1845–1850), 500,000 Irish farmers were evicted from their properties and 20 percent of the entire population died. As a result, Irish immigration to America spiked markedly going from a yearly average of 4,000–5,000 to 37,000 in 1847. By 1890, one-twelfth of the total population of America was Irish. (Sources: "Troy Irish Genealogy Society" and Bryant University.)

Chapter One

1. William J. Ryczek, *Blackguards and Red Stockings: A History of Baseball's National Association, 1871–1875* (Jefferson, NC: McFarland, 1992), p. 24.
  Organized on August 2, 1859, the Victorys of Troy was one of the strongest baseball teams in the New York Capital District in 1859–1862. They won over 80 percent of their games against local competition with often impressive wins over clubs from Albany, Cohoes, Green Island, Port Schuyler, West Troy (Watervliet), Whitehall, and Yorkville as well as defeating Troy rivals the Alerts, the Stars, Empire, Niagara, Hudson, and Zouaves [Troy Civil War Veterans of the 165th New York Volunteer Regiment]. The Troy club also tackled the best clubs of the day, playing the New York Knickerbockers. However, their most notable game of this period was a 7–13 loss at Weir's Course Ballpark to the touring powerhouse Brooklyn Excelsiors on July 3, 1860. This was the closest game of the Brooklyn's victory march through Upstate New York, which included routs of Albany (24–6), Buffalo Niagaras (50–19), Rochester Flour Citys (21–1), Rochester Live Oaks

Notes—Chapter One

(27–9), and Newburgh (59–14). As was the custom of the day, the victorious Excelsiors were feted—"[They were] well-entertained at the Troy House"—and were awarded the game ball. (Charles Peverelly, *The Book of American Pastimes, Containing a History of the Principal Baseball, Cricket, Rowing and Yachting Clubs of the United States.* New York: Privately published,1866; reprinted as John Frazer and Mark Rucker, eds. [Charleston, SC: Arcadia Press, 2005]); and Craig B. Waff, "Games Tabulation: New York State, Capital Area," http://protoball.org (accessed 1/6/2014); Jack "Peerless" McGrath, *Troy Times Record*, 28 February 1939.)

2. Bill Passonno, "Troy's Baseball Legacy: A Bunch of Hicks," *Troy Times Record*, 27 August 2001; cited in *Troy Record*, 10 November 2010, p. 1. http://www.troyrecord.com/articles/2010/11/10/sports/doc4cdae90f055b245614287.prt. (accessed 11/06/2012); and David Pietrusza, "Capital Region Baseball Timeline Part I: 1819–1899," 2. http://www.davidpietrusza.com/capital-reg-baseball-1.html (accessed 06/21/2011); Ray Kim, "When Troy Was a Major League City," 1. http://www.empireone.net/~musicman/troyball.html (accessed 6/15/2011). In its attempt to be first-class in all aspects of the game, the Lansingburgh Unions were the first team to have baseball cards with players' photographs on them, including star players Bill Craver, Steve King, and Bub McAtee. The sponsor was Albany photographer and business owner E. S. Sterry and Company. A complete set of six cards of the 1866 Unions series is listed at $250,000 on Internet auction sites.

Five years later, former Troy player Burr Penfield, the brother of Cal Penfield who was the Lansingburgh Unions' starting third baseman from 1866–1869 and a club member until 1870, created a photographic scorecard for the 1871 NAPBBL season with catcher Mike McGeary on the cover. (Morris, "Union Base Ball Club," in *Base Ball Founders*, p. 17)

3. Richard A. Puff. "Haymakers and Daisy Cutters: Troy and the National Pastime," *Troy's Baseball Heritage* (Troy, NY: Committee to Preserve Troy's Baseball Heritage, 1992), pp.6; "Nineteenth Century Baseball Leagues," 19th Century Baseball (website), www.19cbaseball.com (accessed 11/29/2013). While the NABBP helped organize and standardize baseball, it was a volunteer organization that had no regulatory power to deal with the sport's leading vices: gambling, rowdyism among fans and players, and play-for-pay under the table arrangements. (Richard Tholkes, "Timeline of the Pioneer Era," in Morris et al,, *Baseball Pioneers*, loc. 115-158)

4. Mike Roer, *Orator O'Rourke: The Life of a Baseball Radical* (Jefferson, NC: McFarland, 2005), p.52; William J. Ryczek, *When Johnny Came Sliding Home; The Post-Civil War Baseball Boom, 1865–1870* (Jefferson, NC: McFarland, 1998), p. 34; Puff, p. 6.

Baseball was such a popular pastime in Troy by 1861 that the winter season did not prevent Trojans from playing the game. In a memoir by 1899 world speed skating champion and Troy resident "Skater" Reynolds, the author reveals that baseball on ice was part of the sports calendar: "Baseball was played on ice on skates as early as 1861. Albany and Troy teams were great rivals in those early days. A soft ball was used in these games. The bat was about five feet long. The skates were much longer than those used at present. The blades curved up over the foot. The top of the skate was wood." (*Troy Daily Times*, 6 May 1920).

5. For the information in the discussion of the Victory Base Ball Club of Troy, I am indebted to the scholarship of Craig B. Waff, "Pre-Civil War Base Ball Games Played in the Capitol [sic] Area of New York State," *Retrosheet*; and Peter Morris, "Victory Base Ball Club of Troy," in Peter Morris et al., *Base Ball Pioneers, 1850–1870: The Clubs and Players Who Spread the Sport Nationwide,* Kindle edition (Jefferson, NC: McFarland), 2012, loc. 1540–1614.

6. Other dates that are significant in the organizational history of the Lansingburgh Unions are a supposed match game on July 4, 1865, and August 15, 1866, when the club began play. (Morris, "Union Base Ball Club of Lansingburgh," in Morris et al., *Baseball Pioneers*, loc.1663–1669.)

7. The Great Troy Fire began at noon on the Rensselaer-Saratoga Railroad Bridge between Troy and Green Island when sparks from a passing engine lit the bridge roof. The fire swirled and burnt 75 acres of central Troy that cost the city $2,667,882. By November 1862, all but two of the burned edifices were rebuilt. (William H. Young, *Troy's One Hundred Years, 1789–1889* [Troy: n.p., 1891], in "Troy Irish Genealogy Society")

8. Tom Melville, *Early Baseball and the*

Notes—Chapter One

Rise of the National League (Jefferson, NC: McFarland, 2001), p. 27.

9. Puff, p. 6; "19th Century Baseball Leagues"; Ryczek, *Blackguards and Red Stockings*, p. 92; "Troy Baseball Monument," pp. 1–2 http://projectballpark.org/other/troy/b2b.html (accessed 9/7/2013); Pietrusza, p. 1.

10. Paul Browne, "John Morrissey," SABR BioProject, pp. 1–8. http://bioproj.sabr.org/bioproj.cfm?a=v&v=1&2011)bid=3195&pid=19722 (accessed 6/24/2011); Melville, p. 27; Phelan, p. 87; Don Rittner, *Legendary Locals of Troy* (Charleston, SC: Arcadia, 2012), pp. 65 and 121. An example of John Morrissey's vengeful nature and hardball tactics occurred when he was prevented by Troy's Brahmins from purchasing property on which he planned to build a mansion. His revenge entailed the building of a soap factory that was down wind of the residential district so that the resulting stench was ever-present for the city's social elite. (Phelan, p. 87)

11. Puff, pp. 6–7.

12. "Famed Old Haymakers," *Troy Northern Budget*, 9 April 1896, p. 5, cited in Morris et al., *Baseball Pioneers*, loc. 1693–1700.

13. Peter Morris, "Union Baseball Club of Lansingburgh/Haymaker of Troy Club History," personal website of Peter Morris, http://archive.is/yuZ3V (accessed 12/7/13/2013); Paul Batesel, *Players and Teams of the National Association, 1871–1875* (Jefferson, NC: McFarland, 2012), pp. 88 and 156; Brian McKenna, "Professional Baseball in Chicago: A Shaky Start," Baseball History Blog, http://BaseballHistoryBlog.com/1790 (accessed 1/15/2014).

14. Puff, p. 7; Bill Passonno, "Troy's Baseball Legacy: A Bunch of Hicks," *Troy Record*, November 10, 2010. It was reported that the Brooklyn Atlantics were so impressed by their Lansingburgh opponents that they allowed the team to borrow their cleats for the August 9, 1866, victory over the New York Mutuals. (Morris et al., *Baseball Pioneers*, loc. 1703)

15. Ryczek, *Blackguards and Red Stockings*, p. 118.

16. Puff, p. 7; *Troy Daily Times*, 2 September 1867; *Troy Daily Whig*, 10 October 1867.

17. Morris et al., *Baseball Pioneers*, loc. 1717–1743.

18. Ibid., loc. 1785–1808.

19. Ryczek, *When Johnny Came Sliding Home*, p. 130; *Troy Daily Whig*, 30 September 1867; Morris et al., *Baseball Pioneers*, loc. 1808.

20. Batesel, p. 45; "Troy Haymakers," p. 115. www.baseballhistorian,com/html/americanheroes.php?year=1878 (accessed 12/22/2013).

21. Batesel, p. 45.

22. Geoffrey C. Ward and Ken Burns, *Baseball: An Illustrated History* (New York: Alfred A. Knopf, 1994), pp. 3 and 61; Don Rittner, *Legendary Locals of Troy*. (Charleston, SC: Legendary Locals (Arcadia Press), 2012), p 103; *Auburn (NY) Evening Auburian,* 16 February 1878, vol. 2, no. 205; *Brooklyn Eagle (BE),* 3 June 1878.

23. Morris et al., *Baseball Pioneers*, loc. 1808–1821.

24. Peter Morris, "Union Baseball Club of Lansingburgh/Haymaker of Troy Club History," http://archive.is/yuZ3V (accessed 12/7/2013), p. 14; Batesel, p. 57; "Clipper Flynn," www.baseball-reference.com>EncyclopediaofPlayers> F Listing.

25. Morris, "Union Baseball Club," pp. 15–16; Batesel, p. 80; "Troy Haymaker Franchise Leaders," www.databaseball.com (accessed 1/14/2014).

26. Cited by Morris from *Troy Times*, (4 August 1868) in "Unions of Lansingburgh/Haymakers of Troy," in Peter Morris et al., *Base Ball Pioneers, 1850–1870: The Clubs and Players Who Spread the Sport Nationwide* (Jefferson: McFarland, 2012), pp. 65–66; Puff, p.8.

27. Morris et al., *Baseball Pioneers*, loc. 1821–1841.

28. Batesel, pp. 55 and 14; Daniel E.Ginsburg, *The Fix Is In: A History of Baseball Gambling and Game Fixing Scandals*. (Jefferson, NC: McFarland, 2004), p. 44.

29. *Troy Daily Press*, June 1869, cited by Warren F. Broderick in *Troy Record*, 30 August 1969, p. 43.

30. Broderick, *Troy Times Record*, 30, August 1969, p. 43. The umpire for this game was P. A. Gaffney of the Unions of Cohoes (NY) who appeared to be favoring the Haymakers who scored 12 runs in the first three innings which led to an umpiring controversy in the rematch on August 26, 1869, at the Union Grounds in Cincinnati. There is much still in dispute regarding this game with the attendance being estimated to be upwards of 15,000 spectators, including even the final score which has Cincinnati by winning the game by 2 to 7 runs. (Ryczek, *When Johnny Came Sliding Home*, p. 140)

31. *New York Herald*, 23 June 1869, p. 1.

32. *New York Herald*, 10 August 1869, pp. 11; *Troy Daily Times*, 31 July 1915.

33. Broderick, p. 43; Puff, p. 8.

34. Melville, p. 39.

35. Broderick, p. 43; Marty Appel, *Slide Kelly Slide: The Wild Life and Times of Mike*

Notes—Chapter Two

"King" Kelly (Lanham, MD: Scarecrow,1999), p. 4.
36. Ibid.
37. Puff, p. 9; *Troy Daily Times,* 13 August 1870.
38. Stephen R. Guschov, *The Red Stockings of Cincinnati: Baseball's First All-Professional Team* (Jefferson, NC: McFarland, 1998), p. 79.
39. Guschov, pp. 76 and 78–79; Ryczek, *Blackguards and Red Stockings,* p. 85; John Thorn, *Baseball in the Garden of Eden: The Secret History of the Early Game* (New York: Simon and Schuster, 2011), p. 145; Ryczek, *When Johnny Came Sliding Home,* p. 146; *New York Times,* 18 September 1869.
40. *New York Times,* 29 August 1869, p. 1.
41. *Sullivan (IN) Democrat,* 2 September 1869, p. 2.
42. Morris et al., *Baseball Pioneers,* loc. 1864; *Louisville (KY) Courier-Journal,* 29–30 August 1869, 5.
43. Puff, p. 9.
The citizens of the Capital District were still commemorating the infamous disputed 1869 Haymaker-Red Stocking tie over a century later at the dedication of Carhenger Field in Lansingburgh. ("Jim 'Peerless' McGrath, *Troy Record,* 25 June 1971; *New York Clipper,* 11 September 1869)
44. *New York Clipper,* 18 September 1869; Morris et al., *Baseball Pioneers,* loc. 1939.
45. *New York Clipper,* 17 July and *New York Clipper,* 26 June 1869.
46. "Charlton's Chronology—1869," p. 3. http://www.baseballlibrary.com/chronology/byyear.php?year=1869 (accessed 4/2/2009).
47. *Troy Daily Whig,* 13 July 1870.
48. Passonno, p. 3; "Big League, Small Town," p 1; Puff, p. 10.
49. "The Coming Base-Ball Season," *New York Times,* 7 April 1870; Morris et al., *Baseball Pioneers,* loc. 1955.
50. Ibid.
51. "Charlton's Baseball Chronology—1870" www.baseballlibrary.com/chronology/byyearphp?year=1870.
52. *Madison (WI) State Journal,* 25 May 1870, p. 1.
53. *Fort Wayne (IN) Daily Democrat,* 28 June 1870, p. 11; Pietrusza, p. 4; Peter Morris et al., "Union Base Ball Club of Lansingburgh/Haymaker of Troy" http://archive.is/yuZ3W, p. 11. The extent to which the Haymakers were committed to improving their club for the 1870 season no matter the cost is reflected in the six-week signing of reliable catcher Pat Dockney who was also a noted carouser and serial revolver. (Ryczek, *When Johnny Came Sliding Home,* pp. 143–144.)
54. Guschov, pp. 111 and 122.
55. *Troy Daily Whig,* 8 June 1870.
56. *Troy Daily Whig,* 4 July 1870.
57. *Troy Daily Whig,* 28 July 1870.
58. *Troy Daily Whig,* 8 July 1870.
59. *Troy Daily Times* 6 August 1870.
60. *Troy Daily Whig,* 31 May 1870.
61. *New York Herald,* 27 August 1870, p. 5 and 6 October 1870, p.7.
62. Puff, p.10.
63. Batesel, pp. 175–76, http://verdun2.wordpress.com/2013/01/29/big-league-small-town (accessed 9/7/2013).

Chapter Two

1. Thomas Carroll, "The Rise, Fall, and Rebirth of an American City," p.1 www.visittroyny.com/aboutTroy/history (accessed November 23, 2013).
2. Ibid and Daniel J. Walkowitz, *Worker City, Company Town: Iron and Cotton-Worker Protest in Troy and Cohoes, New York, 1855–1884* (Urbana: University of Illinois Press, 1978), p. 6.
3. Often referred to as "North Troy," Lansingburgh owes its origins to Abraham Jacob Lansing in 1763. The settlement had its first charter in 1791 and remained an independent village until being annexed by its southern neighbor Troy in 1900. (Thomas Phelan, *The Hudson Mohawk Gateway: An Illustrated History* (North Ridge, CA: Windsor Publications, 1985), p. 20)
4. Ibid., pp. 20 and 22–23; Deborah Nazon, *Brownfield's Redevelopment and Competitive Advantage Theory: Urban Revitalization and Stakeholder Engagement in South Troy, NY,* (Ann Arbor, MI: ProQuest (UMI Dissertations Publishing), 2007), p. 33.
5. Walkowitz, p. 6; Don Rittner, *Remembering Troy: Heritage on the Hudson* (Charleston, SC: The History Press, 2008), p. 71.
6. Carroll, p.19; Nazon, pp. 31 and 37.
7. Arthur James Weise is the author of *Troy's One Hundred Years* (Troy, NY: William H. Young, 1891); and Rutherford Hayner is the author of *Troy and Rensselaer County, New York: A History* (New York: Lewis Historical Publishing Company, 1997), cited in Nazon, pp. 40–41.
8. George Baker Anderson, *History of Troy, New York, Landmarks of Rensselaer*

Notes—Chapter Two

County (Syracuse, NY: D. Mason and Company, 1897), pp. 15-16.

9. Carroll, pp. 24-26; Nazon, pp. 37-38";A History of Troy," p. 2-3, http://www.uncle-sams-home.com/troyhis2.html. (accessed 2/15/2014).

10. Don Rittner, "I'll Take Troy for $500, Alex" (Originally *Troy Record*), pp. 1-3, http://www.rootsweb.ancestry.com/-nyrensse/articlez.html (accessed 6/24/2011);"Troy, New York," p. 3, http://www.princeton.edu/-achaney/tmve. (accessed 11/25/2013); and Margaret Burden Proudfit, *Henry Burden: His Life and a History of His Inventions Compiled from the Public Press.* (Troy, NY: Pafraets Press, 1904), pp. 1-3.

11. Rittner,"I'll Take Troy," pp. 2-3; Carroll, p.2; Proudfit, p.2.

12. George Baker Anderson, "History of Troy, New York," p. 2; http://history.rays-place.com/ny/ren-troy-ny2.htm (accessed 3/9/2014).

13. Don Rittner, *Legendary Locals of Troy* (Charleston, SC: Legendary Locals (Arcadia Press), 2012), pp. 12 and 58; Peter Morris et al., "Union Baseball Club of Lansingburgh/Haymaker(s) of Troy Club History," p. 14. http://archive.is/yuZ3V (accessed 12/7/2013).

14. Gerald Zahavi and Susan McCormick (revision of original text by James S. Corsaro and Kathleen D. Roe), [Department of History—University at Albany], "Labor and History in Troy and Cohoes: A Brief History," p. 2, http://www.albany.edu/history/Troy-Cohoes (accessed 11/25/2013). Detachable collars and cuffs are reputed to have been invented by Trojan Helen Montague in 1827: "She became tired of washing her husband's shirts every day because only the collars were dirty … she decided to cut off a collar, wash it, and sew it back on. The first detachable collar was made at her home at 139 Third Street." The collar and shirt industry grew in Troy to "employ over 15,000 launderers, starchers, bleachers, and ironers—over 85 percent of them women." (Rittner, *Legendary Locals*, p. 72-73)

Many observers were sanguine about the nature and value of Troy's textile industry:

Unlike many branches of the industry there is no trust or combination the collar business, but the freest competition. Many grades, from the finest of linen—and part linen and cotton, to all cotton, are produced, and the workmanship in all grades has been brought up to the highest standard of excellence. The wages paid to both men and women are good, and the industry, taken as a whole, is a splendid illustration of modern American skill, integrity and indomitable energy and enterprise. With the branch factories which some of the Troy concerns maintain in other places, such as Glens Falls, Mechanicville, Ballston Spa and Greenwich, and other towns even further away, the value of the annual production of linen and cotton collars and cuffs alone by the Troy concerns is about $5,500,000, besides the value of the immense quantities of men's shirts and women's shirt-waists. (George Baker Anderson, p. 8)

15. *Daily (Herkimer, NY) Telegram*, 24 August 1913.

16. Rittner, "I'll Take Troy," p. 3 and *Legendary Locals*, p. 32; Nazon, pp. 44-45 and 49.

17. Walkowitz, pp. 259-260. Organized labor developed as Troy became an industrial center with the two strongest unions being the iron molders ("Iron Molders' International Union #2") and the laundry workers ("Collar Laundry Workers") whose founder was 19-year old Trojan Kate Mullany who oversaw the country's first all-women union in 1864. Mullany led her striking union on February 24, 1864, arguing for (and receiving) a 25-cent an hour wage increase; in 1868, the Trojan was the first woman appointed to a labor union's national office (National Labor Union). Craft unions and service worker unions were soon to follow suit as Troy became a center of labor activism. (Zahavi and McCormick, pp. 3-4 and 12)

18. Rittner, *Remembering Troy*, p. 91

19. Carroll, p. 2; Rittner, "I'll Take Troy," pp. 1-2; Rittner, *Legendary Locals*, pp. 85 and 91. In 1895, Emma Willard's school for women was renamed as the "Emma Willard School" and the old Troy Female Seminary reopened in 1916 as "Russell Sage College" which was provided initial funds by Olivia Slocum Sage, the widow of Congressman Russell Sage. Both educational institutions are leaders in their respective fields to this day.

A final observation on Emma Willard's writing and teaching careers can also serve as a brief summary of her widespread national influence on nineteenth century education, especially for young women:

She was a born teacher. Never content to follow others slavishly and always striving to get her pupils and teachers

Notes—Chapter Two

away from the deadening monotony of memorizing mere words and facts, she eagerly explored untried paths in education. She was one of the outstanding progressive educators of her day. Aside from all this, more than all this was the satisfaction of having done her country a great service. One of the great ambitions of her life was to see disproved all the prophecies of European statesmen regarding the inevitable fall of the Republic of America [The title of her history of America is "Republic of America"] and instead to see her country, steadfast, prosperous, true to its ideals, an object lesson to Europe. This could be accomplished, she felt, only by proper education of America's youth, the barometer of future generations. It warmed her heart to think what love of country and what zeal for noble citizenship her book would inspire in the youth of America. (Alma Lutz, *Emma Willard: Daughter of Democracy*, (Washington, D.C.: Zenger Publishing, 1929), pp. 126–27.

20. Phelan, p. 85; Rittner, *Legendary Locals*, p. 93; Rittner, *Remembering Troy*, p. 119.; "A History of Troy," pp. 6–7.

21. Nazon, p. 39.

22. Troy had a special love for boxing and the colorful stories that were a part of the sport's appeal.

Troy had two heavy weight of America boxing champions in the mid to late 19th century: John Morrissey who won the crown in 1853 (and whose major importance in the Troy Haymaker narrative is discussed in full in Chapter One) and Paddy Ryan who won the crown in 1880 and lost it to John J. Sullivan in 1882. Ryan fought Sullivan a dozen more times and never won a match. (Rittner, *Local Legends*, pp. 121 and 125).

Paddy Ryan's reputation also took a beating in his many contests with John L. Sullivan and this competitive relationship ended in Ryan's retreat from the ring: "It has leaked out that he [Ryan] was imposed upon, as the arrangement was that the fight should be stopped in the second round. Sheedy and "Boss" Buckley had matters fixed, however, and when John L began to slug the Troy champion in the second round, Capt. and his corps of police were too much engrossed in the science of the exhibition to see any illegal brutality in it. The result was that Paddy lost his reputation as a slugger." (*The Sporting News*, 20 November 1886, p. 2)

In the following month, Paddy Ryan was beating a hasty retreat from the ring and the Capital District: "Mr. Patrick Ryan, once the hero of Troy, is now engaged in keeping a saloon in San Francisco. Recently he was offered $500 a week to travel with the [John L.] Sullivan Combination. The position required him to stand up before Mr. Sullivan every night, the latter trying to knock him out in four rounds. Mr. Ryan declined this tempting offer as he is still a young man, and wants to live for a while longer." (*The Sporting News*, 31 December 1886, p. 4)

These John L. Sullivan-Paddy Ryan boxing matches were so brutal that such contests were banned in many United States locales and fanned the movement to abolish the sport altogether:

Two ruffians engaged in a prize fight Tuesday on the shore of the Gulf of Mexico. It is gratifying evidence of the efficiency with which the laws against such exhibitions of brutality are executed that, although one of these ruffians lives in Troy and the other in Boston, they were obliged to go all the way to the State of Mississippi to find a place where they could fight with a fair chance of escaping arrest. The affair will doubtless cause the Legislature of that State to supply the deficiency in its statutes by passing a stringent law against such encounters. The fight lasted about half an hour and demonstrated that Sullivan, the Boston ruffian, could strike harder and endure more pounding than Ryan, the Troy ruffian, and is therefore the greater brute of the two. No peculiar human quality is displayed in prize-fighting. A man must have physical courage and endurance to be a pugilist, but any bulldog possesses these attributes to a higher degree than the best fist-fighter that ever lived.—New York Herald. (*Wellsville (NY) Allegheny County Reporter (WADR)*, 26 February 1882.)

23. Steven M. Gelber, "Working at Playing: The Culture of the Workplace and the Rise of Baseball," *Journal of Social History*, 16, 4 (Summer 1983), p. 10.

Chapter Three

1. *New York Herald*, 4 July 1870, p. 7.
2. David Pietrusza, "Capital Region Baseball Timeline, Part I: 1819–1899," p. 4; John Thorn, *Baseball in the Garden of Eden: The Secret History of the Early Game* (New York: Simon and Schuster, 2011), p. 149.
3. Roy Kim, "When Troy Was a Major League City," p. 3. http://www.em[ireone.net/.mjusicman/troyball.html (accessed 6/5/2011); Bill Passonno, "Troy's Baseball Legacy: A Bunch of Hicks," *Troy Record*, November 10, 2010; Paul Batesel, *Players and Teams of the National Association, 1871–1875* (Jefferson, NC: McFarland, 2012), p. 175.
4. *Troy Daily Times*, 3 May 1871, cited by Kim, p. 3.
5. Richard A. Puff, "Haymakers and Daisy Cutters: Troy and the National Pastime," *Troy's Baseball Heritage* (Troy, NY: Committee to Preserve Troy's Baseball Heritage, 1992), p. 11. Haymaker Grounds was surrounded by a racetrack with a short porch in left field with a very deep right and right center field(s). This ballpark was still in existence in 1880–1881 and served as the home field for the NL Troy Trojans. (Batesel, p. 175)
6. *New York Times*, 20 April 1871, p. 8.
7. *New York Times*, 26 April 1871, p. 2.
8. Puff, pp. 11–12; Passonno, p.3.
9. *Fort Wayne Daily Sentinel*, 13 June 1871, p. 8; *Seymour (IN) Times*, 27 June 1871, p. 2.
10. Puff, p. 12; Passonno, p 4.
11. *New York Times*, 4 July 1871, p. 1.
12. "Baseball," *New York Times*, 14 July 1871.
13. *New York Herald*, 14 July 1871, p. 10.
14. *New York Times*, 14 July 1871.
15. On July 11, 1871, the Orangeman Riot occurred between Irish working class Protestants and Roman Catholics. On July 13, 1871, the day of the game between the Mutuals and the Haymakers, a crowd of 20,000 gathered at the morgue at Bellevue Hospital. Tensions were running high, especially in Irish Catholic neighborhoods in Queens and Brooklyn. (Edwin G. Burroughs and Mike Wallace, *Gotham: A History of New York to 1898* (New York: Oxford University Press, 1999), pp. 1003–1008.
16. *New York Herald*, 14 July 1871, p. 10; *Troy Daily Whig*, 18 July 1871, p. 3, cited by Tom Melville, *Early Baseball and the Rise of the National League* (Jefferson, NC: McFarland, 2001), p. 62.
17. *Troy Daily Whig*, 8 July 1871.
18. *Troy Daily Times*, 14 August 1871.
19. *New York Herald*, 3 October 1871, p. 4.
20. *Troy Daily Times*, 29 July 1871.
21. *Troy Daily Times*, 10 August 1871.
22. "1871—National Association," *Sean Lahman Baseball Archives*, www.sean-lahmans-baseball-archive.com (accessed 12/12/2013); James L. Terry, *Long before the Dodgers: Baseball in Brooklyn 1855–1884* (Jefferson, NC: McFarland, 2012), p. 99; John Thorn, *Baseball in the Garden of Eden: The Secret History of the Early Game* (New York: Simon and Schuster, 2011), p. 152; William J. Ryczek, *Blackguards and Red Stockings: A History of Baseball's National Association, 1871–1875* (Jefferson, NC: McFarland, 1992), p. 64.
23. Pietrusza, 4; David Nemec, *The Great Encyclopedia of 19th-Century Major League Baseball*, 2nd edition (University of Alabama Press, 2006), p. 21; "Lip Pike," www.baseball-reference.com/players/p/pikeli01/shtml (accessed 1/16/2014).
24. Cited by Robert H. Schaefer, "Lip Pike," SABR BioProject, p. 1. http://sabr.org/bioproj/person/7a6a0655 (accessed 12/31 /2013). (Sources also include "1866," *The Baseball Chronology*, p. 16; *The Biographical History of Baseball*, p.362)
25. Cited by Schaefer, p. 2. Sources include *The National Association of Base Ball Players, 1857–1870*, pp. 114–115 and 298; "1871," *The Baseball Chronology*, p. 19.
26. Schafer, p. 4; Richard Worth, *Baseball Team Names: A Worldwide Dictionary, 1869–2011* (Jefferson, NC: McFarland, 2013), entry #33 "Adrian, Michigan."
27. Schafer, p. 5.
28. *The Sporting News*, 14 October 1881, cited in Schaefer, p. 5.
29. Batesel, pp. 177 and 14; David Fleitz, *The Irish in Baseball: An Early History* (Jefferson, NC: McFarland, 2009), p. 28; Terry, p. 99.
30. Batesel, p. 90; "Mike McGeary," www.baseball-reference.com; "1871 Troy Haymakers," www.fangraphs.com/leaders.aspx? (accessed 1/14/2014).
31. Batesel, p. 92; "John McMullin," www.baseball-reference.com (accessed 1/14/2014); "John McMullin," www.retrosheet.org (accessed 1/14/2014); "Dickie Flowers," http://www.baseball-reference.com/players/f/flowedi01.shtml (accessed 1/22/2014).
32. Pietrusza, p. 5; Fleitz, p. 28; Kim, p. 3.
33. Rafael Rua who pitched for the 1868 Troy Haymakers and has been often credited with possessing baseball's first effective screw-

Notes—Chapter Three

ball attended the same prep school— St. John's School in the Bronx—that produced the Haymakers' Steve Bellàn.

34. Brian McKenna, "Steve Bellàn," SABR BioProject (pp. 1–6), http://bioproj.sabr.org/bioproj/person/78dbf37d (accessed 112/6/2012); Robert L. Tiemann and Jose de Jesus Jimmenez, M.D., "Esteban Enrique (Steve) Bellàn," Robert Tiemann, editor, *Nineteenth Century Stars* (Phoenix, AZ: Society of American Baseball Research, 2012), p. 21; Esteban (Steve) Bellàn, "Nueva New York, 1613–1945," *New York Historical Society*, pp. 2–3, *http://abclocal.go.com/wabc/feature?section=resources/lifestyle community*; "Baseball Fever in Cuba," *Syracuse Sunday Times*, 14 September 1879.

35. "Tom York," www.baseball-reference.com; "To Be Hissed and Hooted at in the East is Too Much," Baseball History Daily, pp. 8–11 http://baseballhistyorydaily.com/tag/troy-haymakers/ (accessed 9/212/2013); Batesel, p. 136.

36. William J. Ryczek, *Blackguards and Red Stockings: A History of Baseball's National Association, 1871–1875* (Jefferson, NC: McFarland, 1992), pp. 184–185; *Troy Daily Times*, 2 February 1872.

37. Batesel, p. 176. As a result of the lasting effects of the devastating Chicago Fire in October of 1871, the White Stockings did not field a NA team in either 1872 or 1873.

38. *Charlton's Baseball Chronology—1869* www.baseballlibrary.com/byyearphp?year=1869 (accessed 1/5/2014); "Alphonse Martin," www.baseball-reference.com (accessed 1/5/2014); Batesel, pp. 86 and 162; "Doug Allison," www.baseball-reference.com/bullpen/Doug_Allison; www.baseball-reference.com/players/a/allisodo01.shtml (accessed 1/22/2014).

39. Joseph M. Overfield, Robert Tiemann, ed., *Nineteenth Century Stars* (Phoenix, AZ: Society of American Baseball Research, 2012), pp. 94–95; Batesel, pp. 58–59; *Chicago Tribune*, 24 October 1875, cited by Dean A. Sullivan, editor, *Early Innings: A Documentary History of Baseball, 1825–1908* (Lincoln: University of Nebraska Press, 1995), pp. 91–92.

40. Batesel, p. 177; Ryczek, *Blackguards and Red Stockings*, pp. 31–32 and 80–81.

41. "Count Gedney," www.baseball-reference.com>EncyclopediaofPlayers>G. (accessed 1/18/2014); Ryczek, *Blackguards and Red Stockings*, pp. 42 and 51; "Candy Nelson," http://www.baseball-reference.com/players/n/nelsoca01.shtml (accessed 1/22/2014).

42. *New York Sun*, 30 May 1872, p. 3; *Troy Daily Times*, 3 May 1872; *Troy Daily Whig*, 17 July 1872.

43. *Boston Daily Globe*, 20 July 1872, p. 8.

44. *Boston Daily Globe*, 22 July 1872, p. 8.

45. *Troy Daily Times*, 31 July 1872.

46. Peter Morris et al., *Baseball Founders: The Clubs, Players and Cities of the Northeast That Established the Game* (Jefferson, NC: McFarland, 2013), pp. 174–175.

47. Kim, p. 3; Puff, p. 12; Nemec, p. 34; Ryczek, *Blackguards and Red Stockings*, p. 134; "Jimmy Wood," http://www.retrosheet.org/boxesetc/W/Pwoodjl06.htm. (accessed 1/19/2014).

48. "Offered Him $1,000 to Throw the Game" *Troy Haymakers Archive*, pp. 1–4 http://baseballhistorydaily.com/tag/troy-hay makers (accessed 9/21/2013); "George Zettlein," http://www.baseball-reference.com/players/z/zettlge01.shtml (accessed 1/18/2014); "1871," *1871—The Baseball Chronology*, www.baseballlibrary.com/chronology/byyear.php?year=1871 (accessed 1/18/2014).

49. *New York Times*, 31 July 1872, p. 8; *Troy Daily Times*, 31 July 1872.

50. *New York World*, 31 July 1872, p. 5.

51. *New York Herald*, 31 July 1872, p. 5.

52. "1877 Troy Haymakers" and "Mike McGeary," www.baseball-reference.com; Roy Kerr, *Buck Ewing: A Baseball Biography* (Jefferson, NC: McFarland, 2012), p., 22.

53. *Troy Daily Times*, 10 August 1877.

54. *Troy Daily Times*, 14 September 1877. From its first game in midsummer, the 1877 Nolans-Haymakers series was met with enthusiasm by the partisan fans of both cities for both the quality of play and the local bragging rights that would go to the winning club. The sporting press fanned the flames of the rivalry as hyperbole reigned supreme: "The Albany club evidently came to this city [Troy] yesterday with the idea that they were to vanquish the Haymakers as the sons of Achilles are reported to have overcome the forces of ancient Troy, but in this they were soon undeceived." The double play of Lawton, Dunn, and Smith was "beautiful" and the battery combination of McManus and Brady "were almost perfect." (*Troy Daily Times*, 15 August 1877).

55. *Troy Daily Times*, 16 September 1877.

56. *Troy Daily Times*, 19 September 1877.

57. *Troy Daily Times*, 8 October 1877.

58. *Logansport (IN) Chronicle*, 23 March 1878, p. 1.

59. *Atlanta Daily Constitution*, 9 August 1878.

60. *Syracuse Standard*, 21 August 1878, p.4;

Utica (NY) Daily Observer (UDO), 20 August 1878; *Utica (NY) Morning Herald*, 7 October 1878.
61. *Syracuse Standard*, 12 September 1878.
62. *Syracuse Herald*, 6 December 1878.
63. Kerr, *Buck Ewing*, p. 23.
64. Kim, p. 4.
65. Michael Haupert, "William Hulbert," *SABR Biography Project*, pp. 1–3 http://sabr.org/bioproj/d1d420b3 (accessed 12/31/2013).
66. William E. Eakin, "William A. Hulbert," Robert Tiemann, ed., *Nineteenth Century Stars*, (Phoenix, AZ: Society of American Baseball Research,2012), pp. 135–136.
67. Haupert, p. 4.
68. Ibid., pp. 5 and 7.
69. Haupert, pp. 4–7; Eakin, p. 136.
70. Ray Kerr, *Big Dan Brouthers: Baseball's First Great Slugger* (Jefferson, NC: McFarland, 2013), p. 16.
71. *Troy Daily Times*, 14 September 1878.

Chapter Four

1. "1878," www.baseballlibrary.com/chronolgy/byyear.php?year=1878; *New York World*, 17 March 1879.
2. Richard A. Puff, "Haymakers and Daisy Cutters: Troy and the National Pastime," *Troy's Baseball Heritage* (Troy, NY: Committee to Preserve Troy's Baseball Heritage, 1992), p. 12; *New York World*, 13 April 1879; *Chicago Inter-Ocean*, 9 May 1879; *Troy Daily Times (Troy Daily Times)*, 22 September 1908, p. 10 and 16 April 1879.
3. *Poughkeepsie Daily Eagle*, 3 April 1879.
4. *Albany Evening Journal*, 24 April 1879; *Syracuse Standard*, 24 April 1879. Troy Trojans shortstop John Shoupe played that position for the 1878 Troy club, but, though described as "an acrobat and comedian of the Arlie Latham type," he hit only .091 in 11 games for the 1879 NL Trojans and was soon replaced by Ed Caskin.
(*Troy Daily Times*, 22 September 1908)
5. *Auburn (NY) Evening Auburian*, 26 May 1879.
6. *Albany Daily Evening Express (ADE)*, 1 June 1879.
7. *Troy Daily Times*, 22 September 1908, p. 10.
8. *Syracuse Sunday Times*, 4 May 1879
9. *Syracuse Daily Courier*, 29 June 1879.
10. *New York World*, 23 June 1879.
11. *Syracuse Standard*, 24 June 1879.
12. *Auburn (NY) Daily Bulletin*, 26 June 1879.
13. *New York Clipper*, 28 June 1879.
14. *Daily Kennebec (ME) Journal*, 17 May 1879.
15. *Syracuse Sunday TimesT*, 18 May 1879.
16. Puff, p. 13; *Syracuse Standard*, 17 May 1879, p. 4 and 3 July 1879, p. 4.
17. *Syracuse Daily Journal*, 31 July 1879
18. *Syracuse Sunday Times*, 13 July 1879.
19. *Batavia (NY) Daily News*, 26 July 1879.
20. Ibid.
21. *Troy Daily Times*, 22 September 1908, p. 10.
22. *Syracuse Sunday Times*, 10 August 1879.
23. *Syracuse Daily Journal*, 5 and 7 August 1879; *Brooklyn Daily Eagle (BDE)*, 12 August 1879.
24. *ADT*, 26 August 1879. The Trojans were looking for a reliable change pitcher for the entire 1879 season, starting with Pat McManus who was "studying law so that he may be able to 'kick' legally and appeal from the decision of the umpire." (*Oswego (NY) Morning Herald*, 18 December 1878). The Trojans then tried Gid Gardner who was found wanting; they then acquired Fred Goldsmith who went 2–4 late in the season with a sparkling 1.57 earned run average.
25. *BDT*, 19 September 1879: *ADT*, 24 September 1879.
26. Kim, p. 4; Nemec, p. 133; Jim Overmyer, "City of Diamond Heroes," *Troy's Baseball Heritage* (Troy, NY: Committee to Preserve Troy's Baseball Heritage, 1992), p. 25; Puff, p. 12; "The Chronology—1879." www.baseballlibrary.com/chronology/byyear.php?year=1879 (accessed 2/8/2014); "Troy Trojans Results—1879," http://www.justsportsstats.com/baseballresults.php?team=TRN&year=1879 (accessed 2/10/2014).
27. Roy Kerr, *Big Dan Brouthers: Baseball's First Great Slugger* (Jefferson, NC: McFarland, 2013), pp. 3–15.
28. Ibid., pp. 17–25; "The Baseball Chronology—1879," p. 4.
29. Mike Roer, *Orator O'Rourke: The Life of a Baseball Radical* (Jefferson, NC: McFarland, 2005), p. 96; "Dan Brouthers," www.baseball-reference.com,>EnclopediaofPlayers>BListing. (accessed 1/21/2014).
30. *Troy Daily Times*, 22 September 1908, p. 10.
31. Kerr, *Buck Ewing*, p. 25; Brian Mc Kenna, "Bob Ferguson," SABR BioProject, p. 5, http://sabr.org/bioproj/person/df8e7d29. (accessed 12/31/2013).

32. Fleitz, p. pp. 29–30.
33. McKenna, pp. 1–2.
34. Robert Tiemann, ed., *Nineteenth Century Stars* (Phoenix, AZ: Society of American Baseball Research, 2012), p. 88; McKenna, pp. 3 and 6.
35. Tiemann, pp. 88–89; *The New World (NW)*,1887, cited by McKenna, pp. 8–9.
36. *ADT*, 2 September 1879; *New York Evening Express (NYEE)*, 28 August 1879.
37. *Troy Daily Times*, 22 September 1908, p. 10.
38. Eric Miklich, "First Players Reserve List: 1880," www.19cbaseball.com/players-first-players-reserve-list.html. (accessed 12/28/2013).
39. Reserve Clause," www.baseball-reference.com/bullpen/reserve_clause. (accessed 1/9/2014).
40. *Troy Daily Times*, 8 May 1880.
41. John R. Husman, "Lee Richmond," SABR BioProject (pp. 1–4). http://www.sabr.org/bioproj/person/cd8979a0 (accessed 12/31/2013); "Lee Richmond," http://baseball-reference.com/players/r/richmle01.shtml (accessed 1/29/2014).
42. Nemec, pp. 143–144; Overmyer, p. 26.
43. David L. Fleitz, *Ghosts in the Gallery of Cooperstown* (Jefferson, NC: McFarland, 2004), p. 166; Roy Kerr, *Roger Connor: Home Run King of 19th Century Baseball* (Jefferson, NC: McFarland, 2011), pp. 2–5; Bill Lamb, "Roger Connor," SABR BioProject (pp. 1–11) http://sabr.org/bioproj/person/4ef2cfff. (accessed 12/31/2013); Jim Overmyer, "City of Diamond Heros [sic]," *Troy's Baseball Heritage* (Troy, NY: Committee to Preserve Troy's Baseball Heritage, 1992), p. 27; "Roger Connor," http://www.baseball-reference.com/players/c/connoro01.shtml (accessed 1/22/2014).
44. Kerr, *Roger Connor*, pp. 19–22 and 32–33; Lamb, pp. 1–2.
45. Overmyer, p. 27 Cited by Kerr, *Roger Connor*, pp. 32–33 and 36.
46. Fleitz, *Ghosts in the Gallery*, p. 166.
47. Lamb, pp. 2–6.
48. Ibid., pp. 6–7.
49. David Fleitz, *The Irish in Baseball: An Early History* (Jefferson, NC: McFarland, 2009), pp. 29–30 cited in Tiemann, p. 171.
50. "Mickey Welch," www.baaseball-reference.com/players/w/welchmi01.shtml. (accessed 1/22/2014). As early as the conclusion of Mickey Welch's extraordinary 1885 season, the diminutive hurler's stamina and overuse by the Giants were called into question:

"Mickey Welch has been weakening for a month past. At that time the Phillies began to pound him and the Chicago finished up the last week. The strain of the season has been too great for the splendid little twirler. Next year it beehoves [sic] the management to alternate their pitchers no matter the situation." (*Sporting Life,* 7 October 1885, p. 3.)
51. *New York Times*, 14 January 1890.
52. Fleitz, P. 37 and 40–41; Kerr, *Roger Connor*, p. 33.
53. *Kingston (NY) Daily Freeman*, 21 July 1941.
54. "Mickey Welch," www.baseballlibrary.com/ballplayers/player.php?name=Mickey Welch (accessed 1/22/2014).
55. Charlie Bevis, "Tim Keefe," SABR BioProject, pp. 1–5, http://www.sabr.org/bioproj/person/6f1dd1b1 (accessed 12/31/2013); Kerr, *Buck Ewing*, p. 28; http://www.baseball-reference.com/players/k/keefeti01.shtml (accessed 1/22/2014).
56. *New York Tribune*, 4 October 1891; *Boston Globe (BG)*, 27 May 1928; *Sporting Life*, 24 February 1906: cited by Bevis, p.4; *Troy Daily Times*, 22 September 1908, p. 10.
57. Bevis, pp. 7–10.
58. "Fatty Briody," http://www.baseball-reference.com/players/b/bfriodfa01.shtml; "Fatty Briody," http://www.baseball-reference.com/bullpen/Fatty_Briody; "Dick Higham," http://www.baseball-reference.com/players/h/highad01.shtml;"Dick Higham," http://www.baseball-reference.com/bullpen/Dick_Higham (accessed 1/22/2014).
59. *Troy Daily Times*, 16 April 1880.
60. *Troy Daily Times*, 21 April 1880.
61. *Troy Daily Times*, 1 May 1880.
62. *Albany Evening Times*, 1 May 1880.
63. *BDE*, 9 May 1880.
64. *Troy Daily Times*, 16 May 1880.
65. *Albany Evening Times*, 24 April 1879.
66. Kim, p. 4; Puff, p. 15; *Troy Daily Times*, 20 April 1880.
67. *Troy Daily Times*, 25 May 1880.
68. *Troy Daily Times*, 17 May 1880.
69. *Troy Daily Times*, 28 September 1880.
70. *Troy Daily Times*, 12 June 1880.
71. *Albany Evening Journal*, 22 July 1880.
72. *Albany Evening Journal*, 17 June 1880.
73. *Troy Daily Times*, 15 July 1880.
74. *Buffalo Evening Courier and Republic (BCR)*, 24 August 1880.
75. *Troy Daily Times*, 12 August 1880.
76. *Albany Evening Journal*, 3 September 1880.
77. *Troy Daily Times*, 28 July 1880.

78. *Troy Daily Times*, 22 September 1880.
79. *Troy Daily Times*, 17 September 1880
80. *Troy Daily Times*, 29 September 1880.
81. *Troy Daily Times*, 12 October 1880. The New York Metropolitans' October 1880 six-game series with the NL Troy Trojans was a high point of the season for the independent club, who tied the Trojans for the New York State championship with three victories apiece. (John J. O'Malley, "The Mets Open in New York," *SABR Research Journal Archives*, http://research.sabr.org/journals/mets-open-in-ny (accessed 3/9/2014).
82. *Troy Daily Times*, 1 October 1880

Chapter Five

1. Richard Puff, "Haymakers and Daisy Cutters: Troy and the National Pastime," *Troy's Baseball Heritage* (Troy, NY: Committee to Preserve Troy's Baseball Heritage, 1992), p. 15; "1881 Troy Trojans Pitching," *Sean Lahman's Baseball Archives*; "1881 Troy Trojans," www.baseball-reference.com; Jim Overmyer, "City of Diamond Heroes," *Troy's Baseball Heritage* (Troy, NY: Committee to Preserve Troy's Baseball Heritage, 1992), p. 26.
2. Kerr, *Buck Ewing*, pp. 25–26; Overmyer, p. 28; "Buck Ewing," pp. 1–2 http://www.baseball-reference.com/players/e/ewingbu01.shtml. (accessed 1/22/2014).
3. Kerr, *Buck Ewing*, pp. 178–179 and 183.
4. Ibid., pp. 32–33.
5. Ibid., pp. 33, 35, and 37.
6. "Buck Ewing," www.baseball-reference.com, pp. 2–6.
7. *Troy Daily Times*, 22 September 1908, p. 10; Kerr, *Buck Ewing*, pp. 180–181.
8. Richard Puff, "Haymakers and Daisy Cutters: Troy and the National Pastime," *Troy's Baseball Heritage* (Troy, NY: Committee to Preserve Troy's Baseball Heritage, 1992), 16.
9. The entire East Coast was experiencing freakish weather in September of 1881: "Eastern papers speak all week of the remarkable condition of the atmosphere throughout the section. The singular effects thus far reported were in Troy, Springfield, Mass., Providence R.I., Boston, and Toronto. At 5 o'clock, the sky presented the appearance of an orange dome of extraordinary beauty. As sunset approached, the orange hue deepened ... and the streets were filled with people gazing at the weird spectacle." (*Decatur (IL) Weekly Republican (DWR)*, 15 September 1881, p. 4.)
10. Puff, p. 16.
11. *Troy Daily Times (Troy Daily Times)*, 28 September 1881.
12. *New York Times*, 25 September 1881, p. 2.
13. *New York Times*, 29 September 1881, p. 2.
14. *New York Times*, 11 September 1881, p.2.
15. *New York Tribune*, 28 July 1881; *New York Herald*, 19 August 1881.
16. *New York Times*, 10 June and August 1881.
17. *Troy Daily Times*, 15 Sept 1881.
18. *Troy Daily Times*, 17 September 1881.
19. *Troy Daily Times*, 19 September 1881.
20. *Troy Daily Times,* 22 September 1881.
21. *Troy Daily Times*, 24 September 1881.
22. *New York Times,* 4 June 1881, p. 4;*Sporting Life*, 22 September 1886, p, 5.
23. *New York Times*, 30 September 1881, p. 5.
24. Kerr, *Roger Conner*, p. 45.
25. *New York Herald*, 5 January 1882.
26. *New York Herald*, 21 February 1882.
27. *New York Times,* 10 May 1882, p. 5.
28. *Syracuse Herald*, 13 June 1882.
29. *Troy Daily Times*, 7 June 1882. In 1882, Cleveland's Jim McCormick went 36–30 with a 2.37 ERA while George Bradley was 6–9 with a 3.73 ERA for the fifth place Blues (42–40).
30. *Troy Daily Times*, 8 June 1882.
31. *Troy Daily Times*, 9 June 1882.
32. *Troy Daily Times*, 10 June 1882. Jim "Pud" Galvin is a Hall of Fame inductee (1965) who had 365 wins, a 2.85 earned run average, and 57 shutouts in a fifteen-year major league career.
33. *Troy Daily Times,* 12 June 1882; *Syracuse Herald*, 9 July 1882; *New York Times*, 10 July 1882; *Syracuse Daily Courier*, 21 May 1882.
34. *New York Sun*, 26 June 1882.
35. *Troy Daily Times*, 11 August 1882.
36. *Troy Daily Times*, 13 September 1882.
37. *Troy Daily Times*, 26 September 1882
38. *Troy Daily Times*, 22 September 1908, p. 10.
39. *Troy Daily Times*, 21 August 1882.
40. Puff, pp. 16–17; Dave Nemec, *The Great Encyclopedia of 19th Century Major League Baseball* (New York: Donald I. Fine Books, 1997), p. 182; Kerr, *Roger Connor*, pp. 36–37 and 44; Dave Walsh, "The Last Major League Season, Troy vs Worcester, 1882," *Troy's Baseball Heritage*, p. 18; http://www.justsportsstats.com/baseballresults.php?team=TRN&

year=1882 (accessed 2/10/2014); *Syracuse Sunday Herald*, 22 October 1882, p. 2.

41. *Troy Daily Times*, 23 September 1882 cited in Roy Kim, "When Troy Was a Major League City," http://www.em[ireone.net/.mjusicman/troyball.html (accessed 6/5/2011), p. 5.

42. Melville, pp. 135–136.

43. *Lancaster (PA) Daily Intelligencer; Syracuse Morning Standard (SMS)*; and *New York Times*, 26 September 1882.

44. *Troy Daily Times*, 8 December 1882.

45. Puff, p. 17; Steve Wulf, "Two Cities with a Claim on Baseball: the National League Owes Both Troy and Worcester," *Sports Illustrated Vault*, July 2, 1990. http://cnnsi.printthis.clickabi;lity.com/pt/cpt?expire=&title=The+National+Leagur+owes+bot (accessed 5/28/2013), p. 1; Kim, p. 5.

46. *New York Times*, 7 December 1882; cited in *Troy Times Record* (1959).

47. *Troy Daily Times*, 7 July 1882.

48. *New York Times*, 11 July 1882, p. 2.

49. *New York Times*, 6 August 1882, p. 5.

50. *New York Sun*, 5 June 1882, p. 1.

51. Paul Browne, "Pete Gillespie," *SABR Biography Project*, pp. 1–4; "Pete Gillespie," http://www.baseball-reference.com/players/g/gillepe01.shtml (accessed 1/22/2014); Nemec, *Great Encyclopedia*, cited by Browne.

52. *Troy Daily Times*, 26 October 1882.

53. *New York Sun*, 10 October 1882.

54. *Troy Daily Times*, 11 October 1882. In a blatant public relations ploy, the players in question made unequivocal statements of loyalty to the Collar City that were never borne out by the facts: "Ewing, Connor, Gillespie, Halbert [Holbert], Keefe and Welch declared that they would remain in Troy another year if the club wanted them, even at a lower figure than at present. Roseman says he would stay also if wanted. But when they were asked to sign they refused to do so." (*New York Sun*, 13 November 1882)

Chapter Six

1. Roy Kerr, *Buck Ewing: A Baseball Biography* (Jefferson, NC: McFarland, 2012), p. 34 and John Thorn, *Baseball in the Garden of Eden: The Secret History of the Early Game* (New York: Simon and Schuster, 2011), p. 175.

2. Dean A. Sullivan, editor, *Early Innings: A Documentary History of Baseball, 1825–1908* (Lincoln: University of Nebraska Press, 1995), pp. 139–140.

3. Jim Overmyer, "City of Diamond Heros [sic]," *Troy's Baseball Heritage* (Troy, NY: Committee to Preserve Troy's Baseball Heritage,1992), p. 27.

4. Roy Kim, "When Troy Was a Major League City," p.6, http://www.em[ireone.net/.mjusicman/troyball.html (accessed 6/5/2011).

5. Leo Bolley, "Sports on Parade," *Troy Times*, 3 February 1938, p. 3.

6. *Sporting Life*, 7 October 1885, p. 3; *Troy Daily Times (Troy Daily Times)*, 20 June 1885.

7. *The Sporting News*, 31 May 1886, p. 5.

8. *The Sporting News*, 19 July 1886, p. 5.

9. *The Sporting News*, 30 September 1886, p. 1.

10. "Jim Devlin," http://www.baseball-reference.com/.../DListing. (accessed 2/6/2014).

11. *Saratoga (NY) Daily Saratogian*, July 1886.

12. *The Sporting News*, 6 November 1886, p. 4.

13. Richard A. Puff, "Haymakers and Daisy Cutters: Troy and the National Pastime," *Troy's Baseball Heritage* (Troy, NY: Committee to Preserve Troy's Baseball Heritage, 1992), p. 17; David Pietrusza, "Capital Region Baseball Timeline, Part I: 1819–1899." p.8 http://wwwe.davidpietrusza.com/capital-reg-baseball-1.html (accessed 6/22/2011); "Troy (New York) Minor Leagues," www.baseball-reference.com.

14. *The Sporting News*, 8 February 1890, p. 5.

15. Brian McKenna, "George Stovey," *SABR Biography Project*, p. 6. www.sabr.bioproj.org/bioproj/person/8ff10f5c (accessed 2/4/2014).

16. *Troy Daily Times (Troy Daily Times)*, 26 June 1890.

17. *Gloversville (NY) Daily Leader*; *Johnstown (NY) Daily Republican*, 14 May 1891; and *New York Sun*, 17 April 1891, p. 4.

18. *New York World*, 17 April 1893.

19. *Buffalo News Courier (BNC)*, 26 July 1894.

20. *Johnstown Daily Republican*, 4 and 11 April 1895.

21. *Albany Evening Journal*, 5 July 1900.

22. *Troy Daily Times*, 18 April 1901.

23. *Troy Daily Times*, 30 Apr, 1902.

24. *Troy Daily Times*, 23 May 1902.

25. *Gloversville (NY) Daily Leader*, 15 July 1902.

26. *Gloversville (NY) Daily Leader*, 27 July 1903.

27. *Troy Daily Times*, 23 July 1910.

28. The odd nickname "Washerwomen" is alleged to be an ironic comment on Troy's

many laundries and its rough and tumble baseball reputation: "Here's what's going to happen. We're going to get your uniforms real dirty—blood, sweat, mud, tears. And then we're going to clean them for you. Because that's what we do. We're the Troy Washerwomen." www.wapc.mlb.com/cutfour/2013 (accessed 1/14/2014).

29. *Amsterdam (NY) Evening Recorder*, 13 January 1916.

30. *Troy Daily Times*, 14 January 1888.

31. Puff, p. 17; "Troy Trojans—Minor League History," www.baseball-reference.com.

Chapter Seven

1. *Sporting Life*, vol. 10, no. 11, 21 December 1887, p. 1.

2. *Troy Daily Times*, 22 September 1908, p. 10.

3. *New York World*, 19 May 1879, p. 8.

4. *New York World*, 27 May 1879, p. 2.

5. *Syracuse Evening Telegram*, 17 June 1901, cited by Peter Morris, "Union Baseball Club of Lansingburgh/Haymaker of Troy Club History," personal website of Peter Morris, http://archive.is/yuZ3V (accessed December 7, 2013).

6. Morris et al., pp. 11–12.

7. Chuck Rosciam, The Evolution of Catcher's Equipment," *Baseball Research Journal* (SABR) 39, 1 (Summer 2010).

8. *Troy Daily Times*, 4 September 1902.

9. *Troy Daily Times*, 6 May 1920.

10. Deborah Nazon, *Brownfield's Redevelopment and Competitive Advantage Theory: Urban Revitalization and Stakeholder Engagement in South Troy, NY* (Ann Arbor, MI: ProQuest UMI Dissertations Publishing), 2007), pp. 45 and 49–50; George Baker Anderson, "History of Troy New York" in *Landmarks of Rensselaer County* (Syracuse, NY: D. Mason and Company, 1897).

11. Steven M. Gelber, "Working at Playing: The Culture of the Workplace and the Rise of Baseball," *Journal of Social History*, 16, 4 (Summer 1983), p. 16.

12. Peter Morris, Union Base Ball Club of Lansingburgh/Troy Haymakers," in Peter Morris et al., *Base Ball Pioneers, 1850–1870: The Clubs and Players Who Spread the Sport Nationwide* (Kindle edition) (Jefferson, NC: McFarland, 2012) loc. 1962–1984..

13. *Troy Times Record*, 6 June 1992; Thomas A. Blair, "A Reminder of Troy's Proud Baseball History," *Troy's Baseball Heritage* (Troy, NY: Committee to Preserve Troy's Baseball Heritage, 1992), pp. 39–40.

Bibliography

Books

Anderson, George Baker. *History of Troy, New York, Landmarks of Rensselaer County*. Syracuse, NY: D. Mason, 1897.

Appel, Marty. *Slide Kelly Slide: The Wild Life and Times of Mike "King" Kelly*. Lanham, MD: Scarecrow,1999.

Batesel, Paul. *Players and Teams of the National Association, 1871–1875*. Jefferson, NC: McFarland, 2012.

Bogen, Gil. *Tinker, Evers, and Chance: A Triple Biography*. Jefferson, NC: McFarland, 2003.

Burroughs, Edwin G., and Mike Wallace. *Gotham: A History of New York to 1898*. New York: Oxford University Press, 1998.

Fleitz, David L. *Ghosts in the Gallery of Cooperstown*. Jefferson, NC: McFarland, 2004.

_____. *The Irish in Baseball: An Early History*. Jefferson, NC: McFarland, 2009.

Ginsburg, Daniel E. *The Fix Is In: A History of Baseball Gambling and Game Fixing Scandals*. Jefferson, NC: McFarland, 2004.

Guschov, Stephen R. *The Red Stockings of Cincinnati: Baseball's First All-Professional Team*. Jefferson, NC: McFarland, 1998.

Hartgen Archeological Associates (commissioned by Rensselaer Polytechnic Institute). *A View of the Past: Excavating the Lives of Troy's Working Class*, Vol. 1. Rensselaer, NY: Hartgen Archeological Associates, July 2004.

Kerr, Roy. *Big Dan Brouthers: Baseball's First Great Slugger*. Jefferson, NC: McFarland, 2013.

_____. *Buck Ewing: A Baseball Biography*. Jefferson, NC: McFarland, 2012.

_____. *Roger Connor: Home Run King of 19th Century Baseball*. Jefferson, NC: McFarland, 2011.

Lowry, Philip J. *Green Cathedrals: The Ultimate Celebration of Major League and Negro League Ballparks* (SABR). New York: Walker and Company, 2006.

Lutz, Alma. *Emma Willard: Daughter of Democracy*. Washington, D.C.: Zenger, 1929.

Melville, Tom. *Early Baseball and the Rise of the National League*. Jefferson, NC: McFarland, 2001.

Morris, Peter. *But Didn't We Have Fun?: An Informal History of Baseball's Pioneer Era, 1843–1870*. Chicago: Ivan R. Dee, 2008.

_____. *A Game of Inches: The Stories behind the Innovations That Shaped Baseball* (Kindle edition). Chicago: Ivan R. Dee, 2010.

Morris, Peter, William J. Ryczek, Jan Finkel, Leonard Levin and Richard Malatzky, eds. *Base Ball Pioneers, 1850–1870: The Clubs and Players Who Spread the Sport Nationwide* (Kindle edition). Jefferson, NC: McFarland, 2012.

_____. *Base Ball Founders: The Clubs, Players and Cities of the Northeast That Established the Game*. Jefferson, NC: McFarland, 2013.

Nazon, Deborah. *Brownfield's Redevelopment and Competitive Advantage The-*

Bibliography

ory: Urban Revitalization and Stakeholder Engagement in South Troy, NY. Ann Arbor, MI: ProQuest UMI Dissertations, 2007.

Nemec, David. *The Great Encyclopedia of 19th Century Major League Baseball.* New York: Donald I. Fine, 1997.

Peverelly, Charles. *The Book of American Pastimes, Containing a History of the Principal Baseball, Cricket, Rowing and Yachting Clubs of the United States.* New York: Privately Published, 1866. (Reprinted as *Peverelly's National Game*, John Frazer and Mark Rucker, Eds. Charleston, SC: Arcadia, 2005).

Phelan, Thomas. *The Hudson Mohawk Gateway: An Illustrated History.* North Ridge, CA: Windsor Publications, 1985.

Pietrusza, David. *Major Leagues: The Formation, Sometimes Absorption and Mostly Inevitable Demise of 18 Professional Baseball Organizations.* Jefferson, NC: McFarland, 1991.

Proudfit, Margaret Burden. *Henry Burden: His Life and a History of His Inventions. Compiled from the Public Press.* Troy, NY: Pafraets Press, 1904.

Rittner, Don. *Legendary Locals of Troy.* Charleston, SC: Arcadia, 2012.

———. *Remembering Troy: Heritage on the Hudson.* Charleston, SC: The History Press, 2008.

———. *Troy Revisited.* Charleston, SC: Arcadia, 2013.

Roer, Mike. *Orator O'Rourke: The Life of a Baseball Radical.* Jefferson, NC: McFarland and Company, 2005.

Ryczek, William J. *Blackguards and Red Stockings: A History of Baseball's National Association, 1871–1875.* Jefferson, NC: McFarland, 1992.

———. *When Johnny Came Sliding Home; The Post-Civil War Baseball Boom, 1865–1870.* Jefferson, NC: McFarland, 1998.

Seymour, Harold. *Baseball: The Early Years.* New York, Oxford University Press, 1960.

Spalding, Albert G. *America's National Game.* Lincoln: University of Nebraska Press, 1992.

Sullivan, Dean A, editor. *Early Innings: A Documentary History of Baseball, 1825–1908.* Lincoln: University of Nebraska Press, 1995.

Sutter, L. M. *Arlie Latham: A Baseball Biography of the Freshest Man on Earth.* Jefferson, NC: McFarland, 2012.

Terry, James L. *Long before the Dodgers: Baseball in Brooklyn, 1855–1884.* Jefferson, NC: McFarland, 2012.

Thorn, John. *Baseball in the Garden of Eden: The Secret History of the Early Game.* New York: Simon and Schuster, 2011.

Tiemann, Robert, Ed. *Nineteenth Century Stars.* Phoenix, AZ: Society of American Baseball Research, 2012.

Walkowitz, Daniel J. *Worker City, Company Town: Iron and Cotton-Worker Protest in Troy and Cohoes, New York, 1855–1884.* Urbana: University of Illinois Press, 1978.

Ward, Geoffrey C. and Ken Burns. *Baseball: An Illustrated History.* New York: Alfred A. Knopf, 1994.

Weise, Arthur James. *Troy's One Hundred Years.* Troy, NY: William H. Young, 1891.

Worth, Richard. *Baseball Team Names: A Worldwide Dictionary, 1869–2011.* Jefferson, NC: McFarland, 2013.

Wright, Marshall. *The National Association of Base Ball Players, 1857–1870.* Jefferson, NC: McFarland, 2000.

Articles

"Base Ball: Haymakers vs. Worcester," *Troy Evening Standard* (1878), http://www.auctiva.com/hosted images/showimage.aspz?gid=610066&ppidf=1122. (accessed 10/27/2012).

Bevis, Charlie. "Tim Keefe," SABR BioProject (pp. 1–14) http://sabr.org/bioproj/person/6f1dd1b1. (accessed 12/31/2013).

"Big League, Small Town" (pp. 1–5). http://verdun2.wordpress.com/2013/01/29/big-league-small-town (accessed 9/7/2013).

Blair, Thomas M. "A Reminder of Troy's Proud Baseball History," *Troy's Baseball*

Bibliography

Heritage (Troy, NY: Committee to Preserve Troy's Baseball Heritage, 1992), pp. 39–40.

Broderick, Warren. "Haymakers Tie Red Stockings in Exciting Game," *Troy Record*. 30. August 1969, p. 43.

Browne, Paul. "John Morrissey," SABR BioProject (pp.1–8) http://bioproj.sabr.org/bioproj.cfm?a=v&v=1&bid=3195&pid=19722. (accessed 6/24/2011).

_____. "Pete Gillespie," SABR BioProject (pp. 1–6) http://sabr.org/bioproj/person/be4016e2. (accessed 12/31/2013).

Carroll, P. Thomas. "The Rise, Fall, and Rebirth of an American City" (pp. 1–2) www.visittroyny.com/aboutTroy/histry. (accessed 11/23/2013).

Cunningham, Kevin J. "The History of Troy & the Giants, or How Baseball Grew Up," *SF Dugout Online Magazine*, p. 3 http://www.sfdugout.com/content.php?1471-The-History-of-Troy (accessed 6/17/2011).

"Esteban (Steve) Bellan" in "Nueva New York, 1613–1945," *New York Historical Society*, http://abclocal.go.com/wabc/feature?section=resources/lifestyle_community. (accessed 9/7/2013).

Ettkin, Brian. "Four Strikes, They Were Out," *Albany Times-Union* (Saturday, March 31, 2007), pp. A1 and A6.

Fyle, Rich. "Troy Amateur Baseball League Could Rival Anyone with Competition and Camaraderie," http://www.troyrecord.com/general-rules/20101111/troy-amateur-league. (accessed 3/14/2014).

Gelber, Steven M. "Working at Playing: The Culture of the Workplace and the Rise of Baseball," *Journal of Social History*, 16, 4 (Summer 1983), pp. 3–22.

Haupert, Michael. "William Hulbert," SABR BioProject (pp. 1–10) http://sabr.org/bioproj/person/dld420b3. (accessed 12/31/2013).

Husman, John R. "Lee Richmond," SABR BioProject (pp. 1–4) http://sabr.org/bioproj/person/cd8979a0 (accessed 12/31/2013).

Kim, Roy. "When Troy Was a Major League City," (pp. 1–6) http://www.empireone.net/.mjusicman/troyball.html (accessed 6/5/2011).

Lamb, Bill. "Roger Connor," SABR BioProject (pp. 1–11) http://sabr.org/bioproj/person/4ef2cfff. (accessed 12/31/2013).

"The Leagues," 19th Century Baseball," pp.1–2. http://www.19cbaseball.com/leagues.html. (accessed 9/6/2013).

McKenna, Brian. "Bob Ferguson," SABR BioProject (pp. 1–12) http://sabr.org/bioproj/person/df8e7d29 (accessed 12/31/2013).

_____. "Dickey Pearce," SABR BioProject (pp. 1–8) http://sabr.org/bioproj/person/db8ea477. (accessed 12/31/2013).

_____, "George Stovey," SABR BioProject, (pp. 1–9). www.sabr.bioproj.org/bioproj/person/8ff10f5c. (accessed 2/4/2014).

_____. "Professional Baseball in Chicago, a Shaky Start," http://BaseballHistoryBlog.com/1790. (accessed 1/15/2014).

_____. "Steve Bellan," SABR BioProject (pp. 1–6). . http://bioproj.sabr.org/bioproj/person/78dbf37d. (accessed 12/6/2012).

Miklich, Eric. "First Players Reserve List: 1880." www.19cbaseball.com/players-first-players-reserve-list.html (accessed 12/28/2013).

Moran, Kevin. "World Series Trophy Headed to Troy," *Troy Record*, 12 December 2009.

Morris, Peter. "Union Baseball Club of Lansingburgh/Haymaker of Troy Club History," (pp. 1–20). http://archive.is/yuZ3V. (accessed 12/7/2013).

"Offered Him $1,000 to Throw the Game," "Troy Haymakers Archives," *Baseball History Daily* (pp. 1–4). http://baseballhistorydaily.com/tag/troy-haymakers. (accessed 9/21/2013).

O'Malley, "The Mets Open in New York," *SABR Research Journal Archives* http://research.sabr.org/journals/mets-open-in-ny. (accessed 3/9/2014).

Overmyer, Jim. "City of Diamond Heros [sic]," *Troy's Baseball Heritage* (Troy, NY: Committee to Preserve Troy's Baseball Heritage, 1992), pp. 21–28.

Passonno, Bill. "Troy's Baseball Legacy: A Bunch of Hicks," *Troy Record*, November 10, 2010.

_____. "Troy's Baseball Legacy: Cutting

Bibliography

Down Perfection—at a High Price," *Troy Record*, August 27, 2001.

Pietrusza, David. "Capital Region Baseball Timeline, Part I: 1819–1899." http://wwwe.davidpietrusza.com/capital-reg-baseball-1/html. (accessed 6/22/2011).

Puff, Richard A. "Haymakers and Daisy Cutters: Troy and the National Pastime," *Troy's Baseball Heritage* (Troy, NY: Committee to Preserve Troy's Baseball Heritage, 1992), pp. 5–18.

Rittner, Don. "I'll Take Troy for $500, Alex" (Originally in *Troy Record*). http://www.rootsweb.ancestry.com/-nyrensse/articlez.htm. (accessed 6/24/2011).

———. "Troy's National League Days." http://www.donrittner.com/his58.html. (accessed 5/28/2013).

Rosciam, Chuck. "The Evolution of Catcher's Equipment," *Baseball Research Journal* (SABR), Vol. 39, no. 1 (Summer, 2010).

Schaefer, Robert H. "Lip Pike," SABR BioProject (pp. 1–7) http://sabr.org/bioproj/person/7a6a0655. (accessed 12/31/2013).

Thorn, John. "The Park in the City," *Our Game* (pp. 1–3). http://ourgame.mlbblogs.com/2011/06/11/thepark. (accessed 6/24/2011).

Thornley, Stew. "The Demise of the Reserve Clause: The Players' Path to Freedom" http://milkeespress.com/reserveclause.html. (accessed 12/28/2013).

"To be Hissed and Hooted at in the East Is Too Much," "Troy Haymakers Archives," *Baseball Daily History* (pp. 8–10). http://baseballhistorydaily.com/tag/troy-haymakers (accessed 9/21/2013).

"Troy Baseball," (pp. 1–13) http://www.classcreator.com/troy-ny-1900/class_profile.cfm?member_id=5087366. (accessed 2/23/2014).

"Troy Baseball Monument," (pp. 1–2) http://projectballpark.org/other/troy/b2b.html. (accessed 9/7/2013).

"Troy Haymakers," Baseball Historian, "Heroes" (p. 15). http://www.baseballhistorian.com/html/american_heroes.cfm?page=15. (accessed 9/7/2013).

"Troy Haymakers (1871–1872) and "Troy Trojans (1879–1882)," *Seamheads.com Ballparks Database*, http://www.seamheads.com/ballparks/team.php?teamid=trn. (accessed 9/7/2013).

"Troy, New York" (pp. 1–4), http://www.princeton.edu/-achaney/tmve. (accessed 11/25/2013).

Walsh, Dave. "The Last Major League Season: Troy vs Worcester 1882," Troy, NY: Committee to Preserve Troy's Baseball Heritage, 1992, pp. 19–20.

Wulf, Steve. "Two Cities with a Claim on Baseball: the National League Owes Both Troy and Worcester," *Sports Illustrated Vault*, July 2, 1990. http://cnnsi.printthis.clickabi;lity.com/pt/cpt?expire=&title=The+National+League+owes+bot. (accessed 5/28/2013).

Zahavi, Gerald and Susan McCormick (revision of original text by James S. Corsaro and Kathleen D. Roe), [Department of History—University at Albany], "Labor and History in Troy and Cohoes: A Brief History," pp. 1–12. http://www.albany.edu/history/Troy-Cohoes. (accessed 11/25/2013).

Newspapers

Albany Evening Journal
Albany Evening Times
Albany Express
Albany Knickerbocker News
Amsterdam (NY) Daily Democrat and Recorder
(Atlanta) Daily Constitution
Auburn (NY) Daily Bulletin
Auburn (NY) Evening Auburnian
Batavia (NY) Daily News
Boston Daily Globe
Boston Herald
Buffalo Evening Courier and Republic
Chariton (IA) Democrat
Chicago Inter-Ocean
Clinton (NY) Courier
Daily (Herkimer, NY) Telegram
Daily Kennebec (Maine) Journal
Decatur (IL) Herald
Elmira (NY) Morning Telegraph
Fort Wayne (IN) Daily Democrat
Fort Wayne (IN) Daily Gazette

Bibliography

Fort Wayne (IN) Daily Sentinel
Freeport (IL) Daily Bulletin
Freeport (IL) Republican
Friendship (NY) Weekly Gazette
Gloversville (NY) Daily Leader
Greenville (PA) Advance
Hamburg (NY) Erie County Independent
Hudson (NY) Evening Register
Indiana (PA) Progress
Janesville (WI) Chronicle
Johnstown (NY) Daily Republican
Kingston (NY) Daily Freeman
Lancaster (PA) Daily Intelligencer
Lockport (NY) Daily Bulletin
Logansport (IN) Chronicle
Louisville (KY) Courier-Journal
Madison (WI) State Journal
New York Clipper
(NY) Commercial
New York Herald
New York Sun
New York Times
New York Tribune
New York World
Ohio City (Cleveland) Argus
Oswego (NY) Daily Times
Oswego (NY) Morning Herald
Oswego (NY) Palladium
Port Jervis (NY) Evening Gazette
Poughkeepsie (NY) Daily Eagle
Rochester Democrat Chronicle
Rochester Union and Advertiser
Rome (NY) Daily Sentinel
Saratoga (NY) Daily Saratogian
Seymour (IN) Times
Sporting Life (Philadelphia)
The Sporting News (St. Louis)
Sullivan (IN) Democrat
Syracuse Daily Courier
Syracuse Daily Journal
Syracuse Herald
Syracuse Standard
Syracuse Sunday Herald
Syracuse Sunday Times
Titusville (PA) Morning Herald
Troy Daily Press
Troy Daily Times
Troy Daily Whig
Troy Northern Budget
Troy Record
Troy Times
Troy Times Record
Utica (NY) Evening Herald
Utica (NY) Morning Herald
Utica (NY) Observer-Dispatch
Watertown (NY) Daily Times
Watkins (NY) Democrat
Wellsville (NY) Allegheny County Reporter
Wellsville (NY) Daily Reporter
Worcester (MA) Spy

Online and Archival Collections

Baseball Almanac
Baseball Library
Baseball-Reference.com
Charlton's Chronology
Chronicling America (Library of Congress)
E. Baseball Websites
Just Sports Stats
Lannan Foundation 84
Library of Congress
Newspaper Archives.com
Old Fulton New York Post Cards
Paper of Record
Protoball—Retrosheet
Seamheads.com Database
Sean Lahman Baseball Archives
Troy Public Library

Index

Numbers in **_bold italics_** indicate pages with photographs.

A and W Orr Company 50
Abrams, Thomas 14–15, 21
Adams, Daniel "Doc" 9
Agricultural Fairgrounds (Worcester) 166
Ahern, Bill 137
Albany Baseball Club (National Association) 69, 124, 129–132
Albany Beverwycks 11
Albany Capital Citys 91–92, 99–100, 107, 132
Albany Champions 10–11
Albany Express 160
Albany Governors 173
Albany (New York) Baseball Club 11
Albany Nolans 87–89, 210*n*54
Albany Senators 177, 179, 181
Albany Twilight League 2, 203*Intro.n*1
Albany Unions 11
Allison, Doug 74–76, 80, 82, 97, 200
American Association 94, 105, 108, 113, 151, 156–157, 167, 176, 188, 192
American Basketball League 2
Amherst College 127
Anson, Adrian "Cap" 92, 101, 106, 110, 119, 147
Auburn (New York) Auburnians 89
Austin, Henry 42

Baltimore Canaries (Lord Baltimores) 20, 25, 82
Baltimore Marylands 35
Baltimore (National Association) 132–133
Baltimore Pastimes 32
Bancroft, Frank 119, 147
bank panics (1873 and 1893) 56, 85, 157
Barnes, Ross 79, 92
baseball: attractions of game 56; batting order value 131; evolution of catching equipment 143–144; gambling 154–155; high salaries 142; newspaper influence 3, 115; rowdyism 63–64, 184
Bellan, Esteban "Steve" 25–26, 39, 42, 66–67, 71, 73–74, 76, 79, 84–85, 200, 210*n*33

Bennett, Charley 146
Bernard, Curt 183
Bessemer steel process 48
Bierman, Charlie 28, 32
Binghamton (New York) Crickets 51, 86, 108
Birdsall, Dave 19–20, 42
Bond, Tommy 113, 120
Bonker, Gene 26
The Boston Herald 153
Boston Nationals 185
Boston Red Caps 110, 133, 140–141
Boston Red Stockings 57–58, 66, 69, 71, 76, 78, 81, 98–99, 133, 170
Boston Tri-Mountains 32, 35
Bradley, George Washington 98, 102–105, 107, 160–161, 201
Brady, Steve 149, 171, 210*n*54
Brainard, Asa 26
Briody, Charles "Fatty" 86, 88, 97, 127–128, 137, 159, 192
Brockway, W.R. 28, 30–31
Brooklyn Atlantics 15–16, 25–27, 33, 35–36, 38, 58–59, 68–69, 111–112, 193, 205*n*14
Brooklyn Bridegrooms 123, 181
Brooklyn Eagle 19–20
Brooklyn Eckfords 26, 32–33, 35, 66–67, 70, 74–76, 78, 81–83
Brooklyn Excelsiors 10, 203*ch*1*n*1
Brooklyn Olympics 81
Brooklyn Stars 65
Brooklyn Unions 69
Brotherhood of Professional Base Ball Players 123, 176
Brouthers, Dan 97, 101–***102***, 105, 107–110, 133, 137, 163, 188, 192, 196, 200
Brown, James 183
Browning, Pete 72
Buck Ewing's Big Giants 121
Buffalo Bisons 98–103–105, 124, 138–139, 142, 150, 152, 161–163, 165
Buffalo Clause *see* "Reserve Clause"

223

Index

Buffalo Courier 162
Buffalo (New York) Baseball Club 32
Bulkeley, Morgan 93
Bull's Head Tavern Field (Lansingburgh) 25
Burden, Henry 48
Burden Iron Works **48**
Burden Water Wheel **49**
Burdock, Jack 133–134, 170–171
Burke, James 162
Burns, Tom 135, 147, 154

Calhoun, Jack 185
Caperoon, John 87–89
Capitoline Grounds (Brooklyn) 15–16, 36, 38, 59, 112, 115
Carbondale (Pennsylvania) Alerts 172
Carbondale Lackawannas 172
Cargo, Chick 183–184
Carhenger Field (Lansingburgh) 206n42
Cartwright, Alexander 9
"Casey at the Bat" (poem) 127
Caskin, Ed 69, 97, 105, 107, 114, 130, 133–134, 136, 138, 145–146, 152, 170, 176, 200–201, 211n4
Cassidy, John 97, 114, 129–130, 133–134, 143, 148–149, 151–152, 154, 157, 159–161, 170–171, 174, 201
Caylor, O.P. (Oliver Perry) 108, 147, 173
Center Island Field (Green Island, New York) 72, 147
Chadwick, Henry 79, 112
Chatham (New York) Baseball Club 11
Chicago Baseball Club 15, 22, 34, 41
Chicago White Stockings 35–37, 40, 64–67, 76, 83, 92, 98, 102, 104, 112–114, 117, 119, 122, 135, 138, 141, 147–148, 150, 152, 154, 164, 191–193, 222n50
Cincinnati Outlaw Reds 105
Cincinnati Red Stockings 13, 23, 25–33, 36, 38, 59, 69, 75, 93–94, 101, 112, 192
Cincinnati Reds 98, 102, 142, 193
Civil War 6, 9, 12, 19, 21, 57, 74, 94
Clapp, Aaron 97, 103, 107, 151, 200
The Clarion 54
Cleveland Blues 98, 102, 105–106, 117, 124, 135, 137, 142, 150–152, 158–161, 164, 167
Cleveland Forest Citys 66, 83
Cobleskill (New York) Baseball Club 179
Cogswell, Ed 97–98, 129–130, 133–134, 136, 201
Cohoes Music Hall 53
Cohoes (New York) Base Ball Club 14
Cohoes Unions 205n30
Cohoes Vanguards 10
Coleman, Rip 5
Connecticut State League 121
Connor, Ned 67, 70

Connor, Roger 97, 111, 114, 117–**118**, 119–122, 126, 129–130, 133–134, 138, 141, 143, 145–146, 149, 151–152, 154, 157–158, 161, 167, 170–171, 174–176, 181, 188, 192, 196, 201, 214n54
Connors, J.P 89
Cooperative Movement 7
Craver, William 12, 14–15, 19–21, **22**–23, 25–28, 30–36, 39, 59, 64–67, 82, 86, 90, 187, 190–191, 204n2
Cuban baseball 71–72
Cuban X-Giants (African American) 183
Cummings, Candy 73–74, 113
Cuthbert, Ned 35

Daley, Hugh (Daily) 132–133, 141
Dalrymple, Abner 148
Daly, John 14
Dauchy, C.H. 174
Day, John B. 121, 123, 144, 173, 176
Dealy, Pat 179
Deasley, Pat 170–171
DeForest, D.H. 156
de la Rue, Raphael Julian 21, 23, 209n33
De la Vergne, Ben 191
Detroit Wolverines 128, 149, 154, 164, 168, 186
Devlin, Jim 178, 181
Dexter Park (Chicago) 36
Diach, William 88, 120
Diamond, Jack 196
Dick, Billy 42
Dickerson, Lewis "Buttercup" 97, 130–131, 170, 188, 201
Dockney, Pat 206n53
Doherty, Mike 184
Dolan, Tom 162
Donovan, Tom 181
Dorgan, Jerry 97, 102, 104, 114, 130, 145
Doscher, Herm 97, 103, 128, 130, 139, 152, 159–160, 201
Doyle, John 158
Drive Park (Worcester, Massachusetts) 166
Dubuque (Iowa) Red Stockings 106
Duffy, Hugh 110
Dungon, F.C. 89
Dunlap, Fred 134, 137–138, 151, 161

Earl, Gardner 167
Eastern Association 5, 180
Eastern League 5, 180–181
Eastern Park (Brooklyn) 181
Eaton, Amos 52
Egan, Jack 163, 170
Egolf, Colonel 28, 73–74
Eight Hour Movement 8
Elmira (New York) Colonels 185

224

Index

Elysian Athletic Field (Hoboken, New Jersey) 16
Erie (Pennsylvania) Baseball Club 2
E.S. Sterry and Company 204n2
Evans, Jake 97, 114, 141, 149, 151, 188, 192, 201
Evers, Johnny 7, 183–185, 196
Ewing, William "Buck" 101, 109, 117–118, 120, 125–127, 137, 140–141, 143–**144**, 145–146, 148–150, 153–154, 157–163, 165–166, 170, 173–177, 181–182, 192, 196, 201, 214n54

Falls River (Connecticut) Indians 121
Farley, E. 89
Farrell, Jack 102, 104
Farrow, John 149
Ferguson, Bob "Death to Flying Things" 27, 59, 77, 97, 106–114-**115**, 119, 122, 128–131, 133–134, 137–140, 144–145, 147, 152, 154, 157–158, 160, 162–165, 174–175, 186, 201
Fisher, William Charles "Cherokee" 25, 28–29, 34, 37, 42–44, 193
Flint, Silver 148
Flowers, Dickie 39, 42–43, 65–67, 70–71, 200
Flynn, Clipper 15, 22, 25–26, 35, 39, 59, 63–66, 85–86, 191–192, 200
Foley, Curry 134, 162
Foley, Tom 34, 192–193
Foran, Jim 39, 42–43
Force, Davy 74, 76–77, 79, 82, 97–98, 138, 153, 162, 200
Forster, Tom 164–165
Fort Wayne (Indiana) Kekiongas 51, 59–60
Fourth Coinage Act (1873) 85
Fulmer, Chick 84

Gaffney, R.A. 205n30
Galvin, James "Pud" 137–139, 153, 161–162, 165
Gardner, Gideon 105–106, 211n24
Garfield, President James 154
Garnet, Rev. Henry Highland 53
Gedney, Alfred "Count" 42, 74, 76–78, 80, 82, 163, 200
Gibson House (Cincinnati) 30
Gilbert Car Company 48
Gilded Age 6–7, 115
Gillespie, Pete 97, 111, 114, 118, 130, 133–134, 138, 146–147, 150–152, 154, 157–158, 164, 171–**172**, 173–174, 177, 188, 201, 214n54
Glasscock, Jack 158–160
Goldsmith, Fred 97, 105–107, 114, 147, 154, 192, 211n24
Goodwin, Art 183–184
Gore, George 154
Gould, Charlie 79, 83, 112
Granville (New York) Eurekas 11
Great Chicago Fire (1871) 15, 64, 67, 92

Great Railroad Strike (1877) 85
Great Troy (New York) Fire (1862) **10**, 12, 204n7
Greenback Movement 7
Griffith, Clark 147
Griswold, John 48–49
Guelph (Ontario) Maple Leafs 51

Hackett, Mert 179
Haddock, George 179, 181
Hall, Al 90, 97, 201
Hamilton (Ontario) Mountaineers 179
Hankison, Frank 97, 146, 149–151, 171, 177, 192
Hanlon, Ned 135, 164–165
Harbridge, Bill 114, 128–129, 133, 163–165, 188, 201
Harlem (New York) Clippers 108
Harmony Conference 176
Harrell, Billy 5
Harrisburg (Pennsylvania) Islanders 185
Hartford Dark Blues 83, 113, 122, 128
Harvard College (Cambridge, Massachusetts) 27, 40, 99
Harvard University 127
Hatfield, John 84
Hawkes, Thorny 97, 200
Haymaker Grounds (Lansingburgh) 57–58, 147, 166, 209n5
Higham, Dick 63, 97, 128, 164
Hilley, Ed 183
Hodes, Charlie 35, 74, 79
Holbert, Bill 100–101, 106, 120, 127–128, 130, 133, 137, 139, 141, 151–153, 157, 159–160, 162–165, 177, 192, 201, 214n54
Holyoke (Massachusetts) Shamrocks 69, 111, 114, 119, 122, 172
Hoosick Falls (New York) Baseball Club 180
Hornesville (New York) Baseball Club 109
Hornung, Joe 170
Hotaling, Pete 170
Hotchkin, A.L. 167, 169, 174, 187–188
Houck, Sadie 133–134
Houston Astros 186
Hudson (New York) Baseball Club 108
Hudson River League 5, 177
Hudson State League 177
Hudson Valley Community College 186
Hulbert, William **77**, 92–94, 98, 132, 148, 153, 156, 164

International Association 5, 21, 86, 90, 100, 172, 178–179, 187–190
International League 179

Joe Bruno Stadium (Troy) **196**
Johnson, Frank 190

Index

Johnstown-Gloversville (New York) Baseball Club 179
Junior Association of Base Ball Players 44

Keefe, Tim 117, 120–122, 124–**125**, 126–127, 130, 137, 141, 143, 147, 150–152, 154, 157, 161–166, 174, 177, 181, 188, 192, 196, 201, 214n54
Kelly, Andy 190
Kelly, John "Kick" 72, 102
Kelly, Mike "King" 7, 98, 99, 144, 146, 196
Kern, James A. 191
King, Marshall "Mart" 15, 22–23, 25, 32, 35, 74, 187, 191–192
King, Steve 12, 14, 22–23, 25, 32, 35–36, 38–39, 41–42, 58, 66, 74, 79–80, 85–86, 88, 187, 191, 200, 204n2
Knickerbocker Club (Albany) 11
Knickerbocker Park (Lansingburgh) 196
Knight, Lon 64, 165
Knox, Tom 180

Lajoie Napoleon 192
Lansing, Abraham Jacob 206n3
Lansingburgh Griswolds 11
Lansingburgh National Baseball Club 9, 12
Lansingburgh Unions 1, 9, 12, 14–16, **17**–19, 22, **24**, 26, 30, 57, 70–71, 189, 204n2, 204n5
Larkin, Terry 121, 128, 130, 133, 137–138
Latham, Arlie 138–139, 211n54
Laureate Grounds (Lansingburgh) 181, 183, 185, 188
Lawler, M. 89
L.E. Gurley Company 48
League Alliance (1877) 1, 5, 86, 157
Leavenworth, Sonny 14
Lexboro Committee Investigations 14
London (Ontario) Athletics 51, 90
London (Ontario) Cockneys 178
London (Ontario) Tecumsehs 106
Long, W.H. 182
Louisville Colonels 72
Louisville Grays 20–21, 93, 189
Lynch, Jack 177
Lynn (Massachusetts) Live Oaks 51, 172

MacGamwell, Ed 185
Mack, Connie 147
Maloney, J.D. 182
Manhattan College 105
Mann, Francis N. 166
Mansell, Tom 97, 104, 106, 192, 201
Marsh, P.G. 18
Martin, Alphonse "Phonney" 32, 43, 66–67, 74–75, 79, 80–81, 200
Matthews, Bobby 170

McAtee, James "Bub" 12, 14–15, 25–26, 32, 35, 74, 76, 79, 85, 191–192, 200, 204n2
McCormick, Harry 88, 103–104
McCormick, James 138, 158–160, 192
McDonald, Dan 35, 64, 112
McGeary, Mike 39, 43–44, 58–59, 65, 67, 70, 73, 86, 97, 98, 200, 204n2
McGraw, John 147
McGuiness, John 104
McKeon, James 29
McKeon, Peter 14
McKinnon, Alex 100
McLean, D.R. 134
McManus, Pat 89, 105, 210n54, 211n24
McMullin, John "Lefty" 37–39, 43–44, 59, 65, 70–71, 73, 200
McNally, Dave 114
McNeely Bell Company 48, **50**
McQuide, Andrew 14–15
McVey, Cal 29, 92, 97
Meachem, Lewis 92
Meir, Angeline 120
Melville, Herman 52
Messersmith, Andy 114
Messit, Tom 181
Meteca (Attleboro, Massachusetts) Baseball Club 162
Meyerle, Levi 35, 61
Middletown (Connecticut) Mansfields 81
Mills, Charlie 43
Mills, Everett 43
Milwaukee West End Club 25
USS *Monitor* 49
Moore, Clement 52
Morrill, John 98, 170
Morrisania (Bronx) Unions 19, 35, 39–41
Morrissey, Jack 130
Morrissey, John **13**, 14, 30, 32, 205n10, 208n22
Muldoon, Mike 160
Murnane, Tim 147
Mutrie, Jim 124, 147, 177

National Agreement 176
National Association (minor league) teams (1879) 96–97
National Association of Base Ball Players 1, 5, 9, 12, 204n3
National Association of Professional Base Ball Players (National Association) 24, 31, 33, 44, 57, 65, 70, 91–92, 105, 111, 172, 204n3
National League: clubs (1879) 96; expulsion of Troy-Worcester (1882) 167, 169–170, 175–176, 189, 192; pitching rules changes (1863–1883) 197–198; poor fan support 86, 92, 94, 113; uniforms 156

Index

Nelson, John "Candy" 67, 74, 76, 78, 80–81, 177
New Bedford (Massachusetts) Whalers 119, 124
New England League 121
New Jersey Irvingtons 68
New Jersey Skeeters 179
New York Clipper 73–75, 113, 120
New York Flyaways 44
New York Giants 121–122, 124–125, 127, 173, 180–181
New York Gothams 113, 120, 122, 146, 169, 173, 176–178
New York Green Stockings 176
New York Herald 147
New York Knickerbockers 203ch1n1; rules 9
New York Maroons 146
New York Metropolitans 69, 72, 100, 120, 125, 140–141, 148–150, 154, 157, 163, 171, 174, 176–177, 213n80
New York Mutuals 1, 16–17, 21, 25, 27, 33, 35–36, 43–44, 57, 61, 66, 68–69, 73, 75, 83–85, 111, 189
New York–Penn League 6, 186
New York State League (Baseball Association) 5, 90, 182, 185, 188
New York Times 184
Newark Little Giants 178
Niagara (New York) Baseball Club 2
Nichol, Hugh 148
North Adams (Massachusetts) Club 11
Northwestern League 176

O'Brien, Tom 28, 183–184
Ogdensburg (New York) Pastimes 51
O'Neill, Mike 185
Orangeman Riot 209n15
O'Rourke, James "Orator" 98, 121, 126, 133, 147
O'Rourke, John 134
Osterhut, Charlie 102

Pabor, Charlie 42–43
Partridge, Laud 183
Pearce, Dickie 84, 112
Penfield, Burr 204n2
Penfield, Cal 14, 39, 204n2
Pfeffer, Fred 145, 157, 160, 162, 165, 167, 171, 188, 201
Philadelphia Alerts 68
Philadelphia Athletics 22, 25–26, 33–36, 57, 60–61, 66–68, 73, 76
Philadelphia Inquirer 104
Philadelphia Keystones 38, 60
Philadelphia Phillies 121, 127, 169, 212n50
Philadelphia Quakers 72, 167, 178
Philadelphia Roths 81

Philadelphia White Stockings 83
Philbin, Thomas 185
Phillips, Bill 151, 158, 161
Phillips, Horace 106, 108, 111, 145
Pike, Lipman 24, 27, 39, 60, 66–**69**, 73, 97, 130, 176, 200
Pinkham, Ed 35
Pittsburgh Alleghenys 108
Players League 6, 113, 125
Poland, Phillip 185
Polo Grounds (Bronx) 72, 119, 141, 148–150, 157, 171
Post-Civil War Speculation Bubble 85
Powell, Abner 179
Powell, Martin 165
Powers, Mike 25, 35
Powers, Phil 133–134
Providence Grays 72, 98, 107, 131–132, 134–136, 141, 152–153, 174
Purcell, William "Blondie" 104, 153, 162
Putnam Grounds (Troy) 98

Quigley, John 108

Rabbit, William 182
Radcliffe, John 61
Rafter, Jack 183–185
Rankin, Thomas 88
Raub, Jimmy 183
Reach, Al 61
Reconstruction 57
Reilly, Charlie 98, 103, 200
Rensselaer Park (Lansingburgh) 16, 21–22, 58
Rensselaer Polytechnic Institute (Troy) 47
Reserve Clause 6, 93, 114–115, 142, 176
Reynolds, "Skater" 204n4
Richardson, Danny 181
Richmond, Lee 115, 117, 120, 140, 159, 166
Rochester Hop Bitters 100, 145
Rochester (New York) Flour Citys 90
Rock Island (Illinois) Argus 160–161
Rockford (Illinois) Forest Citys 28, 37, 41, 51, 66
Roseman, James "Chief" 97, 145, 149, 158–160, 163–165, 171, 173–174, 177, 188, 201, 214n54
Rowe, Jack 137, 139, 153
Rusie, Amos 181
Ryan, Paddy 208n22

St. John's College (Rose Hill) 71
St. Louis Brown Stockings 104–105, 123, 126
St. Louis Browns 178
Salisbury, Harry 105
Saratoga Springs (New York) Baseball Club 178

227

Index

Saratoga Springs Racetrack Island Park 14, 188
Schafer, George "Orater" 151, 159
Schenectady Frog Alleys 184
Schenectady Mohawks 11
Schenectady (New York) Ancient Citys 14, 27
Schoefield, John W. 57
Scranton (Pennsylvania) Indians 180
Second National Agreement 176
Seitz, Peter 114
Shoupe, John 137, 211*n*4
Smink, Bill 183
Smith, Arthur 183–184
Smith, John 158, 160–163, 171, 210*n*54
Spalding, Albert 92
The Sporting News 147
Spotten, James H. 16
Springfield Hampdens 16
Springfield (Massachusetts) Baseball Club 69, 117, 121
Springfield Ponies 121
Start, Joe 65, 111
Staub, Joe 137
Stottsville (New York) Baseball Club 108
Stovey, George 186
Stovey, Harry 140
Sullivan, John L. 208*n*22
Sullivan, Ted 179, 187
Sullivan, Yankee 13
Sutton, Ezra 83, 98, 133, 170
Sweazy, Charlie 26
Syracuse Courier 103
Syracuse (New York) Central Citys 190
Syracuse Stars 91, 97–98, 102–106

Tamsett, James 184
Taylor, Billy 128, 151
Taylor, J. 89
Taylorville (Illinois) Noisy Nine 51
Thayer, Ernest 127
Tighe, Edward 61
Tobin, Bill 137
Treacy, Fred 35
Tri-Cities ValleyCats (Troy) 6, 186, 196
Tripartite Agreement 176
Trott, Sam 164
Troy (New York): arts 53–54; baseball's importance 54–55; communications 48; economy 45, 51–52, 54, 157, 193; geography 45–47, 52, 91; Hall of Fame Monument 196; industry 46–47, 50; Irish immigration 51, 203*ch*1*n*4; labor movement 52; natural resources 46; technical-educational institutions 46–47, 52; textiles 50–51, 207*n*14
Troy Amateur Baseball League 5
Troy City Baseball Association 137
Troy Citys (minor leagues) 180
Troy Citys (National League) 1, 98–101, 103–108, 110, 118, 128–129, 132–133, 135–138, 140–142, 148–149, 152–153, 161, 165, 180, 192, 199
Troy Haymakers 1–3, 5, 7, 14, 16–20, 22–23, 32–33, 35, 44, 49, 51, **58**, 61, 81, 83, 85, 89–90, 95, 179, 185–186, 188–193, 195–196, 199, 203*n*1—Preface, 205*n*30, 206*n*53, 210*n*54
Troy Music Hall **53**
Troy Priams 9–10, 12
Troy Public Library 74
Troy Putnams (Juniors) (1870) **44**, 81, 85
Troy Trojans (minor leagues) 124, 173, 177–185, 187–188
Troy Trojans (National League) 1, 77, 95, 97–98, 101–106, 114, 117, 120, 122, 128–130, 137, 139–141, 143–145, 147–152, 157–158, 160, 162–163, 165–168, 170–171, 176, 188–189, 192, 199, 211*n*4, 213*n*80
Troy Vanguards 10
Troy Victorys 10–12, 191, 203*ch*1*n*1
Troy Washerwomen 180, 185, 215*n*28
Troy Zouaves 203*ch*1*n*1
Tweed, Boss 13

Underground Railroad 53
Union Association 105
Union Baseball Club of Rensselaer County *see* "Lansingburgh Unions"
Union Base-Ball Grounds (Chicago) 65
Union College (Schenectady) 128–129
Union Grounds (Cincinnati) 205*n*30
Union Grounds (Williamsburg) 38, 43, 62–63, 65, 75, 83–84
Utica (New York) Utes 11, 90

Vail's Lot (Lansingburgh) 88
Van Horn baseballs 39–40

Wachter, Lew 185
Walker, Oscar 103
Wappingers Falls (New York) Actives 107
Ward, James 14, 26, 97
Ward, John Montgomery 98, 121, 123, 126, 135, 147, 176
Washington (District of Columbia) Mutuals (African American) 86
Washington Nationals 35, 90, 117
Washington Olympics 22, 35, 66, 74
Waterbury (Connecticut) Monitors 119
Waterbury Pirates 121
Waterbury Rough Riders 121
Weir's Course (Lansingburgh) 9, 203*ch*1*n*1
Welch, Mickey 111, 114, 117–118, 121–124, 126, 128–130, 133–136, 138, 140–141, 143, 145–

Index

146, 149, 153–154, 157–163, 165, 167, 171–174, 176, 181, 188, 192, 196, 201, 212n50, 214n54
Weldman, George "Stump" 164–165
Werden, Percy 179
West Troy Champions 14
West Troy Dalys 127–129
West Troy Excelsior Club 10–11
West Troy Grounds 166, 168, 177, 181–182, 188
Wheaton, William 9
White, Deacon 92, 102, 167
Whitney, Jim 170
Willard, Emma 52, 207–208n19
Williams College (Williamstown, Massachusetts) 14, 182
Winslow, William Henry 117
Wise, Sam 170
Wittsie, Hooks 184

Wolters, Rynie 34
Wood, Jimmy 35, 74, 79, 82–83, 140, 192–193, 200
Worcester (Massachusetts) 90–91
Worcester Grays 95, 115–**116**, 140, 172
Worcester Red Stockings 95
Worcester Ruby Legs 69, 115, 120, 137–139, 149–150, 153, 163, 166, 168, 171
Worcester Worcesters *see* "Worcester Grays"
Wright, George 28, 76, 79, 98, 112
Wright, Harry 28, 38, 59, 92

York, Tom 39, 67, 72–73, 200
Yorkville (New York) Champions 11
Young, Nicholas 57, 72

Zettlein, George 27, 74, 79, 82–83, 112, 187, 200

www.ingramcontent.com/pod-product-compliance
Ingram Content Group UK Ltd.
Pitfield, Milton Keynes, MK11 3LW, UK
UKHW041946140426
5217IPUK00014B/673